June Goodfield has a doctorate in the history of medicine and is an internationally renowned medical writer and broadcaster. Her 1985 series *From the Face of the Earth* told the story of modern medical achievement and proved a worldwide television success.

She devised, researched and wrote the television documentary *The Planned Miracle*.

For
Frances —
affectionately .

June

THE
PLANNED
MIRACLE

June Goodfield (signature)

June Goodfield

CARDINAL

A Cardinal Book

First published in Great Britain in 1991 in Cardinal by
Sphere Books Ltd, a Division of
Macdonald & Co (Publishers) Ltd
London & Sydney

The publishers and author would like to gratefully acknowledge
Thurston Clarke and Century Hutchinson Publishing Ltd for
granting permission to quote an extract from *Equator: A Journey Round
the World* by Thurston Clarke.

Photoset in North Wales by
Derek Doyle & Associates, Mold, Clwyd
Printed and bound in Great Britain by
Cox & Wyman Ltd, Reading

ISBN 0 7474 0933 1

Sphere Books Ltd
A Division of
Macdonald & Co (Publishers) Ltd
Orbit House
1 New Fetter Lane
London EC4A 1AR

A member of Maxwell Macmillan Pergamon Publishing Corporation

TO
Margaret
and
Alison, Caroline, Gillian,
and also
Will and Jim, Ann and Christopher, Richard, Henry and
Edward

Contents

'Weeping, I know, solves nothing; morality is an activity, not a sentiment.'

Peter Marin, 'Coming to terms with Vietnam',
Harpers, Dec. 1980, p.56

'I pondered how men fight and lose the battle, and the thing they fought for comes about in spite of their defeat, and when it comes turns out not to have been what they meant, and other men have to fight for what they meant under another name.'

William Morris, before listening to a sermon from John Ball, in his vision of the lost past.

The Planned Miracle

Preface and Acknowledgements

Amongst its many scientific successes the twentieth century counts improvements in health and medicine as its two most signal achievements. Yet as we approach the millennium any complacency we might feel should be shattered by these statistics. The atom bomb on Hiroshima killed 180,000 people; every three days a silent Hiroshima occurs in childhood deaths. Globally, children are dying at somewhere near the rate of 270,000 per week, 14 million a year; 217 million will not reach their fifth birthday; one death in every three in the world today is the death of a child.

In 1983, a group of people of truly audacious vision decided to mount a major onslaught on this silent epidemic. Their project has been dubbed 'the planned miracle'; their story is told in this book.

Since 1983 I have followed closely the campaigns to give every child in the world a healthy headstart in life and a chance to live. I was to find that, like any human saga, this story was compounded of heroics and jealousies, of poignant endeavours and difficult choices. Every triumph carried a price; every problem solved generated fresh dilemmas. The problems were wide ranging: from the spectre of over-population, to the ethics of intervention into the lives and cultures of others, to whether a quick medical success was more desirable than slow progress towards a firm structure of health care. So emotionally charged were these issues that during the years it took to complete this work, I have often felt like a ball being bounced between the strongly held views of committed men and women, all of whom have a passionate concern for the future of the world and its children. So, as I wrote, cocooned in the security of my home and the warmth of my friends, I have constantly had to remind myself: the result of the continuing debates is not a logical point won, but a practical outcome that will affect the lives of every one of those young, vulnerable faces I have seen in the *favelas* of Rio, on the red earth of Africa and the lush, tropical hills of Southeast Asia.

This book is divided into three parts. Part I gives the background to the story and shows what had to happen – and what still has to happen – in order that a protective vaccine, manufactured in an industrialized developed country, can be delivered to a baby in the rural heartland of a developing one.

Over 100 countries in the developing world would participate in the planned miracle. There was no way I could visit them all, and equally when you've seen one measles shot you've seen them all. However, there were major differences between their various experiences. The countries whose tales I recount in Part II were chosen both because I had first-hand experience of the people and places involved and because they illustrated varying aspects of this saga: Turkey, a massive country, provided the quintessential example of the UNICEF approach in a campaign that would mobilize every sector of its society for a three months' immunization onslaught; Lebanon, where in a magnificently futile or magnificently heroic effort, depending on your point of view, the warring factions were persuaded to halt for a short space of time so that the children could be immunized; Brazil, where efforts to eradicate polio were ambushed just when we were on the verge of success; Uganda, where the opportunity to protect the children was seized as a simultaneous opportunity to reunite a war-torn nation but where the differences between the agencies' approaches would be played out against the background of AIDS.

Part III looks to the future and to what we might expect by the turn of the century, when other vaccines, such as those against malaria, may be added to our protective armamentarium; when polio, perhaps measles too, may be eradicated; when the lives of all children might be supported by an adequate system of health care provided political will permits.

I have many debts and my first is to my three collaborators, Michael Johnstone, Tony Jones and Angela Dyer. Michael was responsible for researching the scientific content of this book as well as the background to the present situation in Uganda. The results of his considerable skills can be especially appreciated in the chapters where, using the example of polio, I describe how nature continues to challenge us. Tony, a superb science writer, analysed my first draft, suggested a more logical order, then researched further for me. Angela, my editor, worked with me patiently and painstakingly through successive drafts. I am deeply grateful to all three friends.

This book has taken many years to research. There were many people to interview many times over, many countries to visit, many conferences to attend. Three organizations made this possible: the Carnegie Corporation of New York, the Rockefeller Foundation and the Merck Foundation. I am deeply grateful to Dr David Hamburg, Dr Adetokunbo Lucas, Ms Jill Sheffield, Mr David Devlin-Foltz and Dr Kenneth Warren for their encouragement and critical advice. I must also place on record a debt of gratitude to the Commonwealth Fund. Many years ago they supported me for a fresh assessment of C.P. Snow's *Two Cultures*, focusing especially on the contribution that he believed science could make to the solution of global poverty. Though I never managed to capture my conclusions in a distinct book, these have permeated my work during the past six years and greatly influenced what I have written here.

Many others helped me, notably the scientists whose work I reflect and whose names are to be found in the text, as well as the staff of UNICEF, WHO, the Task Force for Child Survival, Save the Children Fund, the Pan American Health Organization, the Canadian Public Health Association, the United States Agency for International Development and the Rotary Foundation of Rotary International. Whether at headquarters or working in the field, all have been unsparing with time and hospitality. My enormous regard for these people derives from the demanding work they selflessly do, their patience with my persistent presence and questions, and their encouragement. Any criticisms which follow in no way diminish my admiration.

My gratitude extends equally to a multitude of people in the numerous countries I visited. This is really their story. The success of 'the planned miracle' is above all due to the efforts of people working on behalf of the children in their own nations. Their numbers run into thousands; I met hundreds and cannot possibly name them all. I hope that they will accept my thanks here. Memories come as vignettes – the villagers of Gokkoy, high on the mountains above Sardis, Turkey, whose Imam and Muhtar, like two friendly Pied Pipers, led me around their glorious land with the village children following behind; the aged rice farmer in Thailand's southeastern province, who invited me up the ladder to the one room of his house where his entire family welcomed me and where his youngest grandson – may blessings rest upon his head for evermore – was the *only* baby in the whole of my travels who didn't scream when placed in my arms; the mother of the sick child in rural Brazil who held my hands tightly while her child was examined for polio by a woman doctor who was close to exhaustion; the dignity of the village head in a rural settlement in eastern Gambia, who welcomed us to a formal village meeting with the words, 'Colour is of no consequence'.

This book is one half of a major project, a three-part television series being the other. This brings a fresh set of debts: to the British charitable trusts who quietly and anonymously make many good things possible and who helped to get the venture off the ground; to colleagues of InCA – the television production company; to my two friends and colleagues, who accompanied me on the research trips, especially Charlotte, whose breathtaking comments, regularly uttered, in a beguiling mixture of perception and assertion, kept me honest and self-critical. For five months, from Brasilia to the Mekong, our travels were exhilarating, compounded of exhaustion, travail and fun. They were the best of companions, though I have never recovered from their capacity to start at dawn, work a fourteen-hour day and still not need to eat until eleven o'clock at night. We all had different jobs to do and sometimes I was caught between the conflicting demands of the book and the films. Once I rebelled, when my need to get humanly close to the people about whom I would write conflicted yet again with the necessity to visit the 104th, or was it 105th, health centre – we finally stopped counting – whose staff were most anxious to welcome us. My friends told me firmly when I was being unreasonable and then made me laugh. I shall remember those days with nostalgia.

Then there are those who are always there: my secretary Ann Wickens, and her husband Robin, stalwart and loving supports; my agent Hilary Rubinstein; Cheryl Lutring; Quentin Crewe, whose hospitality at Le Grand Banc enabled me to meet my deadline; Connie Stone, who kept up a constant flow of cheerful encouragement throughout; my friends and colleagues on the Board of International Health and Biomedicine in both England and America, who have given me wonderful support; my publishers, especially Nick Webb and Julia Bunton of Macdonald, who have achieved their own miracle in getting this book out in time to match a changed television broadcast.

Finally, I must thank my family to whom this book is dedicated: my sister, her children and grandchildren.

PART I

Prologue: With Camera, Credit Card and Typhoid Shot

'Ah, take the Cash, and let the Credit go,
Nor heed the rumble of a distant Drum!'

Edward Fitzgerald, *The Rubaiyat of Omar Khayyam*

In centuries past few people journeyed more than ten miles from their homes. In this century, the jet aeroplane has shattered the confining walls of traditional existence and millions of people regularly journey ten hundred to ten thousand miles. We travel well armed, of course, with cameras for future nostalgia, credit cards for deferred payments, typhoid shots for present protection. Moreover a familiar environment awaits us: Coke and concrete are everywhere, showers with clean water, ice-cubes in our drinks and steaks for dinner. Nevertheless the varieties of language, culture, costume and custom presented to us appear as a romantic and exotic contrast to our humdrum daily lives. But in most cases such local colour is no more than a thin veneer carefully stuck on to a country's surface for the benefit of the tourist. This veneer is generally all we ever encounter, and we return home, in truth, as ignorant as when we left.

The places we visit may be romantic to recall, but for many they are hell to inhabit. The true facts of their existence – an abundance of poverty, hunger, unemployment, disease – we see only on television, though not too often since this would severely depress the ratings.

3

The cheeky, local kids we find so adorable – provided, of course, they are not importunate – who shine our shoes or polish the car's windscreen, are in reality tough survivors. More likely than not they are homeless, come from large families, and many of their brothers and sisters will already have died.

The facts are these: during the last fifteen years of this century, two billion children will have been born, 87 per cent of them in the developing world. Yet 217 million of them will not reach their fifth birthday, for they are dying at a rate equivalent to one Hiroshima every three days: nearly 250,000 a week, 14 million a year. One death in every three in the world is the death of a child under the age of five. By any measure such mortality is an affront. For a child to be born only to die, for a mother to go through pregnancy after pregnancy in order that one or two children may survive, represents a colossal human waste. The personal and economic price is intolerable, whether exacted from a mother or an emerging nation, both of whom need every possible healthy human resource as they struggle to survive in today's harsh world.

Stark the facts may be, but the temptation to romanticize is still insidious. When, ten years ago, I began travelling extensively in the Third World I knew about this silent epidemic of childhood deaths, but even one medical triumph was enough to make me dewy-eyed. In the winter of 1984 I was in Bangladesh taking part in a television series about contemporary biomedical research and its impact on global disease. The final episode celebrated the greatest success ever achieved in medicine, the global eradication of smallpox, and during the filming I came face to face with the last person in human history to have been infected with *Variola major*, the most lethal virus of smallpox.

When Rahima Banu was born in 1972, on Bhola Island in the Ganges Delta, the war against this virus had already been raging for six years. Of the many global armies fighting smallpox, the one in Bangladesh faced the most difficult task. Time and again, in a country the size of Florida, teeming with 82 million people, the disease had regularly been pushed to the very edges of survival only for it to surge back in wave after wave of epidemics, spearheaded by civil war, floods, assassinations and a consequent turmoil which frustrates relief activities. Three years later Rahima Banu succumbed to the virus. Her parents, anxiously wondering whether their firstborn would live or die, could not know that the war was almost over, that the front was just a few miles away, that the people who would finally liberate mankind from one of the worst scourges in human history were converging on their hut. For the virus that over aeons of time had brought down kings and emperors and had changed the course of human history, was making its final stand in the body of their tiny three-year-old child.

Rahima Banu survived the disease. When I met her nine years later this history was etched on her face – the pitted scars of smallpox. The skins of her brother and two sisters, however, were clear: by the time they were born the virus had finally been consigned to history.

I was deeply moved, even overwhelmed, by the encounter. To me, this child seemed to symbolize all that was best in science, technology and human co-operation. Perhaps this was indeed the dawn of a new era: the age of the great infections was passing; all tropical diseases would be conquered; and now the growing recognition that poverty and over-population posed a far greater threat to the world than nuclear war would surely lead to a fairer economic deal all round. With this one giant step, the vicious circle of deprivation had been cut. If Hollywood had been in charge – we were making a film, after all – heavenly choirs would have provided background music as Rahima Banu marched into a glorious sunset.

Then I glanced at Drs Nick Ward and Stan Foster, who for four years had led the campaign in Bangladesh – and my mood dissolved. I had just learnt that the bright sari worn by Rahima Banu was an agreed gift before the family would consent to be filmed. They were bitterly ashamed of their rags. Their house had no walls. Their only land and two skinny cows had disappeared in the floods of last year: as with millions in this grossly over-crowded, low-lying country, they live where they can find land – on temporary sandbanks in the rivers or the shifting shorelines by the ocean – places where no one would ever choose to set up home. After the monsoon had finished with them, they had to borrow in order to eat, so their lives had become the property of a money-lender. As I watched, subdued, the children began plucking at their mother's arm. They were hungry; they almost always are.

So, as Nick Ward insisted when months later we met again in London, far from an end, smallpox eradication marked only the first, minuscule step towards a better life for those in the developing countries. Many problems remained to challenge human skills and human compassion – from AIDS, to aid, to over-population – and there was no magic wand. Human disasters occur suddenly and may quickly alter the course of history. But human progress, whether towards political liberty or more equitable lives, occurs only as the result of small, incremental steps, that demand permanent commitment, professional expertise, compassionate detachment and a recognition that to be moral means not just to think, but to act. Nick and his colleagues would now tackle the other major diseases that wreck children's lives in the Third World. The tools already existed, and one day perhaps polio, measles, whooping cough, even malaria, would go the way of smallpox.

Rahima Banu is now eighteen and will soon be married – that is, if her father can scrape together her dowry. By the turn of the century she will have her own children. This book is the sequel to her story and describes what happened next, when smallpox had finally been eradicated and those concerned with global health decided to give the children of the world – Rahima Banu's children – a chance to live. They had a fair idea of the difficulties they would face. But their campaign nearly foundered at the very start, on rocks of dissension they had not foreseen.

1
Why Children Die

> 'No-one in his senses would choose to have been
> born in a previous age unless he could be certain
> that he would have been born into a prosperous
> family, that he would have enjoyed extremely good
> health, and that he could have accepted stoically the
> death of the majority of his children.'
>
> J.H. Plumb

Children should not die: they should grow up to have
children and grandchildren of their own. Why doesn't
everyone live to a ripe old age?

Though in the industrialized, rich, developed countries of the world most people do, this is a comparatively
new development in history. Demographic research on
French communities in the seventeenth and eighteenth
centuries has revealed a picture which mirrors many
Asian or African communities in the twentieth. The
average length of life was a third of ours today, and
because frequent pregnancies and childbirth wreaked a
dreadful toll, it was significantly less for women. When
harvests failed, cycles followed of a form now distress-
ingly familiar in Africa, as starvation, disease and
epidemics killed off the children, the old and the
debilitated.

As recently as 1906, the infant mortality rate (IMR) in Birmingham, England, was higher than in all but about three countries of the world today: 200 in every 1000 children died. But within forty years this had dropped to 46 per 1000, thanks to a combination of better food, housing, sanitation, clean water, education and maternal and child care. In developing countries too, the infant mortality rate has steadily fallen by nearly a third since the Second World War: from 164 per 1000 births, it averaged 100 by 1980, and in many individual countries it is now much lower than that.

Nevertheless in the very poorest countries the situation today is still as it always has been: in 1983, 14 million of the 15 million children under five dying each year, 93.3 per cent, lived in the developing world. In some countries a quarter of all children never live to see their fifth birthday; in some pockets, such as two arrondissements in Central Mali, half do not. They die not of accidents but of well-known natural causes; the reason such heavy mortality occurs in poor countries is because the contributing conditions of poverty put infants at great disadvantage when infections – whether viruses, bacteria or parasites – strike.

Viruses cause diseases such as polio and influenza. They are the simplest and smallest forms of life, being little more than a solid core of genetic material covered with a protein coat. Invading the body's cells they hijack the DNA by splicing their own genes into the cell's nuclei and assuming genetic command, forcing the cell to become a factory making more virus. In the process the cell dies, bursts open, and the virus, now multiplied millions of times, continues its invasion of other cells.

Bacteria are more complex and specialized organisms. They parasitize the body systems, seeking the special conditions they require. Accordingly they all have different effects. Salmonella, the bacteria that cause food poisoning, thrive in the gut; the mycobacteria of leprosy thrive in the lymphatic cells. Tetanus and diphtheria bacteria kill by producing lethal poisons – toxins – that cause muscular or breathing spasms; those of cholera cause a functional breakdown in the lining of the intestines.

The final group of infectious agents are the parasites, the most specialized of all. The single-celled malaria parasite that causes millions of childhood deaths is a highly sophisticated organism exquisitely adapted for survival in specific parts of the body. Such parasites pose an enormous challenge to medicine and so far the weapons we possess to fight them are very limited.

Yet children in the affluent West, too, are constantly meeting infections but generally they survive and do so because various contributing environmental conditions work in their favour. These conditions determine first whether pathogens are around in great numbers, and secondly, whether a child's immune system is strong enough to resist their attacks. Poor hygiene, rarely a problem in the West, is associated with more than half of all childhood deaths, for insanitary conditions allow pathogens to flourish and gain easy access to infants. Malnutrition is a second contributing condition that compounds infant mortality. This does not mean rank starvation of the type caused by the famines in Ethiopia, the Sahel and most recently the Sudan; these account for less than 2 per cent of all deaths. But even in countries where there are no famines, thousands of people die *every day* from malnutrition. Yet there is a close relationship between malnutrition, infection and childhood mortality, which was discovered only thirty years ago.

This discovery was just one of many that resulted from research into tropical diseases during colonial times, a period when various imperatives came to bear on health – the most obvious being that the colonialists themselves were dying in huge numbers. Yellow fever and malaria cut swathes through the builders of the Panama Canal. Throughout the nineteenth and twentieth centuries, right up to the Korean and Vietnam Wars of the seventies, as many if not more soldiers fell to malaria as they did to enemy action. Administrators, too, were felled in their thousands: a third of all Europeans who settled in West Africa in the great days of the Empire died prematurely from disease. With few exceptions, scientific and medical research concentrated on diseases of adults – for after all, they provided the work force. Little was known, few people cared, about the children.

But after the Second World War, matters were to change as agencies like WHO began to focus on tropical diseases such as malaria and smallpox, and received political support from their nation states for this, in great part because their much-travelled citizens were also catching these debilitating infections. UNICEF was founded to work on behalf of children. Gradually they, and their potential for a country's future and well-being, were placed on the political agenda. Finally came an interest in their health.

But there was woeful ignorance of the real dimensions of the problems. As late as 1976, and even after smallpox had been dealt with, the true extent of childhood diseases was still not appreciated. Polio, controlled in the West twenty years before, was assumed not to be a serious problem; measles was considered to be serious only in West Africa, and neonatal tetanus was totally ignored. Yet within the medical literature articles existed that showed something of the extent of childhood mortality and its relation to children's living conditions and nutrition. One discovery particularly significant for this story was made in a remote village, Keneba, in central Gambia by a Scottish doctor, Sir Ian MacGregor. Working for Britain's Medical Research Council, he had gone there in 1949 to study nutrition and its relation to parasitic disease. His findings turned conventional thinking upside down.

MacGregor's remit resulted from a widespread attitude during the many years of colonial rule; that Africa could become the granary of the world if only its rampant diseases were conquered was taken for granted. But there was a problem – malnutrition – caused, doctors argued, primarily by protein deficiency which led to mortality in children and various debilitating conditions in adults. Africans were unable to work properly because their diet consisted primarily of cassava and other starchy vegetables sadly lacking in protein. The solution offered was twofold. First, WHO launched remedial programmes for infants using skimmed milk powder. But since the only water available to add to the powder was dirty, the milk was soon being described by African mothers as 'the stuff that gives our children diarrhoea'. The second solution was to supplement the diet by growing crops containing more protein. Among many such remedial schemes was the groundnut – peanut – programme of East Africa into which the British government poured millions of ultimately wasted pounds – wasted because the soil was unable to carry sustained cultivation. After extensive studies – some in an Indian village in Guatemala by a Costa Rican scientist, Dr Leonardo Marta, others in Keneba by Sir Ian MacGregor – the premise on which all this action was based was shown to be faulty.

During twelve years of continuous research MacGregor showed that an African baby at birth not only weighed on average half a pound more than a British baby, but irrespective of whether it was born in the dry or rainy season, in times of hunger or plenty, it also grew twice as fast for the first three months, provided it was breast fed. Yet in the second three months growth slowed, and after that went completely haywire, especially during the rainy season. One fact constantly recurred: growth faltered when the child showed signs of infection. For the same rain that brought the harvest also brought disease in abundance – respiratory and diarrhoeal illness, measles, polio and a tide of malaria. Now the child actually lost weight. So whereas a European child would grow in a constant manner from birth on, an African child grew in fits and starts, remarkably well for the first three months, well in the dry season but not at all in the wet. So that between six months and two years of age all African children were underweight compared to their European counterparts.

What seemed to be happening was this: as the protection offered by the mother's antibodies faded during the fourth to sixth months, the child increasingly succumbed to multiple infections. Not just once but time after time its immune system was constantly challenged to defend the body against a series of onslaughts. Moreover, some of the highly endemic infections, such as measles and malaria, actually suppressed the immune mechanisms and compromised the infant's natural defences even further until finally a child's immunity was so weakened that it could succumb even to a common cold. An ill child both loses its appetite and cannot properly absorb even that nourishment it manages to keep down, so it soon becomes malnourished and a vicious circle is quickly set up. The most vulnerable time for an African child is its first five years; the window of death – the period when most children are likely to die – is between six months and two years.

Thus what, in general, determines whether a child survives is not so much the food it eats but its capacity to resist disease. Infection and malnutrition reinforce each other. As MacGregor wrote: 'Malnutrition reduces resistance to infection; infection precipitates malnutrition.' So the child is sucked down into a debilitating whirlpool as repeated cycles of infection, dehydration, malnutrition and immune suppression follow each other. If the mother is uneducated, ignorant of the reason for her child's illness, exhausted or apathetic, if the contributing conditions of dirty water, inadequate sanitation, and poverty are also present, then the infant is well on the way to the grave.

Thus when a child in the Third World dies, it is almost impossible to separate clearly the direct causes from the contributing ones, for the child has probably had several infections simultaneously and also some degree of malnutrition. Nevertheless, in 1990, we do now have a genuine quantitative measure of how many children die, and why. Paradoxically, being born in the first place is one major cause of premature death.

In previous centuries the associated dangers of childbirth were well documented, and many readers have had their withers wrung by novels in which the mother died in childbirth, or the infant died, or both died. Yet even today, *every day*, 1400 women – nearly half a million mothers each year – die in the process of carrying or delivering their babies. They leave behind one million motherless children. In addition five million babies are stillborn, or die within their first week of life. There are basically two causes for this mortality; some affect the mothers, others the children.

Four types of pregnancy are especially risky for both mother and baby. These are summed up in the phrase 'too young, too old, too many or too close': when the mother is under eighteen, or over thirty-five, has already had four children, or is giving birth within two years of the previous child. If these types of pregnancy were avoided, deaths of both mothers and babies could be halved. But studies in Asia show that if a mother dies in childbirth, 95 per cent of her young infants will not live beyond the first twelve months; in Tanzania it has been shown that 85 per cent of the under-threes will also die.

So far as newborn babies are concerned, one infection above all others contributes to their separate mortality. Tetanus, responsible for 0.8 million annual neonatal deaths, is particularly dangerous. In many countries,

Annual Deaths of Children Under Five by Main Causes*

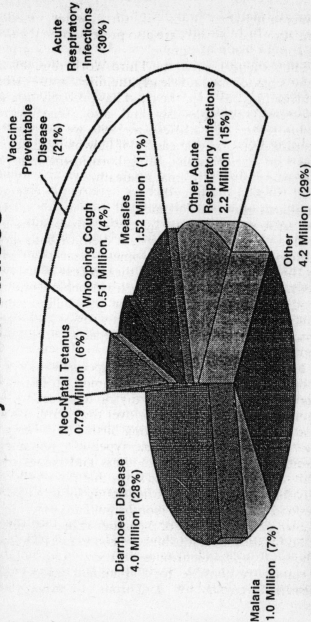

Acute Respiratory Infections (30%)

Vaccine Preventable Disease (21%)

Whooping Cough 0.51 Million (4%)

Measles 1.52 Million (11%)

Other Acute Respiratory Infections 2.2 Million (15%)

Neo-Natal Tetanus 0.79 Million (6%)

Diarrhoeal Disease 4.0 Million (28%)

Malaria 1.0 Million (7%)

Other 4.2 Million (29%)

* In Practice, Children Often Die of Multiple Causes

Source: WHO and UNICEF Estimates

dung or mud – or in India, ghee – is put on the umbilical stump, which has often been cut with a dirty razor blade or even a blade of tough grass. Immunizing a potential mother against tetanus, preferably in adolescence or before pregnancy, and having a trained attendant present at birth to ensure sterile conditions, greatly reduces the risks.

But even if babies survive the first hazard of this world – being born – many other pathogens lurk. As the pie chart (p.15) shows, their next greatest threat comes from diarrhoeal diseases, from which another five million per year will die, and for which we have no vaccines. In poor countries an infant can suffer from diarrhoea for 15–20 per cent of its first two years and a severe attack can kill it in twenty-four hours flat. Diarrhoea is caused by a great range of viruses and bacteria, the nastiest of which is the one that causes cholera. The conditions in which they all flourish are those associated with bad sanitation and polluted water supplies. The aid agencies working in the refugee camps fear floods and overcrowding most of all, for once cholera gets a foothold it spreads with terrifying speed. Deaths come mostly from dehydration, for the infection affects the proper functioning of the intestinal walls and abnormal amounts of salts and water pass from the body. Once again the infant loses its appetite. Traditionally parents withhold foods and fluids, even breast milk, from their sick infants. So the babies become increasingly weak; underweight children have longer bouts and are more likely to die. There is also a synergistic effect between diarrhoea and measles viruses: about a quarter of diarrhoeal deaths could be prevented by measles immunization.

The babies who survive so far then face the risk of acute respiratory infections (ARI), which pick off nearly another three million each year, caused by 300 different viruses and bacteria. Some attack the upper respiratory passages, others the lower, some both. Some, like influenza, cause diffuse disease all over the body, others more localized disease. Those which affect the lungs and bronchial tubes are the greatest killers of children under five years. In 1987, whooping cough (pertussis) alone killed 0.6 million. Then there is diphtheria, an acute contagious infection caused by *Corynebacterium diphtheriae*, a bacillus that produces fever, a swollen throat and severe difficulties in breathing and swallowing. Diphtheria has been virtually eliminated by vaccination in Western countries over the past thirty years, and most physicians have never seen a case.

Vaccines will protect against just two of these respiratory diseases – whooping cough and diphtheria. As for the rest, fifty cents' worth of antibiotics would save most infants, but this presupposes both their availability and parents being able to spot the difference between a bad cold and a life-threatening infection and seek timely help. These infections afflict children in the West almost as frequently as they do those in developing countries, with five to eight attacks a year of seven to nine days' duration. But they cause fewer deaths, especially as children reach school age. A child in a poor country is fifty times more likely to die from bronchitis or pneumonia than is a child in the West.

Measles comes next in the deathly league table, taking out a further two million children each year. Eminently preventable by the use of vaccines, it is far more serious than we in the West can imagine. In Tanzania each of the forty different tribal languages and dialects has a specific word for measles. Without immunization almost all children in the developing world will have caught measles before the age of three, and the poorer their living conditions, the earlier they will be infected. The virus causes fatalities that range from 3 per cent of all infected children to 40 per cent during a famine, or amongst refugees. Children who survive may be permanently blinded, others may develop brain damage.

The deadly effects are enhanced because the virus also suppresses the immune system, thus permitting further infection. So even if a child survives measles, the chances of it dying in the following eight months are increased tenfold. In 1961, while Sir Ian MacGregor was working in Keneba, measles swept through the whole of West Africa. The epidemic struck the village in February and March, a time of year when the children rarely became ill, when, in fact, they were all growing remarkably well. Yet in those two months, *every* child in the village under the age of twelve contracted the disease, and a quarter of all under the age of five died. Most who survived were left blind. Even as late as March 1988, when measles erupted in Dalonguebougou, a small, prosperous village of 600 people in central Mali that had been without an epidemic for ten years, twenty children died, seven alone in one extended family. Many African mothers still say, 'After measles has gone through the village count your children.'

The next cause of this Hiroshima once every three days is malaria, which worldwide takes out a further one million children each year. The single-celled parasite, one of four species of *Plasmodium*, is transmitted by the bite of a female mosquito and wreaks terrible havoc. Nearly 240,000 million people live in areas where malaria is a serious risk; in sub-Saharan Africa, about 750,000 people die each year. We do not have very accurate figures, but informed guesses suggest that in some parts of the world this disease kills 50 out of every 1000 children under five. There is once again a two-way effect with malnutrition, for during each attack of malaria a child loses weight to the equivalent of three days' food. Malaria affects children directly and via their mothers. Pregnant women develop acute cerebral malaria at a rate nearly twelve times that of other women. Since this provokes severe anaemia they give birth to underweight, unhealthy babies who are likely to die.

The very essence of a sophisticated and successful parasite is that it is evolutionally exquisitely adapted to evade anything the immune system can throw at it. So parasitic diseases are notoriously resistant to vaccines and so far we have none to fight *Plasmodium*. Yet in theory one should be possible, for as MacGregor found, people in West Africa can acquire an immunity to malaria.

He was one of the first to notice that for the majority of adult Africans a malarial mosquito bite was nothing at all. In a country with rampant disease, where mosquitoes and malaria were present throughout the whole year and where Europeans were regularly felled, this came as a great surprise. Certainly some individuals – generally very young children – did suffer badly, but although older children and adults could have malarial parasites in their blood, many showed no symptoms and needed no treatment.

Significantly, it was also rare to see an infected child under three months of age, and even after three months the first attack was usually mild with only one child in five needing treatment. But as the infant grew older, the episodes of malaria became more severe and prolonged, till a time came, somewhere between six months and three years of age, when the infant was almost continuously infected and severely ill. Death at that stage was very common. From the data MacGregor gathered it is known that during the last twenty-five years exactly 50 per cent of the children born in Keneba died from malaria before the age of five. However, if they survived their first years, they could ultimately carry without serious effect the same quantity of malaria parasites in their blood that earlier had caused them to be severely ill. The ability to suppress the clinical symptoms of malaria gradually strengthened through adolescence, so by the time they were adults, mosquito bites were of no consequence. People *can* acquire an immunity to malaria but only if they are continually bitten.

These, then, are the major diseases that are still rampant and cause so many childhood deaths. With the exception of the parasitic ones like malaria, all are equally implicated in childhood diseases in the Western world. But here they are kept at bay through deliberate manipulation of conditions – good food, health services, sanitation and preventive vaccination. When we remember that the same causes of infant mortality – diarrhoea, whooping cough, acute respiratory infections compounded by malnutrition – also prevailed in Birmingham in 1906 but no longer do so, there is no doubt that, in theory, the poor countries of the world could similarly hold such infections at bay given improved living conditions and all that this implies. But the economic situation today is truly stark in many developing countries – especially in Africa – with rising populations, environmental degradation, massive debts and world economic recession. Thus development, though highly desirable, will be a very slow solution. Meanwhile, the children are dying.

The outlook is not entirely bleak, however, for we have two weapons not available in earlier centuries – effective medical technology in the form of vaccines, and international compassion. Those people and agencies who worked on smallpox eradication believed that it was possible to break into the vicious circle of poverty and deprivation through medical interventions such as vaccination. The only question now would concern strategy: whether to go for intensive immunization campaigns or introduce immunization slowly, as an integral but developing part of primary health care. Should they in fact target the direct causes – the pathogens – or the secondary ones – living conditions? Would it be possible to hit both at one and the same time?

Whatever the merits of either side in that debate, it has become increasingly clear that immunization has a vital role to play in child survival by preventing six diseases that annually kill or maim so many children. During 1988 measles killed 1.86 million, whooping cough 0.55 million, neonatal tetanus 0.82 million, paralytic polio disabled at least 0.24 million. Though accurate figures for diphtheria are not known, these were certainly high, as were those for tuberculosis, estimated at about 30,000. Two-thirds of the latter came from tubercular meningitis; epidemics of meningitis are now a regular feature of life in the Middle East and sub-Saharan Africa.

Yet cheap vaccines of proven efficacy exist against these diseases, as can be seen in most Western countries. Measles has been virtually eliminated, its control being especially successful in the United States, where vaccination certificates must be presented before children can enter public school. Whooping cough has also been most successfully controlled, though ironically this very success, and the fact that the vaccine can generate unpleasant and on rare occasions disabling side-effects, led to laxity and fear which, in the United Kingdom, has provoked several dangerous epidemics in the last ten years. Tetanus, too, is rare thanks to routine jabs, whether after cuts or in adolescence, and to sterile birth practices. In UK schools all children at fifteen years of age receive booster polio drops and a tetanus shot. Polio is almost completely controlled, as is tuberculosis, in which immunization and improved sanitation have both played a part.

Yet when set against the glamour of high-tech medicine – transplants, by-pass surgery and the like – preventive medicine by vaccination or any other means has a very lowly status, whether in terms of finance, career rewards or government and media interest. But medical prevention has chalked up one major global public health success and will probably achieve several more. More importantly, prevention is likely to be the best path in the future. For even in affluent countries, where people's illnesses come by and large by choice –

from patterns of lifestyle – curative medicine is now
becoming very expensive: in the poorer countries there is
no choice at all. Few people are able to decide to be well.
Even when governments are genuinely concerned with
the health of their entire societies and not just a small
section, few can afford anything more than simple,
cost-effective, preventive measures. So vaccination can
play a unique role, and as research into new and better
vaccines increases, and our understanding of the human
immune system develops, that role will become even
more distinguished.

2

A Lasting Solution

'The Twentieth Century will be remembered
chiefly, not as an age of political conflicts and
technical inventions, but as an age in which human
society dared to think of the health of the whole
human race as a practical objective.'

Arnold Toynbee

The making and delivery of vaccines is just one facet of
the challenge facing those who would immunize the
world's children from diseases that kill. By now this has
been developed to a fine art, for any child receiving a
protective shot is the inheritor of a medical legacy
established nearly two hundred years ago, on 14 May
1796, when an eight-year-old boy was inoculated against
smallpox by Edward Jenner. Since then millions of
children have been – and in ever increasing numbers will
be – protected against some of the worst infections. That
this is possible at all is because of basic research, applied
technology, commercial manufacturing and operational
know-how.

To get a vaccine to the heart of the African bush, ready
to be drawn into a hypodermic syringe and plunged into
a baby's arm, calls for great feats both of scientific
creation and managerial competence. From theoretical
possibility in a scientist's mind to commercial manufacture and distribution, the costs rapidly escalate. Many

stages follow each other: each must be paid for; each depends on efficient organization. The first laboratory phase triggers a series of clinical trials which, if successful and given government approval, lead to commercial development that in turn leads to the production of millions of sterile doses to be shipped across the globe. Stored in central warehouses in strategic locations, these are then transported through rough country until they reach that remote spot where the mother and child are waiting. Throughout the entire journey from manufacturer to child a 'cold chain' must be maintained, for most vaccines will spoil if heated. If they do and this is spotted, the consignment will be thrown away. If not spotted, they will be administered but will not provide immunity.

Contemporary vaccine research has dual roots, in history and the imaginations of scientists. Compared with earlier periods, research in the past twenty years has resulted in a veritable explosion of knowledge, and future historians may wonder why it took so long for this to occur. But vaccination is just one more example of technologies which have worked splendidly for years without anyone understanding why. For aeons the Egyptian priests accurately predicted the flooding of the Nile and eclipses of the moon, knowing nothing of the forces at work. For generations tide tables were written out – and still are – without resort to Newton's mathematical formulae that describe the moon's gravitational pull on the oceans. So too with vaccination: Edward Jenner's discovery that the dead skin of a cow infected with cowpox provided protection against smallpox led to most effective vaccination programmes, even though understanding of what was happening in the body was decades away. Only in the last decade or so have scientists begun to understand the deadly minuet between infectious agents and defending immune cells and so been able to direct research towards tailor-made vaccines, whose blueprints are derived from a detailed knowledge of the molecular structure of infectious agents.

Surprisingly, during the two hundred years that separate our children from Jenner's, only a dozen or so vaccines for humans have been widely applied. The first rabies vaccine was developed by Louis Pasteur, one hundred years after smallpox; those of diphtheria and tetanus followed closely. There was then another gap of over forty years until vaccines against yellow fever and influenza were produced during 1935 and 1945. This slow progress resulted not so much from ignorance of how the immune system works, as from ignorance of the causes of disease. But in the decades since Jenner, scientists did acquire an absolutely essential knowledge of infectious agents.

The earliest ones discovered were bacterial; of these the leprosy bacillus was the very first to be linked to a human disease, by G. Armand Hansen in 1874. Yet a vaccine was not to be created until the 1980s, and still cannot yet be widely applied. Since leprosy is a slowly developing disease it will be many years before the results of present clinical trials in humans are known. A spate of discoveries followed Hansen's, and in the roll-call of the famous two names constantly recur: Louis Pasteur, who discovered the bacilli that cause anthrax, and pneumonia; and Robert Koch, who identified the bacilli of typhoid and tuberculosis, and the streptococcus of throat infections.

The bastion of viruses began to fall at the turn of our century. Viruses causing foot and mouth disease, myxomatosis, cattle plague, sheep pox and fowl pest were quickly discovered, to be followed in 1903 by that of rabies. In 1907 the virus responsible for dengue fever was unmasked, and then came Landsteiner's landmark discovery of the poliomyelitis virus. By 1911 we knew the virus of measles and one that caused cancer in chicks.

Finally, the animal parasites – malaria, sleeping sickness and bilharzia – were revealed and suddenly it was clear why the world was a highly dangerous place.

But the principle behind successful vaccination had already been established by Jenner. Not only does the body defend itself against infection, but because a memory of the attack persists, so, too, does the means for defence. And though there is still a great deal to be learnt, it is evident that 'deception' is the key principle in both infectious disease and protection against it. All infectious agents try to evade the immune system and do so in a variety of ways: some viruses go straight into the nerves, where they are hidden from the patrolling white blood cells (lymphocytes); many parasites keep changing their coats so that the sentinel lymphocytes become exhausted by constantly reacting to new disguises; others again, like the measles virus and the malaria parasite, directly suppress the immune mechanisms; others act in all three ways. Most lethally of all, some such as the AIDS virus actually invade and kill the defending immune cells.

Vaccination, too, is a deceiver, for it hoodwinks the immune system into believing that it is facing a full-scale infection when it is not. Ideally all the defence mechanisms are mobilized just as efficiently as if the full infective challenge had to be met, but without any of the hazards or even the symptoms of disease. The principle of immunological defence is simple and is incorporated into our newest, tailor-made vaccines. If the body is not overwhelmed, counter-attacks are mounted, first through antibodies – very large protein molecules – that quickly latch on to those of the specific invader. Next populations of special lymphocytes are called up which either simply eat foreign invaders or kill by squirting poisons into them.

Between recognition of the invader and counter-attack is a period which may be several days or weeks; recovery from infectious attack depends crucially upon the quality of this counter-attack and the speed with which it is mounted. But if all goes well an immunological memory is left – a memory of the encounter which, when that same agent invades again, evokes the capacity to reproduce the neutralizing antibodies and lymphocytes. The memory comes in the form of a small standing army of cells (B and T lymphocytes) which, when later challenged, rapidly produce platoons of the appropriate cellular defenders. When the vaccine 'takes', the immunity conferred may equal – sometimes surpass – that acquired by the disease itself. Indeed in some cases, as with tetanus, though the disease does not confer immunity, the vaccine does. Even if immunity conferred is only partial so regular booster shots are necessary, again as with tetanus, the possibility of becoming infected is reduced, as is the severity of the disease if later contracted.

The perfect vaccine would have many properties. It would be cheap, less than $1 a shot; would give long-lasting immunity with one dose; be so good that the infection could not be passed to another person; be stable at tropical temperatures; could be administered by primary health workers using cheap and disposable devices that did not require sterilization; would be effective from birth or soon afterwards; would have no side-effects; could be simultaneously administered with other vaccines; would be so pure that no unwanted immunological reactions were produced; would produce a visible scar so that it would be easy to check that the children, indeed an entire population, had all been protected.

The perfect vaccine does not, and may never, exist. But those presently used in the global immunization campaigns are very effective, and prime the immune system in one of four ways. Firstly, virtually identical but perfectly innocuous natural infectious agents can be injected: the live cowpox virus *vaccinia*, for example, was

similar enough to the smallpox virus to provoke a
defence but not the disease. Or one can inject the live
virus itself but in a form so weakened, by having been
passed through several cell cultures, that its virulence is
reduced. Sufficient immune-provoking properties are
retained but none of the dangerous ones. Measles and
Sabin's oral polio vaccine come in this form. Thirdly, the
killed infective agent itself can be injected, as in
whooping cough and the Salk polio vaccines. This is
something of a tightrope, for the vaccine must still be
sufficiently molecularly active to provoke the immune
system, but dead enough not to provoke the disease. Two
further problems arise with dead preparations: first,
extraneous virus materials may provoke unpleasant
side-effects; second, since the injected dead virus cannot
multiply inside a host, as can live vaccine viruses, it takes
more than one dose to evoke a full immune response.
This is also true of vaccines such as tetanus and
diphtheria that are made to stimulate in a fourth way,
from toxins – poisonous substances. Obtained from the
infecting bacteria, these stimulate the body to produce
antitoxins, thus rendering future infections harmless.

Another reason for the two hundred years' gap
between Jenner's first vaccine and our current ones
concerns the commercial process. Enormous quantities
of the infectious agent are needed, and until quite
recently these could only be produced by infecting vast
numbers of laboratory animals. Thus there was much
rejoicing when, in the 1930s, Ross Harrison and Alexis
Carrell developed cell-culture techniques, whereby
embryonic cells could be maintained in the laboratory for
generations. And there was even more rejoicing in 1949
when, in Boston, Enders, Weller and Robbins observed a
strain of polio virus attacking embryonic tissue and
proceeded to grow volumes of the virus in human cells.
Once it was possible to reproduce in a culture dish, or in
large vats, the conditions that viruses and bacteria meet

in the body, the way to commercial manufacture of vaccines was open.

Reproducing the right conditions for bacterial growth is sometimes quite easy. Provided that bacteria are placed in a warm broth stuffed full of nutrients, the process is often straightforward. Many, however, such as the leprosy bacilli, are very fussy: we must still use armadillos – the only animals other than humans to catch leprosy – as the 'factory'. Viruses are even more demanding since they will only grow inside a living cell, so the manufacturer must first grow quantities of the cells that the virus likes and hope the virus will then live in them. In the case of *vaccinia* virus, the skin cells of calves are the host; for measles virus, chick embryo cells or human fibroblasts, the precursors of muscle cells, do the trick; and monkey kidney cells provide the best environment for polio viruses.

Easy or difficult, growing volumes of the infectious agents under carefully controlled conditions is the first step in vaccine manufacture. Much has been written about contemporary monuments of science, whether great linear accelerators in lengthy tunnels under the ground, or exquisitely designed radio telescopes. Comparable monuments of vaccine technology are Merck & Co Inc's plant at West Point, Pennsylvania, or that of the Institut Mérieux in Lyon, France, both large vaccine manufacturing sites. Both are at the forefront of the technology, both foster the production of many unique vaccines. West Point was the pioneering plant for the brilliantly successful vaccine against hepatitis B and liver cancer, as well as that for measles, mumps and German measles. Mérieux's successes include vaccines against rabies, meningitis and the latest dead polio vaccine. Other major suppliers of vaccines for the global programmes, Smith Kline and Beckman in Belgium, Connaught Laboratories in Canada, and Sclavo of Italy, have similar capacities. All their plants are models of applied scientific ingenuity, whose managements take hideously expensive commercial gambles – so much so that, given the spate of lawsuits in the USA when side-effects from vaccination occur, one after another the pharmaceutical companies have dropped out of vaccine development until now only a few remain.

The procedures they follow are, in principle, identical, and so rigid are the safety standards that one may not enter certain areas without a combination of precautions, vaccinations and even medical tests. Their technicians will have been immunized initially, but to ensure that effective protection persists, their blood is tested every six months for antibodies to whatever vaccines are being manufactured. Precautions to ensure sterility are equally scrupulous; a technician merely packing up a culture medium will be completely covered from head to toe in a yashmak with just a slit to see through. The rooms are kept at low temperature to reduce the chance of microbial activity; the packaging of even a culture medium takes place under elaborate, and extremely expensive, laminar flow hoods, each as large as a small garage, in rooms with one-way negative air pressure, so that air can leak out but not in.

Other technicians wash and sterilize any equipment that is not disposable. Dirty apparatus rolls in at one end for a good, old-fashioned scrubbing, then is swept around on a chain of trolleys into the autoclave for sterilization. At the Merck complex an inspector spends a full day every few months by this autoclave and at frequent intervals checks that the temperature and pressure are correct. Another widely used check involves a strip of spores from a particularly hardy bacterium, *Bacillus sterothermophilus*. Regularly this is attached to equipment going through the autoclave and afterwards it is cultured. If live bacteria are found on the strip, the sterilization process is not working properly.

Manufacturing areas at Merck are linked to the vaccine

laboratories by sparkling clean corridors, easy to wash, with high rubber skirtings on each side that prevent trolleys scraping into the walls. In the vaccine laboratories, which no visitor may enter, the walls are covered with another special easily cleaned finish. The tour through most vaccine plants is like a walk through a deep-sea aquarium with everything viewed through double-glazed glass windows. Such quality control services are vital, for vaccines are injected into healthy people. While some inevitable adverse side-effects are acceptable when a drug is given to a sick patient, risks must be minimal during immunization. Thus every single compound, no matter how complicated or how simple, is carefully screened so that no harmful impurities remain.

The first step in making, say, a virus vaccine like measles or polio involves making the culture medium in which can grow the living cells which will be host to the virus. Starting with the raw materials, which themselves have been scrupulously screened, over four hundred different kinds of culture media can be created whose variations reflect the demands of these cells. In large, sterile areas where everybody wears gowns, hair-nets and gloves, the ingredients are mixed – in a small flask if a pilot batch is needed for an experiment, or in 10,000-litre containers for full-scale production. When ready, each culture medium undergoes at least three tests: one to make certain that cells are happy to grow in it, another to guarantee its sterility, a third to confirm its composition. Then the medium is poured into flat, rectangular-shaped bottles, in just sufficient quantity to cover the base, ready to go to the vaccine laboratories.

Two further phases in the making of a virus vaccine now follow: growing the host cells in the culture medium, and adding the virus that will hijack those cells to make more virus. At Merck each phase takes place in its own special room which, along with its equipment, is colour-coded – green for cell culture, yellow for virus culture. Both are surrounded by a cold area.

Cultures of animal cells are grown in the green room. Frozen in liquid nitrogen, stored in two separate depots just in case a disaster destroys one, enough stocks of these cultures exist for the same host cell lines to be used for the next forty years. Consistency is essential. Many of these lines are by now very old, the ancestral cells originating from human or primate tissues first used many years back. Living off the medium, cells from one single ampoule will, in six weeks, have formed enough daughter cells to cover the base of 400 flat bottles, stacked on top of each other in a room maintained at optimum temperature and humidity for maximum growth. Then in the yellow rooms, a virus culture is taken out of its deep-freeze and a small amount is inoculated into every single flask. The virus quickly penetrates the culture cells and soon they become factories whose output is limited only by space considerations. A flat surface of cells offers only so much 'production area'.

The Institut Mérieux has devised a fascinating technique to circumvent this problem and enhance virus production. In their virus culture room, instead of flat, stacking bottles, there are large vats each holding one thousand billion plastic VERO 'micro-carriers' each no bigger than a dust particle, to which the host cells can attach. Once introduced to the vat, the virus penetrates these cells, and when all the cells are all virus, production ceases.

Whichever method is used, the next step in making the vaccine consists of harvesting the virus from the remnants of the cells. These are spun in a centrifuge, then fractionated, and that fraction containing the virus is isolated. Purification comes next, to eliminate any cellular fragments or other impurities which, if allowed to remain, might provoke nasty side-effects when injected. If a dead virus vaccine is being manufactured, substances are now added to kill the virus. Aluminium hydroxide, or antibiotics, may also be put in for sterility or to kill any other living organism that may – though this is highly unlikely – have contaminated the process. Other chemicals may be added as adjuvants, substances that enhance the immune response. Indeed sometimes other vaccines may be added to serve the same function. In the case of leprosy vaccine small amounts of live BCG – tuberculin bacillus – act as a stimulator of the immune system.

The production of just one vaccine may take a whole year, nearly six months of which will be taken up with testing for purity, safety and potency, and in the US, testing by the Food and Drug Administration. Once cleared, however, the final stages of production are fully automated and move extremely rapidly. The amounts put into every ampoule are carefully calibrated and random vials tested for quality. Then, boxed and packaged by individual packers, the millions of doses are ready to be stored or shipped.

From the 1930s, when laboratory cell culture became possible, to the present day, the twin processes of vaccine research and commercial refinement have continued. By the 1950s, preventive immunization for the six childhood diseases was rapidly taking hold in affluent societies, yet it took a further thirty years before this was extensively applied in the rest of the world. Why did it take so long?

There are several reasons, and none was scientific. Of course, the necessary vaccines were always available to the affluent minority. Rahima Banu and her sisters may not have received any sort of immunization until 1975, but children of wealthy Bangladeshis, living in Dhaka, were immunized years before.

Poverty, therefore, was one main reason – and not only of individuals but of governments too. Another was the glamour of high-tech medicine and the hospitals that go with it, which carried for the leaders of newly independent nations a glamour and status similar to that of, say, a nuclear power station or a motorway from the airport. Into the perpetually greedy maws of all three vast quantities of money were poured – mostly aid – in a disproportionate amount of the country's total budget. Health allocations for primary care have generally always been meagre, for those running the economy have seen their people's essentially curative health needs as the first priority and have shown massive indifference to the requirements of the rural population. Even now only 20 per cent of people in poorer countries have access to trained medical care.

If by the early 1990s the situation is rapidly changing, this has little to do with technology but a great deal to do with social change. Throughout the past thirty years, various trends have set in: the agencies of the United Nations such as the World Health Organization (WHO) and United Nations Children's Fund (UNICEF), and donor agencies such as the World Bank, or the United States Agency for International Development (USAID), have slowly begun to place the health of populations on their agenda in a manner foreseen by Arnold Toynbee. Such trends form a strong element in the unfolding story of the Planned Miracle.

Yet there was one medical event which did have a significant impact – the measles outbreak in the village of Keneba, in the Gambia, part of a major epidemic that swept West Africa during the late 1950s that became the starting point of a series of vaccine trials in West Africa. By 1963 measles vaccines were in full commercial production and many American paediatricians planned field trials. Sir Ian MacGregor took part in the crucial planning discussions. Soon the trials began, on a small scale at first. Then in 1966, the Center for Disease Control (CDC) in Atlanta, Georgia – the major epidemiological and public health centre in the USA that analyses all national, and many international, epidemics – mounted a major campaign throughout West Africa to eradicate smallpox, if possible, and control measles certainly. An American team went into the Gambia to run the campaign, using the facilities of the Medical Research Council's Field Station, and so successful were they that both diseases were virtually eliminated from the country.

There was no way, of course, that the Gambia, or any country in West Africa, could sustain such coverage after the foreigners left. As immunization levels quickly dropped, measles returned and child deaths rose in parallel. So, as MacGregor said: 'There was a fair old hue and cry. For you mustn't just walk in, immunize a population, and walk out again' – a view that many were later to reinforce with intense passion. The local governments could not be faulted for they had no money to continue the work, and at that time it was the policy of the US government not to undertake permanent campaigns abroad.

The CDC programme in West Africa did leave, however, one magnificent legacy. The programme's director was an energetic American, Dr Donald A. Henderson, whose flair and skills were quickly recognized. So in 1965, while still immersed in the planning minutiae of this vast operation – management, supplies, recruitment, diplomatic negotiations – he was told to drop everything and go to Geneva. He had been seconded to the World Health Organization and would direct the global campaign for the eradication of smallpox. Under his brilliant leadership, smallpox was driven from one country after another until ten years later, on 16 November 1975, two of his people were converging on Rahima Banu – and this is where our story began.

In the eleven years during which they were in direct contact with the children, giving vaccination over and over again, those in Donald Henderson's teams from WHO reflected: how sad it was that they were not armed with other vaccines, so that the children could have been protected against other diseases at the same time. As a result, in 1974, WHO began an Expanded Programme on Immunization to protect children in the developing world.

3
The Storm Before the Calm

'Charity is never a lasting solution.
At best it alleviates; at worst it subjugates.'

Halfdan Mahler,
Address to the World Health Assembly, 7 May 1985

The World Health Organization (WHO) was founded in 1948, just one among a number of specialist agencies established by the newly formed United Nations after the Second World War. Based in Geneva, WHO is governed, as is the UN itself, by the various member states through appointed delegates, who meet in May every year at the World Health Assembly to discuss general policy. Such policy will have been proposed by the Executive Board – a group of health specialists elected for a three-year term – and the Director-General, elected by the Delegates for a renewable five-year term. He (so far there has not been a she) heads the permanent Secretariat – a staff running into thousands, of many different nationalities. Most of these are based in Geneva; the rest operate from regional offices established on the main continents. Once centralized and centrally controlled, they have in the last decade been given greater independence.

The Regional Officers nominated by their countries, generally through the local Ministries of Health, have been likened to feudal barons, and are quite capable of frustrating the Director-General – and often do – when headquarters' aims are not in tune with local politics. In 1987 Dr Halfdan Mahler, then Director-General, who had granted the devolution of power – an act he now openly admits was a major tactical mistake – would admonish his General Assembly of Delegates in these terms: 'Decentralization, rather than being accepted as delegation of responsibility for the work of WHO and accountability for the use of collective resources, is all too often regarded as a blank cheque for pocket money.' So what was meant to be a sharing of responsibility and accountability, a granting of local autonomy that would lead to greater flexibility, has resulted in the establishment of jealous fiefdoms, whose activities are almost wholly politicized and whose effective operations are correspondingly diluted.

Politicization is not, of course, unique to WHO. Political constraints inevitably determine the actions of every UN agency. The self-preserving properties of all bureaucracies, when added to the political self-interest of UN member governments, lead to considerable operational deficiencies. Flexibility has never been a hallmark of any UN agency, and this can show up in rigid, often ideological plans for tackling the world's problems. In addition, political considerations are manifest in all appointments, whether to positions at headquarters – even that of the Director-General – or those in the field. 'Our turn next' is a national principle that often overrides considerations of professional competence. Another source of contention is the pressure applied by those countries footing most of the bills – until recently the United States. Born out of politics, these agencies operate through politics. Each has its own strengths and weaknesses, each its own successes and failures.

In spite of this WHO has chalked up various signal achievements, and one major success: the eradication of smallpox. But one major failure, that of the malaria campaigns, was so spectacular that the consequences have had a profound and lasting impact on the philosophies of both WHO and the donor agencies. Malaria was WHO's Waterloo; recriminations reverberate even forty years on. Both subtly and obviously the defeat affected not only attitudes within the various divisions of the agency but also the directions and force of their global immunization initiatives, and this has a direct bearing on our present saga. One further, unexpected, consequence was a titanic row between WHO and UNICEF – of such proportions that the infant, Planned Miracle, was nearly torn apart at birth. To understand precisely why, one must reflect a little on history.

When WHO was founded after the Second World War, with a Canadian psychiatrist, Brock Chisholm, as its first Director-General and a mandate 'to achieve the highest possible level of health', its activities reflected a medical philosophy widely prevalent at the time – cure diseases rather than prevent them. If this meant bringing patients to hospitals and doctors, that, for the most part, is what member countries set out to do. Although in the developing world the financial burdens of this approach were major while the benefits to the rural populations minor, there were certain curative initiatives which did make a dramatic impact on the health of the poor. In the 1950s, for example, WHO in collaboration with other organizations such as UNICEF and the Rockefeller Foundation mounted a major attack against yaws. This disease, whose bacillus causes suppurating sores and is transmitted by contact with open wounds, was rampant in Southeast Asia. Sixty-five million people in the Malay Archipelago lived in yaws-infected areas. But the bacillus can be obliterated by penicillin. In Indonesia alone, through a massive campaign lasting two years and costing $1.2 million provided by UNICEF, ten million cases were cured – and not in the five years originally allowed, but in three. The two crucial elements for success were present: a new, cheap and popular drug, which could be easily administered by locally trained health auxiliaries. This success had a major influence on those working in international health care, and other, essentially curative, campaigns followed – against tuberculosis, leprosy and trachoma. But since these diseases are far more complex than yaws, the results were nothing like so spectacular.

Then during the Second World War came the advent of DDT, a substance that apparently was as miraculous for malaria as penicillin had been for yaws. By killing the mosquitoes it broke the chain of parasite transmission and the disease could be eradicated with a single-strategy, vertical campaign, or so it seemed. Traditionally malaria control was based on a multi-faceted, horizontal attack, involving drugs, mosquito nets and draining stagnant pools where the larvae breed. But suddenly this remarkable chemical appeared, and with major spraying of houses and swamps a dramatic drop in malaria occurred in places like Sardinia, southern Italy and Iran.

As a result, in 1955, the World Health Assembly voted for their first major worldwide campaign: to eradicate malaria. Given DDT, all that was required was to mobilize resources, political will and effective management into global spraying. There were a few, lone, dissenting voices, but they were considered obscurantist cranks. Sir Ian MacGregor, who had taken part in brilliantly successful malaria control programmes in Palestine, argued that the existing tools were woefully inadequate for Africa. So certain was he, that when in 1965 WHO actually mounted the global campaign, the Gambia was one of the few governments not to become involved, for MacGregor had convinced them that it could not possibly succeed. Nor did it, on the African continent.

Later analyses revealed several contributing elements to the failure, many of which came down to a grossly simplistic assessment of the epidemiological and bio-logical problems. DDT sprayed on the inside of people's huts certainly killed those mosquitoes that sucked human blood and then rested on the walls. But in West Africa the most dangerous species of mosquito fly into the huts, bite, and then fly straight out again. They could not be controlled even immediately near the settlements; the surrounding land could no more be blanketed with insecticides than could the pools of brackish water on the tracks, or the mile upon mile of mangrove swamps which provide an ideal breeding ground. Moreover, the mosquitoes quickly developed resistance to DDT, though most experts believe this did not come from its medical use, but from agricultural over-use. Then, to crown it all, the malarial parasite itself became resistant to existing anti-malarial drugs.

So although by 1964 WHO reported that 683 million people were now living in areas completely, or nearly, free from malaria, and that two million lives a year, mostly children, were being saved, it was clear that the campaign was stalling. A sharp ceiling was now placed on the escalating costs, and by 1970 most agencies had phased out malaria control as a separate programme. All that was left was a dangerous vacuum. Worse, the early successes with DDT had lulled people into a dangerous state of euphoria: laboratories had been closed, entire research programmes dismantled, and governments ceased to pay for traditional control methods. As Sir Ian MacGregor ruefully remarked: 'Malariologists, not malaria, were eradicated.' Only in a few countries, such as Malaysia and Thailand, was old-fashioned control sustained. The consequences were catastrophic. To give but one example: in India the incidence of malaria had plummeted during the campaigns. When, several years later, the disease reappeared but old control methods had long since vanished, the population was totally unprotected and people died by the thousands. The full complexities presented by malaria were only appreciated at a time when there was no one left to investigate them.

Of the several lessons that were learnt from the malaria fiasco, three came to predominate. First, present research is neglected at future peril. Second, if vertical programmes are not sustained by being based in a firm primary health infrastructure all they achieve is a vacuum, one that may prove fatal. Third, it is folly to raise hopes about eradication unless these are realistic. Even to control a disease needs eternal vigilance. But where eradication is the aim, people fall prey to a seductive will-o'-the-wisp: some day the disease will vanish. If it then doesn't, they become disillusioned and apathetic. No one escaped the traumatic failure of malaria, whether WHO, the donor agencies, local governments and, of course, those who succumbed to the disease.

So when, in 1974, WHO formally established an Expanded Programme on Immunization (EPI), vertical, single-strategy campaigns were emphatically ruled out, in spite of the fact that the agency was in the throes of one such, smallpox. But smallpox was to be the very rare exception. Indeed many within WHO had opposed it initially and still remained sceptical, but could take comfort from the fact that it was not an exclusive WHO operation. Directed and staffed by people only on temporary secondment, to a division that was itself only temporary, the smallpox programme – the 'parachute in then come straight out' exercise, as someone described it – would not either in style or format be the model for EPI. WHO's Director, Dr Halfdan Mahler, was adamant. At a Washington cocktail party he encountered Dr Ciro de Quadros, a smallpox veteran who was to play an equally distinguished role in this present story. Spotting the emblem in de Quadros's lapel, the badge made from a bifurcated needle and given to all who took part in the smallpox campaign, Mahler observed: 'Ah, you're one of those, I see. Let me tell you, there will never be anything like that again in WHO.'

Thus the programme to protect children in the developing countries against measles, polio, diphtheria, tuberculosis, pertussis (whooping cough) and tetanus was begun only after considerable heart-searching. For in many respects it too was a vertical programme, a fact which made its leader, Dr Ralph Henderson, initially most reluctant to take it on. Henderson was a highly motivated perfectionist, who had been one of D.A. Henderson's two deputies (though no relation) in the smallpox campaign. At the beginning, he was the programme's only full-time medical officer and ran the operation with a secretary and a few part-time staff. They held seminars in many countries to encourage governments to provide immunization. But it soon became clear that far more had to be done, for at that level of action nothing effective would ever be achieved. In April 1977, therefore, EPI was the subject of World Health Day, the annual public airing of one of WHO's programmes. By 1990, so the World Health Assembly of 1977 decided, childhood illnesses and deaths would be greatly reduced by vaccination. The wording of the declaration was devised with great care; it always is. No one mentioned universal coverage, for few expected that immunizing *all* the world's children would be possible, and in any case, catching the last few might cost more than it was worth.

Shortly afterwards the programme gained an increased budget, a full-time staff of twelve, and a target. The aims of the staff were realistic; they hoped to achieve a level of immunization high enough to stop transmission of disease but did not expect to achieve globally the almost blanket coverage that exists in rich countries like the United States. In truth, their real objective was as much managerial as medical. They wanted to create delivery systems that would not only provide children with proven immunization but ensure that as new

vaccines became available they, too, could be given. This
ambition presupposed the existence of a solid infrastructure of total primary health care within which many
other aspects of health would similarly be covered.
Where this did not exist, they would not immunize. They
would put equal efforts into other health initiatives for
rural areas, otherwise immunization would eventually
collapse. Immunization did, however, have particular
merits: as it is specific, simple and cheap, failures are
easily documented – an outbreak of polio quickly shows
something amiss. Another attractive feature was that
immunization programmes demand effort at all levels,
from the centre to the periphery, from policy decisions
taken in the capital city to manpower skills that, along
with the vaccines, must be applied in the rural
settlements.

Thus the EPI strategy called for a slow start, a gradual
acceleration and, possibly, a final dash towards 1990.
Unlike smallpox eradication there would be no dramatic
and massive efforts over a short period of months.
Moreover member governments would be required to
make a permanent commitment towards a health care
infrastructure, since without this WHO's efforts would be
a complete waste of time and money. Even with all these
caveats, Dr Ralph Henderson insisted on a small, slowly
moving, step-by-step programme. In fact, Finland once
offered a substantial sum of money to EPI which
Henderson refused; he would accept neither extra funds
nor responsibility beyond that built into his carefully
defined programme. Unlike D.A. Henderson before
him, he was not prepared to go high, wide and handsome
and fervently proclaim that a target date of 1990 could be
reached.

If WHO embraced immunization only cautiously this
was in part because of a dramatic shift in their
philosophy, one due above all to Dr Halfdan Mahler. In
May 1973, in the middle of the smallpox era and one year

before EPI was established, he was appointed Director-General and was to play a major role in this story.

Halfdan Mahler may insist that his Christian name means only 'half a Dane', but he is larger than life. The son of a preacher, brought up in a fundamentalist, Baptist faith, a fact to which he often refers as a 'permanent burden of puritanism', he is a rangy, sinewy person with the face of an aesthete. Though he will sometimes preface his remarks with 'in my humble opinion', he is a man of strong convictions and passionate idealism who speaks vehemently and often abrasively. Reflective and thoughtful, with a burning regard for the white-hot truth, he is as critical of himself as he is of the collective failings of the human race. No one would describe him as the quintessential man of action – indeed his managerial talents have been one source of criticism during his term – but over a decade he was the fount of idealism within WHO, totally committed to a philosophy of 'Health For All' by the year 2000 – where 'all' meant everyone. Nothing was to be allowed to undermine that vision. However, Mahler is not inflexible; he is a man who more than most is capable of learning, and once he has sorted out the difficulties of a particular project, whether bureaucratic or personal, his commitment and support are formidable.

As a physician who took postgraduate training in public health, Mahler specialized in tuberculosis, a disease that was a worldwide scourge before the discovery of antibiotics. He knows all about mass campaigns, and why he dislikes them. In 1950 and 1951 he was an enthusiastic, energetic planning officer for a tuberculosis campaign in Ecuador. With fellow members of the Danish Red Cross he rode on horseback through the mountains taking vaccines to the settlements. Then at the end of 1951 he joined WHO and was posted to India where he worked for ten years as senior officer attached to the national tuberculosis programme. From 1962 until

July 1988 he was based at WHO headquarters in
Geneva. So he knows whereof he speaks, for unlike most
people there, he spent years in the field getting his feet
dirty, experiencing the intractable problems at first hand.
In contrast to the bureaucrats, feudal barons and
important visiting dignitaries who happily roll up
Avenue Appia, Geneva, in black limousines, Mahler has
no pretensions or delusions. One day we were talking
together in his magnificent office on the seventh floor of
WHO headquarters in Geneva. From the window a
panoramic view takes in Lake Geneva with its famous
three-hundred-foot fountain and the Alps beyond. He
turned to me and with a sweep of the hand that ranged
over the luxury carpet, the telephones, the soft
armchairs, the coffee cups and the view said, 'It's too easy
to be taken in by all of this. So many people who work
here, and who visit here, believe that this is the reality.
But the reality is thousands of miles away in the small,
poor settlements around the world.'

Coming as he does from a missionary family, it is
inevitable that Mahler should feel deeply about his
responsibilities to help the advance of human beings both
economically and socially. And gradually he evolved
from holding an authoritarian, paternalistic, curative
approach to Third World medicine, to one of community
health care that started from a standpoint of empathy
with people and their cultures. Absolutely dedicated to
this goal, he can get very emotional about it. Initially,
however, he was a captive, not only of his emotions but of
the bureaucracy under him, the Board above, and his
Regional Directors and the Delegates from member
nations. These Ministers of Health represent the only
political force WHO has, but while they may be powerful
at WHO, traditionally their position within the governments back home is weak. Caught between these
pressures, Mahler occasionally erupted, for once his
mind is made up it is difficult to move him. So far as the

Expanded Programme on Immunization was concerned his heart and his mind were driving him forcibly towards providing not this so much as a truly comprehensive primary medical care for the poor. He believed that concentration on one element alone, whether immunization or population planning, would compromise that goal.

As a result of Mahler's drive and convictions, and after much discussion, conflict and angst, WHO took a fresh direction and in the mid-seventies shifted from a philosophy of curative health care to an essentially preventive one. A situation where, as in Kenya, one hospital alone (the Kenyatta Hospital, Nairobi) consumed 70 per cent of the country's total health budget, was wickedly lopsided. If global populations were to be healthy then medical systems worldwide had to change; their direction should not be decided by physicians at the top, but from communities at the base; the action should come not from professional specialists in Geneva so much as from trained individuals in the villages. Basic health care should be an integral part of all rural development programmes, be made accessible by means that were acceptable to ordinary men and women, entail a community's full participation, and be priced at a cost they and their country could afford.

This philosophy received the collective imprimatur in 1978, at an international conference on primary health care sponsored by WHO and UNICEF. From Alma Ata, the capital city of Kirghizstan in the eastern Soviet Union, at the very top of the world, the famous Alma Ata Declaration was issued: health for all by the year 2000 would be attained through primary health care in a programme whose aspects ranged from improved water supplies and sanitation, to immunization and a variety of social indicators such as literacy and income. Basically, Alma Ata was a declaration about equity, about reducing the disparity between rich and poor, one reflected in their diseases and life expectancy, about health as a fundamental human right, about the first level of contact between people, communities and national health systems.

Delegates from 134 governments and 67 UN organizations attended. Staff members from both WHO and UNICEF wrote working papers. In a speech at the opening ceremony Mahler asked eight questions of his audience, all prefixed with 'Are you ready' . . . 'to reduce the gap between the health haves and the health have-nots . . . to ensure proper planning and implementation of primary health care . . .' etc.

They said they were. But they were not,

For some Alma Ata became a personal crusade, so much so that those who advocated other approaches were condemned as heretics. For others Alma Ata was an impractical, impossible dream. For within the very comprehensiveness of primary health care lay one essential weakness: governments which embraced its concepts wondered just where to begin, for each indicator called for different measures, had different costs and different effectiveness. In fact, many argued that health for all by the year 2000 could not be distinguished from development for all – a complex, expensive and inevitably slow process – and the world was in any case going into recession. Differences were soon to arise over the strategy to be adopted, a timetable that was realistic – over twenty years at least, even over the definition of health for all. Therefore some countries and some agencies wanted to be selective, first identifying those aspects which were immediately possible and devising low-cost strategies to pick off certain health targets systematically, one by one. Mahler strongly disapproved of this vertical approach. But since it was one that, within a few years, UNICEF was to embrace, the seeds of conflict were sown.

By the time this story began, both WHO and UNICEF

had each had only three Director Generals: WHO's were Brock Chisholm, a Canadian psychiatrist; Marcolino Candan, a public health malariologist; Halfdan Mahler, a Danish tuberculosis expert. All UNICEF's Executive Directors have been American: Maurice Pate, a businessman; Henry Richardson Labouisse, a lawyer and civil servant; James Grant, a lawyer and internationalist.

But in contrast to WHO, UNICEF, being largely a field organization, has a highly decentralized structure. Unlike virtually all other UN agencies real power does not reside at the centre, for only 17 per cent of the UNICEF staff are in the headquarters in New York, or in offices in Geneva and Copenhagen. The rest are out in the field. The local representative on the spot is neither a national of the country in which UNICEF is working, nor appointed by that country, and is directly responsible only to UNICEF's Executive Director in New York. Thus local and regional directors can respond quickly as they see fit to changing imperatives and circumstances. One consequence is that what UNICEF terms 'the country programme approach' – where problems are tackled in ways that accord with a country's culture – is both the start and the endpoint of all their initiatives.

Not only is flexibility built into the very heart of UNICEF's system, but in many respects the agency has a far easier time than WHO. Who can resist children? Certainly not Danny Kaye, Peter Ustinov, Liv Ullman and Audrey Hepburn, all of whom have been associated with UNICEF's causes. But besides the compassion that children evoke, UNICEF has another advantage – that of obvious personal caring. A high proportion of Quakers were in the agency from the very beginning, and, as Brian Urquhart, once Deputy Secretary-General of the United Nations, pointed out, Quaker concern has been a major factor leading to greater internationalism over the last three centuries. Many of UNICEF's staff have come in through voluntary service organizations, or the

American Peace Corps, or, as did its Associate Director, Dr Richard Jolly, through pacifism. Some staff members in developing countries joined through UNICEF local protest movements, or from a deep concern with human affairs. All share the common cause of care – a theme emphasized by the national committees of the thirty-six countries who raise funds for the agency.

Since a large proportion – nearly 20 per cent – of UNICEF's funds come from voluntary contributions, UNICEF can disburse these without political pressure from governments. But this also means that they must attract and respond to the public more than WHO does and they have brilliantly cultivated the art of attracting attention. WHO's reports are mostly scientific and extremely technical; UNICEF's annual publication, *The State of the World's Children*, more popular and appealing, and their approach on behalf of children always generates warm human responses. UNICEF is also less bureaucratic, its staff smaller than that of WHO, and it doesn't have so much money. Most people think this is an advantage. If WHO receives $10 million that must be spent on authorized programmes, projects must be developed that demand fast expenditure and rapid importation of materials and people. One likely outcome is that everyone – whether non-governmental organizations, or exporters in the West, or ministries and bureaucracies in the recipient countries – tries to get in on the act. On the other hand UNICEF's grants to any one country rarely exceed $3 million – the average is about $1 million – so the local people have to lend their support, too. UNICEF's strategy is to admit that new, innovative programmes involve risk and uncertainty, but in helping to start them, UNICEF will take the risk and bear the uncertainty. Only later will the country concerned have to underwrite the further finances for the programmes.

There is a real irony in the fact that disagreements were to erupt between WHO and UNICEF because in so many respects their two directors, Halfdan Mahler and James Grant, are so alike. Unique on the global health scene, both are highly articulate and dynamic, idealists and visionaries, both essentially moral people and strong leaders, with a commitment to their mission that inspires others. Neither is afraid to rock the boat, to make radical suggestions, to seize opportunities that seem revolutionary to their colleagues.

However, by contrast with Mahler, Grant is the quintessential man of action, the greatest implementer on the health scene. 'Flying uncle to every needy child' is how one newspaper described him. Other people are nothing like so polite, for he, and UNICEF, have the reputation for exploiting the public relations approach to the limit, skimming off the cream of media attention. Though he has been everywhere, and seen human suffering at its very worst, Grant's key characteristics remain optimism and a total absence of cynicism. Like Mahler he believes fervently in commitment: individuals *can* make a difference and everyone *should* be challenged to make that difference. That he is a man with a mission is not surprising, for both his grandfather and father were medical missionaries in China, where he was born. His grandfather established China's first teaching hospital; his father was on the staff of the Peking Union Medical College established by the Rockefeller Foundation in 1910. Possibly the most influential thing his father ever did for Jim was to take the boy on tours of the rural villages while he was not yet a teenager. Though his father was a pioneer in primary health care, helping to establish health posts in the countryside with simple laboratories and a few trained health workers – the original barefoot doctors – Grant was not encouraged to take up medicine. This may seem surprising, but he senses that his father may have seen further even than his grandfather for he convinced Jim that the fundamental

causes of rural health problems were not so much
medical as economic and social – in a word, poverty.
Mahler would totally agree. Grant quickly saw that the
traditional, Western approach to development was both
academic and authoritarian, specifying in theory what
people ought to do in practice. But, again like Mahler, he
came to believe that actions people take on behalf of their
own health are as valuable as any taken by doctors.

So, putting himself through Harvard by taking up a
Coca-Cola franchise, Jim Grant studied economics and
law. Then, after the Second World War, he returned to
China with the United Nations Relief Agency, just before
the Communists took over. He has worked in development all his life: in USAID; as Director of the Overseas
Development Council in Washington; and as President of
the Society for International Development for three
years, before becoming Director of UNICEF in 1980 – by
which time UNICEF, too, had been going for thirty
years.

Grant truly sells UNICEF's programmes. The techniques of marketing which he learned while handling the
franchise at Harvard he now applies to social ends rather
than profit. Marketing means motivation, and once this is
aroused, a demand is created. Social marketing using all
the techniques of social mobilization is also intended to
create a demand – in this case for health interventions,
including immunization.

Like Mahler, Grant, too, was to change the focus and
direction of his agency's activities. Though in UNICEF's
founding resolution a general clause about child health
was inserted – because these services were most sought
after by parents and families – nevertheless the agency's
detailed focus had changed from time to time. In the
1950s UNICEF had been concerned with the starving
and missing children of Europe. The 1960s saw a shift
towards influencing countries to take account of
children's needs; the 1970s to providing basic services,

such as improvements in water supply and education. Grant became Executive Director in 1980, at the start of a period of world recession and severe economic crisis. The oil cartel had been a major factor whereby the external debts of the poorer countries rose to the present point, where much of their national income is used to service liabilities. The recession became deeply entrenched, and momentum towards a more just and workable world economy was lacking. Since there was little hope of any significant increase in the resources necessary for social progress during the remaining years of the decade, children were therefore bound to suffer badly.

Thus, seeking to direct UNICEF towards constructive actions, Grant's guiding question became, 'How can human progress be maintained in the absence of increased economic resources?' So far as health was concerned, he saw only one answer for both the developed and the developing world: prevention. Choosing not to smoke, drinking alcohol only in moderation, avoiding obesity and taking regular exercise would be appropriate measures for richer nations. But for the developing world, there were some very basic needs still to be met; for example, two-thirds of all children under five had no access to clean water. So UNICEF began emphasizing low-cost, eminently practical, immediately effective programmes – simple remedies like oral rehydration salts for diarrhoeal diseases, breast-feeding rather than powdered milk, and immunization against vaccine-preventable disease. Seeking to apply these throughout the world, they launched 'The Children's Revolution', a campaign that, they claimed, by 1990, would save the lives of up to seven million children a year, protect the health and growth of millions more, and, as an added bonus, slow down the world's population growth.

The strategy that was being formulated in the autumn of 1982 was expressed in the acronym GOBI, whose

four elements were: Growth monitoring, Oral rehydration, Breast feeding, Immunization. All were cheap
and, through the spread of education, communications
and social organization, possible in practical terms to
implement. The plan dropped on WHO like a
bombshell.

Grant wasted no time. He wrote to his old friend,
Robert McNamara, asking him to help raise money for
the Children's Revolution. He knew his request would be
received sympathetically, for while he was President of
the World Bank McNamara had extended its interests
way beyond financing grandiose schemes, to combating
poverty. Whereas earlier World Bank reports had rarely
mentioned health, McNamara, who became President on
1 April 1968, took health and poverty as his main entry
point to the developing world and used the platform the
presidency provided to speak on both constantly. This
was in part a response to criticisms that the Bank had
been ignoring poverty's very existence, criticisms similar
to those now levelled over the environment. But in
addition, McNamara was deeply affected by the
deprivation he had personally seen on his many trips
around the world and the fact that by the next
millennium 600 million would be trapped in absolute
poverty.

McNamara told Grant that of course he would help,
but why did UNICEF not start with something
measurable? Then they could assess progress, evaluate
successes, and keep a beady eye on the bureaucrats who
were running – or not running – the show, with a
quantitative measure of what they claimed to be
achieving. He suggested that instead of concentrating
simultaneously on the four-faceted programme,
UNICEF should focus first on immunization.

McNamara had been influenced in this direction by
conversations with another friend, Dr Jonas Salk, creator
of the first successful vaccine against poliomyelitis. While

on a long trip to Egypt Salk had thought a great deal about protecting the world's children. There was, he could see, an urgent need. He and McNamara were aware of WHO's Expanded Programme on Immunization but, along with many others, they believed that it was moving nowhere near fast enough for the children. Though the programme was excellent in quality, over several years only about 10–15 per cent of susceptible children in the world had been immunized. Salk also believed that new developments on a killed polio virus vaccine now provided a rich opportunity to conquer polio globally, one that was being passed up.

Salk and McNamara discussed the matter many times and concluded that for a very small expenditure – $3–5 per child – some 150 million children per year in the developing world could be saved. This represented a large gain for a very modest outlay, modest because the technology was cheap and available. All that was needed was, firstly, to mobilize technical assistance and some portion of the financial costs, and secondly, to generate political will in leaders of the developing countries to undertake programmes. Moreover, if they could tap the competency and support already available in WHO, UNICEF, the United Nations Development Programme and the World Bank, both the political will and financial and technical assistance could be generated. McNamara was approaching the problem from the standpoint of one wanting to attack poverty directly; Salk from the position of a lifetime spent in immunology. Both passionately believed that over-population was one of the two greatest dangers in the world – nuclear war being the other – and that, paradoxical as it might sound, saving children's lives would be one of the best mechanisms for preventing too many births. For if parents saw their children survive, could conceive both a future for their family and a personal security in old age, there would not be the same pressures to have so many children in order to guarantee that some would live.

They began to talk to interested parties, such as A.W.
Clausen, the new President of the World Bank; they
learnt of various private initiatives, such as the group
from the Netherlands who were immunizing children in
Senegal. In the light of the snail-like progress of WHO to
date, they declared that unless positive and rapid action
was forthcoming they would, in a project called FAIR,
with the support of famous figures like Indira Gandhi,
mobilize private initiatives worldwide and ensure that the
job was done, and without the agencies if need be. But
shortly thereafter McNamara received Grant's letter and
discussed UNICEF's ideas with Salk. On the afternoon of
23 May 1983, both men had an appointment to meet Jim
Grant at UNICEF headquarters in New York and discuss
plans. The actors were beginning to assemble on stage.

However, that morning Jonas Salk first went to the
Rockefeller Foundation, an organization that ever since
it was founded in 1913, has played a seminal role in
global health. Salk was to meet Dr Kenneth Warren, the
dynamic Director of the Division of Health Sciences who,
with massive funds to disburse, played a highly
influential role on the global health scene. Like Mahler
and Grant, Warren is a man of overpowering energy and
enthusiasm, another idealist and visionary, who, also like
them, attracts admirers and enemies in equal proportions. Warren will not admit that something cannot be
done, and his obvious impatience with passive mediocri-
ties and his sense of urgency are deeply rooted. A
diagnosis of the deadly skin cancer, melanoma, usually
carries a death sentence, as Warren well knew when he
received it in the 1970s. Today, at sixty, he glows with
vitality and health. In addition, he was, he once confessed
to me, amongst those people who seriously doubted that
smallpox could be eradicated, but he was happier than
most to acknowledge how wrong he had been when
people of energy and vision achieved the impossible.
This triumph influenced Warren profoundly: he

determined that his criteria in funding health initiatives should be not the safe route of certainty of success, but the more hazardous one of possible failure. He would seek out people who combined professional skills with vision and enthusiasm even in the face of others' scepticism. Warren, too, was to play a major role in the Planned Miracle.

Salk recognized a convergence of interest between others and Warren. As aware as UNICEF of the declining resources available for health, the Rockefeller Foundation had embraced the idea of selective strategies to reduce childhood diseases, with priority given to those approaches that would bring about the greatest effect for the smallest cost. So Salk invited Warren to join the meeting at UNICEF that afternoon.

The discussions took place in Jim Grant's office overlooking the East River. Some of Grant's staff were also present. McNamara suggested that they should convene a major meeting at Bellagio, Italy, where the Rockefeller Foundation maintains a conference centre in the Villa Serbelloni. Representatives from the unilateral and bilateral agencies would be invited to devise strategies that would assure immunization of all newborn children in the developing countries. A small working group should meet in October 1983 to plan the conference. One objective would be to influence WHO to develop priorities within primary health care; a second to accelerate the pace of their immunization programme with a series of major global campaigns. As he was speaking the door opened and an aide interrupted. A telex had just come over the wires of Mahler's annual speech to the General Assembly of the World Health Organization, delivered in Geneva earlier that day. This speech came to be known as Mahler's 'parachute–red herring speech'. When Grant read it aloud he, and the others, were stunned.

While warning WHO's delegates not to allow the

primary health care movement to degenerate into 'a mere facade constructed by the Secretariat, or a gigantic exercise in bureaucracy' – a wise and timely warning indeed – Mahler also told them to beware of red herrings offered by other agencies. He did not mince his words; there were neither diplomatic niceties nor bland euphemisms.

I am all for impatience if it leads to better and speedier action along collectively agreed lines. But I am all against it if it imposes fragmented action from above. I am referring to such initiatives as the selection by people outside the developing countries of a few isolated elements of primary health care for implementation in these countries; or the parachuting of foreign agents into these countries to immunize them from above; or the concentration on only one aspect of diarrhoeal disease control without thought for the others. Initiatives such as these are red herrings that can only divert us from the track that will lead us to our goal. They belong to the distant past of international meddling with national health affairs that I mentioned at the beginning of this address. Such meddling failed then and it will fail now. Indeed, it was partly a reaction to the ultimate ineffectiveness of such action in relation to its cost that the very concept of primary health care was developed. Without building up health infrastructures based on primary health care, valuable energy will only be wasted, and you will be deflected from your path. I have no doubts whatsoever about the good intentions of these would-be benefactors and this makes it all the more difficult to reject their overtures. But I am afraid that is what we have to do – and more, we must try to channel their energies along agreed lines of action.

And reject their overtures they would. If there were to be a meeting at Bellagio to plan a major global immunization campaign, it seemed unlikely that WHO would be represented; if there were to be any influencing, it should be WHO influencing UNICEF rather than the other way round.

As Mahler himself ruefully admits, on this issue he has been variously cast in the role of spoil-sport, obscurantist, *the* major obstacle standing in the way of a great humanitarian initiative. This is grossly unfair, and it is important to understand the source of his reservations. To start with, at that time he was under considerable pressure from four different directions – from his Board, his bureaucracy, his critics and his emotions. Then there was UNICEF apparently ready to tackle an urgent situation with WHO seeming to drag its feet. Equally there were genuine issues of territorial imperatives. Health was the *raison d'être* of WHO; they alone of all the United Nations agencies had the health mandate. Many of Mahler's staff now felt threatened. For years they had, somewhat patronizingly, regarded their counterparts at UNICEF as hewers of wood and drawers of water, while they provided the brains, the expertise and the vision. But when Jim Grant imported into UNICEF a bunch of very bright and capable people, a major challenge was unexpectedly mounted to WHO, who watched a portion of its territory being annexed by a professionally competent and energetic elite.

Over and above all the pressures he was experiencing as Director-General, Mahler was remembering his personal experiences in Ecuador, when he and his colleagues passed through the countryside with cures for tuberculosis and then vanished, just as the measles control teams in the Gambia had done thirty years before. When Mahler returned to Ecuador two years later it was as if they had never been there. He echoed Sir Ian MacGregor who, recalling the hue and cry that followed when the teams left, had said, 'You can't go in and vaccinate a population and then just walk out and leave them.' To make any genuine impact programmes had to be sustained, but how could they be without a primary health care infrastructure in place?

Equally, as Director-General of WHO he was remembering the agency's biggest failure, malaria eradication – the massive vertical campaign that failed in part because the long-term control measures, based firmly in the community, were allowed to lapse in the face of a promise of quick success.

But whatever was going on in Mahler's mind, the group in Grant's room had to decide how publicly to react – if at all – and what practically to do. Some of Grant's staff were all for going it alone. McNamara and Salk were certainly still prepared to mobilize political leaders and galvanize the private sector if the agencies failed to act quickly. But Ken Warren was worried. While understanding both Mahler's position and Grant's intentions, Warren knew it was vital that the agencies co-ordinated their activities, for it would be disastrous for the credibility of future global health initiatives if WHO was left behind or ignored. In any case UNICEF would be concerned with global immunization for a relatively short period. Once the principle of universal childhood immunization had been put into practice, Jim Grant would be seeking new priorities and fresh objectives for children. But WHO was in health for ever.

While equally appreciating the value of Grant's high-profile, dramatic approach, Warren also knew that Mahler too was right. If vaccination programmes were to be sustained they had to be integrated into a permanent primary health care system. But to many people WHO did not appear to have a viable strategy for immunization. UNICEF certainly did: through Grant, UNICEF was superb at communication and mobilization, generating publicity which had enormous political impact. Grant would galvanize presidents, prime ministers, even the Pope – as later he was to do – to the extent that priests giving confession would ask parents if their children had been immunized. Such paths were closed to Mahler. But the dissension between the two agencies, that now threatened to deepen even further, was dangerous. Some way had to be found to co-ordinate what UNICEF planned to do with WHO's methodical, step-by-step approach that built immunization into primary health care.

Thus Warren argued for caution and dialogue. His views prevailed, and Robert McNamara agreed to fly to Geneva to try to persuade Mahler to come to the preliminary planning meeting at least.

During his first hours in Geneva McNamara was engaged in 'one hell of an argument' with Mahler's staff. Finally Mahler arrived and the mutual affection and deep respect that already existed between the two men worked its magic. Though Mahler was prepared to concede that immunization might be a way of breaking into the vicious circles of poverty and over-population, again and again he argued forcibly that such vertical programmes could drain away support – in terms of both finance and manpower – from the task of developing primary health care infrastructures, thus proving only a temporary substitute for a more comprehensive attack on the health problems of the poor. Still he agreed to talk further: he would come to the pre-conference meeting that autumn.

Why, many people have asked, given his unrelenting opposition to the strategies proposed by UNICEF, did Mahler agree to do so? Why indeed would he later support them in part? In one sense he was on weak ground, for like it or not WHO already had a vertical programme in operation – albeit a small one – the Expanded Programme on Immunization – that had received the blessing of the WHO General Assembly of Delegates some five years before. So how could Mahler disown UNICEF's immunization programme without disowning WHO's? In addition, if Grant felt obliged to extend UNICEF's hand of friendship, Mahler felt obliged to take it, or risk WHO being frozen out from what the world would regard as a great humanitarian initiative.

4

The Birth of the Planned Miracle

God: 'I'll just r'ar back an' pass a miracle. Even bein'
Gawd ain't a bed of roses.'

Marc Connelly, *The Green Pastures*

On 24 October 1983, a group of people met in the
Mahogany Room of the Harvard Club in New York City.
From the walls of this famous institution, conveniently
sited on 44th Street just west of Fifth Avenue, the
portraits of past presidents and distinguished alumni
seemed to gaze benignly down at the influential
gathering. The distinction of those present certainly
matched that of any comparable meeting in that famous
location, for the company included Dr Halfdan Mahler,
Mr James Grant, Dr Kenneth Warren, Dr Jonas Salk,
The Honorable Robert S. McNamara, Dr William Foege,
Director of the Center for Disease Control, Atlanta, who
had played a seminal role in the eradication of smallpox,
and Dr Philippe Stoeckel, physical scientist and epidemiologist, one of the most influential people in France in
the field of preventive medicine, with extensive
experience of vaccination programmes in Africa.

The group's visions were cosmic. They had come
together that day to see whether it would be possible to
co-operate on a major international initiative to protect,
by 1990, all the world's children through immunization, a

63

task both humanitarian and daunting. For in 1983 the number of children under five in the world ran into hundreds of millions and was increasing by over eighty million newborn each year. By 1987 that rate of increase would have risen to eighty-five million and most would suffer, many die, from preventable diseases. Whereas in the developed countries immunization coverage was satisfactory, in some countries only 7 per cent of children under five were receiving any vaccination at all. So this task was, Jonas Salk insisted, a moral commitment.

Many discussions had preceded this meeting. McNamara had spent time with Sir Gustav (Gus) Nossal, a famous immunologist and Director of the Walter and Eliza Hall Institute of Medical Research in Australia. He believed the research aspects of such a vaccination programme should be guided by a Technical Advisory Committee which Nossal should head. Ken Warren had exchanged long letters with D.A. Henderson of smallpox fame who, drawing on his unique experience, uttered several words of caution. If there were to be an initiative he was not convinced that merely augmenting the resources of WHO or UNICEF would be the best way to proceed. Though he had an immense respect for both agencies, and knew that world health would be better served if both were stronger, they were, inevitably, both creatures of member governments and thus politically constrained in what they could achieve. Moreover, both experienced difficult management problems that impeded their ability to foster national programmes: WHO's limitations came from an unwieldy bureaucracy, especially in its regional offices, while UNICEF's highly decentralized structure meant that it relied very heavily on outside technical assistance to implement its programmes.

So Henderson recommended one of two approaches: establish either a major consortium to do the job, or a wholly independent enterprise that would collaborate closely with both agencies and provide complementary technical assistance and material support. However, a consortium would itself be unwieldy and equally susceptible to bureaucratic deficiencies and temptations. So he recommended setting up an independent foundation, directed by someone who understood the limitations of both agencies but who was able to work with their officials. It had, he wrote, been just the same with the smallpox campaign, which would not have succeeded without strong backing from entities outside WHO, such as CDC and USAID.

The group had first met the previous evening at Jim Grant's house, when Gus Nossal, too, had been present. He could not stay on for the next day's discussions. In spite of the conviviality induced by a fine dinner in a smart Manhattan apartment, there were strong undercurrents of tension. Mahler was edgy, even testy, it is recalled, but those present knew that he and WHO had been forced into a corner – given, though not explicitly, an ultimatum. The particular group of actors who had now taken centre stage for the child survival problems had made it clear that while they hoped WHO would join in, if it didn't, private organizations and UNICEF would proceed without it. Consequently Warren, for one, was not surprised at the eruption that occurred: it was an inevitable catharsis, he says. An argument developed between Mahler, the missionary humanitarian, and Nossal, the scientific researcher, one of such intensity – fists banging on the table to emphasize points, views reiterated with passion – that Philippe Stoeckel, sitting at the end of the table near them both, wished he could crawl under and hide. For Mahler, hitting at the core of Nossal's work, was saying forcefully, even brutally, that he didn't see the value of spending vast sums on molecular biology and vaccine research; at this time the money could be put to better use, with better results for global health, by delivering basic health care.

Things had calmed down considerably by the next
morning, when Jim Grant opened the proceedings at the
Harvard Club. Diplomatically, he reminded everyone
about primary health care and the landmark decision
taken at Alma Ata, then set UNICEF's immunization
initiatives within its framework. But in order to achieve
an immediate and dramatic reduction in child mortality,
three factors were now essential: advocacy to foster
political will; more dollars and more flexible funding
particularly from 'laggard' countries such as the USA,
France, Germany and Japan; research into vaccines;
improved delivery. Initially he would like to see major,
nation-by-nation immunization programmes organized,
that would later be consolidated by adding other
important technologies, such as growth monitoring and
oral rehydration. An executive body, led by the
sponsoring organizations – WHO, UNICEF and the
World Bank – and a Secretariat headed by a senior
experienced person, would significantly strengthen their
combined efforts.

McNamara, vastly relieved that everyone was at least
sitting down in the same room, felt that this was the way
to proceed. All the main donor agencies should, he
insisted, pledge long-term support to countries willing to
develop major immunization programmes. Salk observed
that if dramatic results were to occur in countries where
UNICEF had already planned campaigns, such as
Colombia and Senegal, the initiatives would sell
themselves. Both men made a prediction: as these
evolved, from immunization, through oral rehydration
into all components of primary health care, and children
survived, the campaigns would become a major influence
in population control.

The first practical step was to call a major conference.
They decided to hold this in Bellagio, Italy, on 12–16
March 1984. No more than thirty-nine people would
attend. In addition to those now present at the Harvard

Club, others to be invited would include D.A. Henderson; A.W. Clausen, the President of the World Bank; representatives of nine bilateral agencies from America, Canada, France, Germany, the United Kingdom, Holland, Japan, Australia and the Nordic countries; several foundation representatives; one delegate from the European Community's Commission for Development in Brussels; and representatives from three countries who were about to start national immunization programmes. Grant and McNamara would divide up the invitation list and make personal telephone calls to all. Kenneth Warren, Ralph Henderson of WHO and Stephen Joseph of UNICEF would draft a letter to sponsors who might fund the meeting – USAID and the Rockefeller Foundation; Gus Nossal would prepare a paper on biotechnology and new vaccines, Bill Foege on the management strategies necessary, and Donald Henderson on the value of childhood immunization as an impetus to primary health care.

A second task was to find an Executive Director for the proposed Secretariat. This needed to be a truly outstanding person who had the confidence of all parties. With Mahler taking the lead a consensus developed that Bill Foege would be ideal for the job – a recognized giant from smallpox eradication days, he knew the problems only too well. Foege, a giant indeed at six foot five, is a most gentle man of great integrity and mischievous humour, who combines professionalism with compassion. Above all he had the vision to see and act beyond the interminably detailed discussions of management, scientific research and international co-operation; other factors in the human equation meant that everyone working for the campaigns might run hard but still remain in the same place. As he would later warn, the dual thrusts of immunization and family planning were essential and simultaneous components of primary health care. While to some this might seem too cold-blooded an approach, it was Foege who never allowed anyone to forget that the initiative *had* to succeed, because 'Behind every one of our failures lies a human face.'

In a closing address Grant told the group they were on the crest of a great wave, with a movement that would make an overwhelming impact on childhood illnesses and deaths. If successful, the effects would ripple outwards and influence many other elements essential for the well-being of the developing world, from population to agriculture and economics.

Five months later, they were all together again in the Villa Serbelloni for the first Bellagio Conference – just. WHO had nearly withdrawn. USAID, whose Administrator, M. Peter McPherson, was to attend the conference, had already committed millions of dollars to oral rehydration therapies – as their main thrust in global health – and he wanted at least half the time devoted to strategies against diarrhoeal diseases. One Trojan horse, one vertical programme – immunization – was difficult enough for Mahler to absorb; two intolerable. It took all Ken Warren's efforts to get McPherson's demands reduced to a one-hour paper and WHO back in place. This time he was not diplomatic so much as dogmatic, with emphatic ultimatums directed to Joshua Cohen, Mahler's deputy: 'You either don't come and we cancel the entire meeting or you come.' They came.

For three days the delegates discussed, argued, resolved. They decided to establish an *ad hoc* Task Force for Child Survival, which Bill Foege would head as joint consultant to both WHO and UNICEF. But the atmosphere throughout was cautious, and some agencies were downright sceptical, especially the potential donors. How could the financial targets possibly be achieved? McNamara had said, 'If the world could raise $100 million a year for immunization, we could really do something significant.' But they, and the health ministries, believed there was no way this kind of money could be found: the world economy was in deep recession; people in the aid agencies and governments were very cost conscious; this was a new activity and existing funds could not be diverted to it. Immunization should certainly be undertaken and perhaps they would help eventually but first they would reserve judgement while keeping a watching brief on the campaigns to see how they developed. Time alone would tell whether the overall plan could be institutionalized and the rhetorical objectives of UNICEF and WHO turned into real ones.

For Dr Ralph Henderson had been frank: WHO's Expanded Programme on Immunization could not possibly meet its 1990 goal. The obstacles to be faced were more subtle and intractable than those of technology or money: they embraced political will; lack of both trained people and effective delivery systems for an immunization protocol which required mothers and children to pay three visits to the health centres; the problem of side-effects of some vaccines; and the fact that in developing countries, as in developed ones, curing diseases still took priority over preventing them.

But Foege would grasp all these nettles. He had spent the previous six months working on *Strategies for Attaining the Goal*, a comprehensive survey in which he identified ten countries, from India to Brazil, that accounted for 55 per cent of all infant deaths in the world, as well as 70 per cent of deaths attributable to vaccine-preventable diseases. It was in these ten countries that Foege recommended accelerated programmes. China was excluded because the Chinese were already active in immunization and would not be calling on any external resources.

Bill Foege returned to Atlanta with few illusions, however. As Director of the Task Force for Child

Survival he would need all his political courage and professional skills. The situation he faced was not promising. True, there were a number of favourable factors: Western societies were becoming more aware of the situation in developing countries; there was greater appreciation, both generally and from business leaders and bankers, that given the present economic troubles a deep recession in the poor countries could rebound to hurt the rich ones; organizations such as Rotary International were belying their 'fuddy-duddy' image of men holding nostalgic reunions, and were now identifying with global health problems such as polio and taking formidably effective action to help solve them. So the time was ripe for all those concerned with child survival and immunization to rethink their attitudes and begin co-operating.

Set against this, however, were several negative factors. Many people concerned with global immunization were showing deep frustration: the science and technology required to meet the 1990 target were clearly available and their effectiveness had been amply demonstrated in Western countries, so why was it so difficult to apply that same science and technology in the developing world? Thus Foege saw one of his first tasks to defuse this frustration by channelling the initiatives in ways that would reinforce everyone's efforts rather than frustrating them. However, inertia might remain a real hurdle, for there had actually been much reluctance to establish the Task Force, notwithstanding the consensus at the Harvard Club meeting and the Bellagio Conference. Neither UNICEF nor WHO were totally convinced of its necessity, and in spite of the evidence still believed that they could co-operate without help from a supernumerary organization. Such attitudes in part dictated the final nature of the Task Force: it would be strictly temporary, designed to co-ordinate efforts, get the job finished, then self-destruct.

A second problem factor was that the profound differences in strategic approach between UNICEF and WHO were already spilling over to the staffs, who had closed ranks around their respective Director-Generals. Unless matters were diplomatically handled, friction could intensify and then only lip-service would be paid to co-operation. This polarization was also a source of frustration to equally committed outsiders. They argued – as did Foege himself – that if primary health care was really to work in the way WHO believed it could, then the health agencies had to show that they were able to deliver immunization as UNICEF believed they would. Because if immunization couldn't be delivered it was unlikely that anything else from the total health care package could be delivered – whether oral rehydration therapy, family planning or pre-natal care.

Thirdly, the Task Force didn't have much money, since the scepticism of certain donor agencies was mirrored in their reluctance to put up the cash. This was especially true of the World Bank, which would be called on for most of the funding. The Bank sided with WHO: they disliked the whole notion of a Children's Revolution; they neither appreciated nor welcomed the setting of health priorities with implied vertical programmes, for almost all agencies were emphasizing horizontal ones. So finally it was the Rockefeller Foundation – one of the very few foundations whose key officers have significant discretionary grants – who alone gave seed money to get the Task Force underway. With their $35,000 Bill Foege rented offices and hired staff. In a year or so the World Bank, UNICEF, WHO and the United Nations Development Programme (UNDP) would all generously support the Task Force. Finally, President Jimmy Carter became involved.

Shortly after Carter lost the presidency to Ronald Reagan in 1980, he founded the Carter Center in Atlanta. Here a programme called Global 2000 was established which focused on health and agriculture in the developing world. Within two years Foege was invited to join. He resigned from the Center for Disease Control but remained as Director of the Task Force for Child Survival, as well as being Executive Director of both the Carter Center of Emory University and the Global 2000 Foundation. From a little suburban office in a central shopping centre in Atlanta, he and his staff moved into beautiful accommodation in the Carter Center.

This small group of people was to have an enormous impact on the programme without once becoming entangled in the strategic argument. Indeed, Foege believes that while the origins of the mutual angst had much to do with the earlier malaria failure, the intensity of feelings provoked had even more to do with frustration. In the days of smallpox, he recalled, it was only the people *not* involved who were arguing about why eradication couldn't happen and why it wasn't a good idea. Those doing the job were far too busy to argue. So though he suspected that in all manner of ways the strategic battles might rage to the very end, getting on with the job was what Bill Foege intended to do right now. And he would reapply some lessons from smallpox.

As we have seen, this campaign had succeeded brilliantly, and as someone who had played a central role in that success, Foege knew its elements well. Certainly one was the fact that, unlike the malaria parasite, the smallpox virus had no natural reservoir other than man to maintain a pool of infection. But, even more importantly, the people directing its eradication took three significant decisions. First, they would never congratulate themselves on any success but rather would analyse scrupulously any failure and take whatever compensating action necessary. Secondly, an effective communication network would be established, of newsletters and regular visits to the field by leaders from headquarters, so that all felt a vital part of the campaign and knew the state of progress. Thirdly, a major research component had been built into the campaign, though D.A. Henderson had to fight hard for this. As with malaria in 1955, so too with smallpox in 1966: when the World Health Assembly voted for their second global campaign they questioned why any research was needed – just as Mahler was now questioning Nossal. Since there were effective vaccines, so the argument went, all that was necessary was to mobilize resources, political will, effective management, etc. But Henderson had made a research component one condition for his taking on the job. Though a reluctant WHO gave him a mere $40,000, worldwide many laboratories and epidemiologists gave time and effort. As a result, within a few years the strains of smallpox vaccine were changed along with their production methods, and were being delivered with tools never used before, the bifurcated needle and the jet-gun. Most significantly, following fresh insights into the pattern of smallpox within populations as a result of research, the whole strategy of the eradication programme altered.

Foege was now equally adamant about the importance of research, and through the Task Force he applied all three measures used in the smallpox campaign – analysing failures, communications and vaccine research.

Though Foege had no executive authority – only the authority that comes from experience and reputation – and could neither urge UNICEF to hold back nor WHO to push on, he could, however, take a number of helpful practical steps. Three aims seemed to him to have high priority: two were achieved, the third turned out to be unrealistic. The first was to create a structure whereby it was mandatory for the leading groups to get together regularly. So every three months for the next five years, without exception, leading figures from WHO, UNICEF, the World Bank and the Rockefeller Foundation met in Atlanta, New York or Washington. Some, like Ken

Warren and Ralph Henderson, never missed a meeting.
As time went on others joined – from USAID, United
Nations Development Programme, the Canadian International Development Agency – and over the months
Foege's role as a moderator yielded results. Warren now
says that the most exciting single thing that happened to
him during all his years at the Rockefeller Foundation
was to attend these meetings and watch the major
agencies work together. Foege is, he insists, a true
professional and idealist, a very intelligent man who
knows exactly what he wants and, given the divisiveness
at the beginning, was able to obtain an extraordinary
degree of consensus. Yet all the time, Foege was careful
to confirm, by word and deed, that the Task Force was
merely a temporary channel whereby the official
organizations could co-operate.

On each occasion they would review the progress of
the preceding quarter. The issues discussed covered not
only the practical, logistic and research details of the
programmes, and what problems were arising and how
these might be solved, but how to handle the money now
pouring in. Over the years the Italian government would
give UNICEF more than $120 million for the pro-
grammes in sub-Saharan Africa; Rotary International
would ultimately provide nearly $230 million for global
polio vaccine, over twice their original target; Save the
Children Fund played an ever increasing role both in
fund-raising and in immunizing in the field. The
Canadian government, which initially gave $25 million
for immunizing within Commonwealth countries, was
soon providing massive funds, as was USAID – $184.5
million in 1987 alone – for child survival programmes.

Foege's second priority was communication. The Task
Force must be active in finding out what was going
wrong, and then help the agencies put it right. Jim Grant
suggested that they should issue a regular newsletter on
global progress. *World Immunization News* now appears

every two months, in French, English and Spanish. The Task Force was soon organizing all the major conferences, seminars and working groups on immunization; then providing personnel who would evaluate the successes of individual country campaigns by listening to all opinions and criticisms.

Next Foege organized a questionnaire to all field workers asking them to specify the main impediments to immunizing the children in their area. Hundreds of replies came in, and as the answers were analysed a whole series of issues appeared, for no one had been systematically looking at the area of applied research. The practical problems that, as a result, the Task Force now set the agencies to solve were many and varied: how to improve the cold chain; how to make more stable vaccines so that temperature was not so critical; how to develop non-reusable syringes so that the risk of AIDS transmission was reduced. This systematic analysis eventually developed into a whole new programme, Applied Vaccinology, which WHO finally adopted as an essential part of their EPI division in Geneva.

Existing resources were also examined and files developed listing experienced individuals who could be seconded to the programmes on short- or long-term contracts. For example, six consultants were quickly recruited to help WHO develop strategies in Botswana, the Congo and Madagascar.

At Bellagio I Foege identified ten countries where special initiatives seemed urgent, with special emphasis on India, Senegal and Colombia. So his third and final priority was to initiate campaigns there, in which the Task Force would play a major role. But though someone from the Task Force was seconded to the UNICEF campaign in Senegal, and though plans in all countries accelerated rapidly, the danger of becoming another independent agency, with its own bureaucracy and territorial imperatives, was deemed too great and the idea was dropped. Better for WHO and UNICEF to figure out how to channel technical and other assistance to the campaigns directly, and for the small and flexible Task Force to aid and abet them.

So Foege began his work for the Task Force, determined not to be trapped in the middle of the strategic argument but to try to co-ordinate UNICEF's intensive campaign approach with the methodical step-by-step approach of WHO. By the time the Bellagio meeting ended the division of labour between the two agencies had been established. To WHO would fall the task of programme planning, management and evaluation; they would develop teaching manuals, and train health staff at global, regional and national levels. They would also create and manage systems for information and surveillance to establish numbers immunized, be responsible for research and development of the cold chain equipment, as well as the technologies that would monitor the efficacy of the vaccines. They would develop and evaluate the tools for vaccine administration, whether hypodermics or jet guns, as well as the solar equipment for refrigeration. UNICEF would be responsible for raising money – for supplies, vaccines, cold chain equipment and Land Rovers, which they would purchase directly. They would also concentrate on communication projects to mobilize governments, health workers and the general public and in specific countries they would be the implementers by helping the Ministries of Health. Compared to the human problems the practical tasks were both solvable and expected, but nevertheless these presented formidable obstacles that had to be overcome at every stage of a vaccine's journey to a child.

This journey begins with an order to the manufacturer from UNICEF, the major purchaser for the campaigns. In 1983, the year before Bellagio I, UNICEF had already spent $5 million on vaccines for 35 million doses each of

DPT – the vaccine against diphtheria, pertussis and tetanus – 24 million doses of oral polio and 22 million doses of measles vaccine. The cost of delivering a full course to a single child is the price of a double gin and tonic, $5, of which $4.30 goes on wages, refrigerators, cold chain maintenance and transport. The cost of the vaccine is a mere 50 cents.

No manufacturer could make a commercial return at 50 cents a dose given that – to take the example of the hepatitis B vaccine now just beginning to be used in some EPI programmes – this had entailed fourteen years of development and over $80 million. Development costs of even greater magnitude will be incurred before malaria vaccines are ready to be added to the programme. The innovative companies that put up these sums will require a high commercial rate of return, yet the countries that most need the shots are the ones least able to pay.

The clues to the low price that UNICEF and the Task Force finally negotiated with the vaccine manufacturers lay in more than the fact that these were bulk purchases that were rapidly increasing. Certainly the orders were huge: by 1986 the agencies had paid $25 million for 468 million vaccine doses; by 1987, 600 million doses were purchased; by 1990 and beyond the projected doses are one billion per year, to remain at this level as a steady state of vaccine use is reached. But more to the point, the vaccines used in the global campaigns have been in widespread use for nearly two decades so their research and development costs have already been recovered. Moreover, since they were initially developed for industrial countries, where a permanent market and excess production capacity already exist, the costs of additional doses are minimal, even if these run into the millions. So all the Task Force wanted was agreements with manufacturers to sell the vaccines at the most favourable prices, even if they continued to charge the developed world the going market rate. Such agreements came very easily.

Cheap or not, the bulk purchases involved a large capital outlay for UNICEF, who also had to find money for the trucks and other transport and for refrigerators. So where did it come from? Basically from direct fund-raising from the general public, governments and agencies. In Central and South America the Pan American Health Organization (PAHO) set up a Revolving Fund, a centralized purchasing system to ensure the lowest prices. The countries of the region tap into this to purchase vaccines in bulk, or supplement those they manufacture at home. Some Asian countries – Thailand, the Philippines, Vietnam, China – manufacture certain of their vaccines and UNICEF gives them the rest. UNICEF also purchased, or registered as gifts, all vaccines for Africa.

Of those countries which supported the immunization campaigns, the United States, through the Agency for International Development (USAID), and Canada, through the Canadian International Development Agency (CIDA), head the league table, with massive donations to UNICEF or PAHO. Italy, an outstanding contributor for Africa, comes next. Private organizations help too, and here the work of Rotary International represents the pinnacle of initiative. They undertook to supply all the polio vaccine needed globally through fund-raising and a whole series of events like lunches, golf tournaments, barbecues, car boot sales and carol services at Christmas.

UNICEF and WHO are ultimately publicly accountable, so they are careful how they spend their money. Soliciting contracts with the best qualified, lowest-bidding vaccine manufacturers in Europe, Japan and North America, they buy from at least two firms to avoid a monopoly, pool their purchases and have various methods of protecting against production failures. The vaccines must meet specific quality-control requirements laid down by WHO, and there are several collaborating laboratories which are regularly called on to test their potency and sterility.

In some of the earliest campaigns vaccine supplies had to be garnered – or even appropriated – from a variety of sources, but now, provided sufficient lead time is given, the commercial manufacturers have no trouble in meeting the needs of the global programmes. A country's requirements are calculated well ahead of time and orders sent in advance for anything from nine to twenty-four months ahead. Then the appropriate plant procedures are opened up for a production run.

But the cold chain always presents a formidable obstacle of another kind, whose demands are inflexible and dominate all those involved in childhood immunization, especially since the journey of the vaccine from manufacturer to child may take at least a year. If purity rules the production process, temperature rules from now on. So important is this challenge that a special Cold Chain Division was set up as an integral part of WHO's EPI programme. Its staff keep a careful watch on all procedures and are constantly seeking ways to make the system foolproof. If a campaign has failed locally, or a major epidemic occurs after immunization, failure of the cold chain is always the first suspect. Thousands of hours have been spent devising checks and procedures to keep the chain intact.

Every step of the way from manufacturer to child, a monitor card accompanies the vaccine. Printed in five languages and five different colours, the card carries heat-sensitive indicators, activated by removing a tab. As the shipment leaves the factory, the tab is pulled off, showing three ovals labelled A, B and C, and a circle, D. If the consignment is ever exposed to temperatures above 10°C, a blue colour slowly spreads across the ovals. The higher the temperature the further the colour travels; at 20°C, all four letters will be blue within eleven days. This monitor card is known as 'the spy in the fridge', because the blue colour is permanent. The only way to keep the card from turning blue is to keep it cold; if the card is kept cold then the vaccine is kept cold also. Many warnings are sent down the system to reduce the risks of a break in the chain: notices on the fridge door: '<u>STOP</u> . . . Do you really need to open it?'; or a reminder to check the maximum temperature of the fridge each evening and its minimum overnight temperature each morning.

When the vaccine is first sent on its way details are filled in at the bottom of the card by the manufacturer: 'Vaccine supplied, 25 November 1984, oral polio'. Months later, when the shipment reaches a country's central store, a technician writes in the new date and place. When perhaps three months later the package arrives in a regional depot, again the date and place are written on the card. So as the vaccine travels down the chain, a full record of its journey and temperature history is there for all to see. By now if oval A is blue, polio vaccine must be tested before using. If both A and B are blue, polio vaccine must be tested and measles vaccine used within three months. If A, B and C are all blue, then both polio and measles vaccine must be tested before using, and DPT and BCG must be used within three months. Tetanus and diphtheria vaccine, however, can still be used. But if all four sections are blue then all vaccines must go back for testing.

Testing is a huge and complex operation, because the vaccine has to be kept cold all the way back to the laboratory that does the tests. In the case of bacterial vaccines testing can often be done in the overseas country, but viral vaccines must go right back to the beginning. The costs are then so high that testing is only cost-effective if a large amount of vaccine is involved – at least 2000 doses of polio vaccine and 200,000 doses for diphtheria and tetanus. Otherwise it is cheaper to throw the stuff away.

A shipment destined for a UNICEF campaign is taken by truck to an airport from a producer's shipping dock, and flown either direct to the country or via UNIPAC. This is a UNICEF depot in Copenhagen: the land and the building were donated by the Danish people as a free port. The area appears desolate but the warehouse is exquisite, the most beautiful architecturally designed storage place in the world.

The next stages follow an agreed procedure devised by the agencies and dictated by the demands of the cold chain. Vaccine is shipped on precise shipment days, never without prior and specific arrangement. A campaign director in a tropical country doesn't want to get home after work on a Friday night to find a telex announcing that a million doses of polio vaccine will arrive next day, for he can only deal with that shipment on the following Monday. While this might not matter in Europe, in Africa the temperature could be nearly 40°C and the vaccine ruined by the time it was picked up.

So there are several rules: prior telexes; no shipment to arrive on a Muslim or Christian weekend – that means no shipments for arrival on Fridays, Saturdays or Sundays; trans-shipment to be avoided wherever possible. Where trans-shipping is inevitable, reliable airports, airlines and personnel must be used. This is mandatory: vaccines are freight and freight always has low priority, so the consignment can easily be offloaded at some god-forsaken spot to sit round, deteriorating. Above all, someone must *always* be available to receive a consignment and get into the cold store as quickly as possible. So all documents for customs clearance are prepared well in advance.

Once cleared through customs, vaccines are quickly shifted to the central storage depot in a country's capital city, typically a large, cold room subject to the numerous problems that recur time after time, along every stage of the journey: power cuts; power fluctuations, which quickly destroy the cooling units; shortages of spare parts and skilled technicians; unreliable fuel supplies. The further along the cold chain the less likely are there to be electricity supplies. In a rural health centre there may be no electricity at all, so gas, kerosene or solar energy feed the equipment that keeps the vaccine cool.

Several hundred solar refrigerators are now in use in thirty different countries. WHO's Cold Chain Division established and maintained close contact with the British, French, Italian, American and Zairean manufacturers, helping them to develop systems suitable for immunization programmes. The companies are encouraged to compete with each other so that no firm has a monopoly. As a result prices have dropped dramatically over the years. Nevertheless solar refrigerators are twenty times the price of other refrigerators, and since they rely on sophisticated electronics there are serious difficulties in servicing them. When they do break down in rural outposts no one can repair them, even if the cause of the failure is known. So it is far cheaper simply to replace a solar panel than attempt to get it repaired. Despite this, solar refrigerators are invaluable – and cost-effective – in hot countries since their maintenance needs are few.

So, too, are the maintenance needs of another link in one particular section of the African cold chain – camels. In the Sahara it is now commonplace to see camels with a solar panel strapped across their saddles to keep cool the vaccine pack boxes strapped on either side. So remarkable is the sight that the oil giant British Petroleum (BP) features them in one of its TV commercials.

So while UNICEF concentrated on ordering, supplying and paying, WHO focused on the other half of the vast operation that takes the vaccine to the baby, assisting directly those health authorities in countries committed to expanding their programmes of immunization, by helping to build and strengthen the primary health care infrastructure with both staff and equipment. WHO's responsibilities covered the whole gamut from teaching and training to management and maintenance. They produce detailed booklets written in various languages which are handed out at training courses held all over the world; just like service manuals for cars, these specify schedules of tasks and checks for every procedure connected with immunization. 'Vaccines and When to Give Them', 'Preparing for an Immunization Session', 'How to Conduct an Outreach Immunization Session', 'How to Control Quality of Stocks', 'Syringes, Needles and Sterilization' and, of course, 'Manage the Cold Chain System', are just a few of the scintillating titles. There are so many procedures to master: how to calculate the quantity of vaccine needed during the next year; what to do when this runs out or when there is too much; what to do when the vaccine *has* become too warm; how to keep the stores, and how to keep records. For each procedure WHO has held a corresponding training course, and with so many countries now undertaking immunization, a multitude of people underpin this enormous support system. So many are there that when asked just how many, WHO's EPI staff couldn't begin to guess. Nor could they guess the number of those people they had trained, directly or indirectly, for in 1983 and 1984 they ran courses in Geneva and in a few selected countries for health personnel who would manage local programmes. These people then returned home and started courses in other areas, and by now thousands have been so trained.

Determining an optimum immunization schedule forced WHO into something of a compromise. Shots are best given at a time determined by two biomedical factors: the age at which the child's immune system is fully functioning, and the number of doses that must be given. A breastfed child is protected by its mother's antibodies for the first three months; thus if immunization is given too soon, they neutralize the protective agent – whether a dead virus or a chemical – and no immune reaction is mounted. Yet if immunization is delayed, the child is vulnerable to infections. The compromise time is the period when maternal antibodies are waning and a fully functioning immune system has not yet appeared.

The recommended schedule is at birth a BCG injection against tuberculosis just under the skin and the first polio vaccine – two or three drops on the tongue; at six weeks the first injection of DPT, against diphtheria, pertussis and tetanus, and the second oral polio; at ten weeks the second DPT jab and the third oral polio; at fourteen weeks the third DPT and fourth oral polio, and at nine months a measles shot into the arm. But this is an ideal only and presupposes five contacts with mother and child and conveniently sited, fixed health centres – conditions that certainly do not exist in Africa's rural heartland. So, if the 1990 target were to be met, the schedule would have to be modified to accommodate the realities of people's lives. If mobile travelling clinics could make at least three contacts then it would be BCG at birth, the first DPT and polio at three months, the second at six months, the third DPT, and polio and a measles shot, at nine months. In very difficult settings contacts might be only two, when the first two shots would be as before, but to the jabs given at six months would be added measles. In such circumstances a dead polio vaccine injection, rather than polio drops, is recommended.

WHO strongly emphasizes flexibility as a crucial part of management and maintenance. The three-man crews who deliver vaccines to remote areas in West Africa double up as immunizers and fridge mechanics. In Zimbabwe the Ministry of Health decided not to employ full-time repair technicians, because they would soon be lost to the private market. In tropical countries repairing air conditioners and fridges is a very valuable skill and though WHO doesn't teach people how to do this, the alert, ambitious technician will soon learn – and then leave. So the Ministry took thirty drivers and trained them as repair technicians with increased status. They continue to drive and to repair their vehicles, but one day a week also repair refrigerators.

Other technical developments initiated by WHO reveal the same imaginative flexibility. Under their aegis the British firm Prestige, manufacturers of pressure cookers, has made a small sterilizer for hypodermic syringes; a Danish company designed special single-dose syringes of sterilizable plastic. Whether people actually do sterilize their syringes is of course another matter, and their training, motivation and supervision is yet another management problem that worries WHO, one that has called for still more training courses. The dramatic spread of AIDS in African countries has made the development of safe jet injectors, or non-reusable or self-destruct syringes, even more urgent. In the simplest design, once the vaccine is drawn up and the injection given, the mechanism jams. Tugging breaks the hypodermic in pieces. But if human ingenuity is smart enough to invent something new, then human ingenuity will be smart enough to get round it. So the battle to ensure a thoroughly sterile, non-infectious delivery system is never ending.

Though the vast, interlocking operation assembled by WHO, UNICEF and the Task Force is as complicated as any underpinning military campaigns, this one stretches right around the globe. So complex is it that the WHO staff have their own variation on Murphy's Law. The original had concluded, 'If anything can go wrong, it will'; theirs is 'If anything can go wrong, it already has.'

But sometimes things go wonderfully right, and of all the anecdotes this one is most often recalled. In a small mountain village high in the Andes the children were waiting. But the pilot of the small plane bringing in vaccines radioed: fog had delayed his departure and he expected to arrive at dark and would need landing lights. So the older children ran round the village, knocking on all the doors. 'The pilot is bringing the vaccines,' they said. 'Come and be a torch.' Carrying kerosene-soaked sticks, the villagers lined up and the plane, flying along the line of human lights, landed safely on a grass strip. Thirty minutes later the peace of the mountain night was shattered by the furious cry of an outraged baby protesting vigorously as a hypodermic needle shot a dose of vaccine into its arm. Another child had been protected.

5

No Turning Back

'Every gun that is made, every warship launched,
every rocket fired, signifies in a final sense, a theft
from those who hunger and are not fed, those who
are cold and are not clothed. This world in arms is
not spending money alone. It is spending the sweat
of its labourers, the genius of its scientists, the hopes
of its children.

This is not a way of life at all in any true sense.
Under the cloud of war, it is humanity hanging on a
cross of iron.'

Dwight Eisenhower

The delegates to the Bellagio Conference were to come
together twice more before 1990, the year when it was
hoped universal childhood immunization would be
reached. They would meet first in October 1985 in
Cartagena, Colombia, and again in March 1988 at
Talloires in France. The main question at their first
conference had been: was universal immunization
realistic? At their second the delegates heard what
actually was being achieved as many people told of
successes in their own countries. There were many new
faces: the new President of the World Bank, A.W.
Clausen; some ministers from countries represented at
Bellagio I had been replaced while others from fresh
countries came for the first time – from China, Egypt,
Japan, Burkina Faso, Senegal, El Salvador.

President Betancur of Colombia was invited to give the opening address. This was not merely a gracious gesture towards the host country but an opportunity for delegates to hear about the huge success of Colombia's National Vaccination Crusade – one which would have a major influence on other campaigns being planned. In a massive mobilization of all sectors of society, from the Catholic Church to the media, a major drive to immunize the children had been mounted.

Country after country was scaling up. India – vitally important because of the numbers of children involved – had, the delegates learned, developed a national immunization plan as a memorial to the late Indira Gandhi and on her birthday, 19 November, that year would launch an intensive programme in 30 districts; by 1988, 250 districts would be covered; by 1990, it was claimed 450. Accelerated programmes had already started in Senegal, Burkina Faso, Nigeria; Turkey had a monumental effort in progress, trying to reach five million children in a three-month campaign to be later described as a model for a miracle.

Within the next eighteen months, nearly 40 more would undertake major EPI accelerations, from China to Mexico to Bangladesh. Their approaches would be widely diverse: some would adopt a UNICEF-style, hard-hitting countrywide campaign; others the WHO strategy, starting in one district and then radiating out, taking in more areas as the infrastructure expanded; others would adopt a combination of both approaches – high profile initial campaigns tied in solidly to the slow expansion of health infrastructures. Many African countries would face special difficulties, from stark poverty, the debt crisis, civil war, to thousands of refugees and no infrastructure as in Sudan, to enormous numbers of children as in Nigeria, or the total destruction of a country's spirit as in Uganda. All would eventually face AIDS.

Latin America was the most rapidly advancing region with regard to immunization – it had been the first area in the world to eradicate smallpox – and now the Pan American Health Organization (PAHO) declared that they would eradicate polio there, too, but use the control of polio as *the* motive force for improving the entire immunization programme in the region.

El Salvador had been a very special case. Here had been demonstrated the validity of UNICEF's famous axiom: 'Children are a peace zone', a notion long established in the agency but a truth which two years later would again be demonstrated in Lebanon. In a most remarkable effort, involving UNICEF, WHO, PAHO and the International Red Cross, nearly a quarter of a million children received three courses of immunization on three Sundays in 1985 (3 February, 3 March, 21 April) designated 'days of tranquillity', when the only shots fired were those into the behinds of small children. Jim Grant was quick to announce: 'This was the first time on record that a countrywide conflict gave way to a health intervention for saving the lives of thousands of children'; and appropriately it was Grant who captured the essence of El Salvador in a remarkable photograph. A nurse at a rural health post is giving vaccine to a small baby. The left-hand side of the picture is dominated by a tall, tough soldier in jungle fatigues, with rifle and bayonet. But he is using the bayonet to open a bottle of Coke that he will give to the exhausted nurse.

There were other pieces of welcome news: Foege reported a massive, and unexpected, increase in resources. Some were political. The single act of President Betancur in launching Colombia's campaign by immunizing a child on television provided one such. Many other political leaders, having seen him capture the attention of the world's press, were now taking an interest. Others were finally convinced that investing for the future first meant investing in their children.

Financial resources had also increased. During Bellagio I, the estimated costs of universal immunization were between $1 billion and $1.5 billion per year, of which $300–500 million would be required very quickly. Most had doubted that such support would be forthcoming. By Bellagio II, however, the money was pouring in: Rotary International, through their fund-raising PolioPlus programmes in member countries, had undertaken to provide $160 million for the elimination of polio from the world by the year 2005; by 1988 they would have raised nearly double the amount. The government of Italy promised $100 million to UNICEF for immunization programmes in the sub-Sahara; by 1988, they had provided $120 million. USAID now massively increased their financial grants, as did CIDA, both for the development of new tools for immunization and programmes to deliver the vaccines. The Inter-American Development Bank then gave PAHO $5.5 million for polio eradication in Central and South America and suddenly cash was no longer an obstacle. Success depended solely on the development of sound programmes in each country to use these resources to the best advantage by mobilizing sufficient managerial skills to deliver immunization effectively.

But the conference was not without worrying moments and Kenneth Warren, always sensitive to internecine strife, was concerned as to its likely outcome. The main agencies were certainly working together but UNICEF was getting all the publicity and most of the money. The Italians had specified that their considerable donations were not only to be channelled by UNICEF for sub-Saharan Africa, but were to be spent in eighteen months, mainly on Italian vaccines and other Italian materials such as solar power units. Such targeted donations threatened to break the spirit of co-operation between the agencies. A second problem was that one particular UNICEF representative, some way down the hierarchy from Jim Grant, was suffering from delusions of grandeur. Having money and clout, he was beginning to push people around and treating Foege like a lackey, which upset many people.

In addition, Warren knew that Mahler was still anxious. Certainly, he was not only being extremely co-operative but was trying to ensure that his people were too. For a start, on 19 July 1985, he had written to all his senior staff at WHO enclosing a memorandum that Jim Grant had sent to all *his* senior staff. Grant had written about the need to build a sustainable structure of immunization that would serve as the cutting edge for a wide range of primary health care actions – a policy Mahler emphasized that was in line with WHO's. He added: 'We obviously must do all we can to support our member states in reaching the target of universal immunization by 1990', and asked his staff to let him know as a matter of urgency how they intended to respond to that challenge.

But one week before Bellagio II, so powerful had been the current of UNICEF's actions to date, so successful the results of their publicity, that rumours were circulating and doubts being raised: did UNICEF think the Task Force redundant? Did they want to continue with it? Such rumours revived Mahler's worries. Were the immunization campaigns still being considered as an end in themselves, Mahler agonized, rather than the means to primary health care? Would the Task Force remain to hold the line? Because if they did not, the whole initiative might collapse. Warren pinned his own hopes on his personal suspicion that in the last analysis, everybody would realize they had much to lose if they dropped the Task Force.

However, Bellagio II turned out to be a genuine success, thanks to the usual diplomatic niceties but, more importantly, to the determination of the main protagonists to make the initiative work. The confidence of the agencies in Foege and status of the Task Force were greatly enhanced; indeed, so positive was the atmosphere that, somewhat prematurely, people began to speak about the disappearance of disputes over vertical versus horizontal approaches. One UNICEF staff member prophesied that in three years time they would wonder why they ever argued about 'campaign' versus 'infrastructure', with such theological fervour.

The two Generals were at great pains publicly to reassure each other. Jim Grant quoted Mahler: they must not be colonial actors, but must remember that primary health care, not EPI, was the only goal. Mahler was equally fulsome. He wanted to express gratitude to 'UNICEF itself, symbolized by Jim Grant, [which had demonstrated] how much can be accomplished when one becomes fully committed to a goal'.

Yet there were critics who presented some forceful opinions on various aspects of the whole initiative. Dr Fred Sai from the World Bank was insistent: the single-minded application of one technology alone would not – could not – yield any lasting improvement. Since, thanks to the present efforts, more children were surviving, greater emphasis had now to be placed on family planning. But though everyone always agreed about this, and nodded their heads sagely, there had been, and always was a striking lack of commitment and action. Why was everyone so chary of the issue? Was it because of a possible political backlash, or fears that the ideological and theological attacks aroused by family planning would create difficulties for the immunization programmes, or that adding family planning would increase the costs and complexity of the programmes? The questions were not answered.

Then several senior representatives from the major agencies questioned yet again the need for further expenditure on research. Had they not just been told that the major obstacles to attaining higher levels of immunization coverage were not technical, but political, social and managerial? Years of experience with smallpox eradication had given Donald Henderson a magisterial experience which could not be denied. He now made full use of this authority as he met these criticisms head on.

At Bellagio I, he reminded them, the hope of reaching at least 90 per cent of the world's children with six vaccines by 1990 seemed Utopian. By Bellagio II it was clear that, though formidable, the task was feasible. So what was there left to discuss? A number of considerations which would extend way beyond 1990. First, the goal was not vaccinating 90 per cent of the world's children but preventing six diseases. What worried him was that no system had yet been devised for establishing whether or not the vaccinations actually *were* preventing the illnesses in the countries in question. If they were, did this then mean the ultimate goal of this initiative had been reached? The answer was an unequivocal No. The programmes still had to be soundly established, with an exceptional managerial framework from which to develop a permanent structure so other cost-effective interventions, such as family planning, vitamin A distribution, or whatever, could be added.

Next Henderson tackled basic research. He reminded the delegates that it was malariologists, not malaria, that had been eradicated; that even on a minuscule budget, the research programmes established during smallpox eradication had resulted in discoveries that revolutionized the strategy of the campaign and guaranteed success. And he hammered the point home: 'I have no hesitancy in saying that, without that ongoing research programme, all of you here would have had to present valid smallpox vaccination certificates before entering Colombia.'

Yet, Henderson continued, not one of the six vaccines being presently used was fully satisfactory, and none approached smallpox vaccine in the three important key

characteristics – heat stability, efficacy and ease of administration – and where was the research? Moreover, while
the descriptions of the national programmes were heart-
warming, little or nothing was known about the incidence
or the epidemiology of the diseases in question, in the
countries in question. Nature might yet spring some nasty
surprises, as eighteen months later she was to do in Brazil.
So he was astonished that as recently as two months ago, a
senior official was querying why funds were being provided for research in one of his agency's programmes.

Foege reinforced Henderson's arguments as he listed
ten areas needing urgent investigation. Three were in
engineering, directed at simplifying the cold chain and the
jet injectors and finding inexpensive, self-contained,
one-off devices for administering vaccines. Three were
biochemical: finding vaccines of higher potency for diseases like diphtheria, that could be given in one or two
doses rather than three; discovering equally potent but
heat-stable viral vaccines for measles and polio; and discovering improved diagnostic methods for diseases like
whooping cough.

The final four areas were in the field: ways must be
found to give all vaccines at an earlier age; to develop a
two-dose schedule rather than a three-dose one; to
improve methods of management and training, as well as
those of surveillance and compliance; and to find the best
strategies for the eradication of polio. Little professional
glamour was attached to such research, for molecular
biology was regarded as the fastest route to the Nobel
Prize by every science postgraduate. As the excitement in
genetic engineering intensified, competition for resources
became more skewed. Yet, he felt, given only relatively
small amounts of money, much of the research now
required could be done by people in the field. So while the
campaigns continued in the various countries the Task
Force would be looking at alternative ways to accelerate
work in all these areas.

*

Bellagio II ended and the delegates dispersed to their various tasks and excitements. As a group they would not meet again for two and a half years. But at last the earlier scepticism of the donor agencies had now so diminished that Grant could speak of 'a flood tide' in which they, and the world's children, were both caught up. Nothing could stop them.

PART II

6

Model for a Miracle

'It was some time and it wasn't any time, when the
flea was a barber and the camel a street-crier, and I
was rocking my grandfather's cradle . . .'

The Turkish equivalent of 'Once upon a time . . .'

Struggling with fatigue and a windswept sari, surrounded by suitcases and cardboard boxes, Sarojini
Abraham stood in the forecourt of Ankara Airport
waiting for a taxi. Wrenched from her home and job in
Sri Lanka and the Maldives, she had been given
seventeen days' notice to leave for Turkey where she was
to organize a major immunization campaign. Such speed
of decision was, she reflected, typical of Jim Grant, and
even though he would provide every kind of support, the
task was daunting. There were over five million children
under five in Turkey and just five months to get the
campaign under way. One of those was the month of
Ramadan.

Grant had long been attracted to a campaign in
Turkey. He had worked there in the 1960s as Director of
USAID, and now counted amongst his many close
friends the Prime Minister, Turgut Ozal, and Ihsan
Dogramaci, Turkey's leading paediatrician and a strong
supporter of UNICEF. By April 1985, when Sarojini
Abraham was posted to Ankara, immunization covering
between 60 and 80 per cent of the vulnerable population

99

had been successfully accomplished in countries with smaller populations, such as Colombia, Senegal and El Salvador. But to make global immunization a reality UNICEF had to show that a campaign could be equally successful in a large country with an enormous number of children. This is what drew Grant to Turkey.

One cannot understand the dimensions of the challenge set by Grant without appreciating the nature of Turkey, a country stretching one thousand miles from east to west and nearly six hundred from north to south. Although exquisitely beautiful, the terrain is generally rugged and mountainous, arid and difficult. The population is scattered throughout fourteen cities of over 400,000 people, rather more towns, 35,000 villages and 40,000 remote settlements. The climate is extreme: the searing dry heat of summer gives way to mountain blizzards in winter, which in turn yield to the thaws of spring and muddy, impassable roads.

Turkish cultures and backgrounds are equally diverse. Over the centuries many peoples have come together from Europe and Asia, Mongols and Romans, Muslims and Byzantines, to form a remarkable historical mosaic every level of which can be traced and observed, from the Sumerians and Hittites to the Phoenicians and Greeks.

In the 1920s the country was first unified and then modernized by Kemal Ataturk. As instruments of change Ataturk used costume, language, law and women's education: he encouraged Western dress and forbade women to wear the veil; he insisted that everyone speak Turkish rather than Arabic; he banned the religious courts; he sent the girls and young women to school. To promote these changes he appealed to the country's pride and sense of identity. For the Turks of the Ottoman Empire regarded themselves amongst history's rulers, not the ruled, and the people continue to respond to a leader's challenges with loyalty and discipline.

The late 1970s and early 1980s were a traumatic time

for the country. Terrorism was rife, and for months on end some twenty people were being killed every day. Civil disturbance ended with the military coup of 1980 and for a while social and collective life virtually came to a standstill. In 1983, as the result of an election, civilian rule once more displaced the military. The Turkish people, praying that the new calm would last, were ready for a redeeming cause.

When Jim Grant flew to Turkey in February 1985, he was well aware of this situation. He also believed that Turkey and UNICEF could each do something crucially important for the other. With notorious charisma, he advanced all the reasons he could marshal to persuade the President and the Prime Minister to mount a major immunization campaign for their children. In every country Grant visited he would need to use his powers of persuasion to a greater or lesser extent. Of all the arguments he used in Turkey, one was most telling. Turkey hoped to join the Common Market, wanting to add an overlay to its culture at once more modern and developed even as it maintained pride in its ancient past. The Turks were anxious to play a more prominent role on the world stage and move towards developed status not only economically, but in all ways. Using indicators of human resources and humanity rather than economic resources and money, Grant argued that there was a far more telling index of a country's wealth and status than the gross national product. The health of children as reflected in the infant mortality rate was a major indication of progress, and here Turkey wasn't doing too well. Whereas in the western regions of the country 45 babies per 1000 under the age of three died, in the east 160 per 1000 died – one of the highest levels in the world. This rate was far above those of the country's neighbours – Syria, Iraq, Iran, Russia, Bulgaria and Greece, and even matched parts of Africa. The six childhood diseases claimed 80 Turkish babies a day. Yet because the country was disciplined and the required technology was available, this horrific situation could be remedied almost at a stroke.

So Grant invited Turkey to join forces with UNICEF. Together they would face the challenge of those silent deaths and by the end of 1985 the children would be vaccinated. Grant's persuasive magic worked yet again. Time and again, skilfully but gently, he trapped politicians so that despite the low priority they traditionally accorded to health, they had no alternative but to co-operate.

However, many people in Turkey's Ministry of Health had well-founded reservations about the wisdom and likely success of this decision. The idea of a campaign was dropped onto their desks at a time of year when budgets were being decided but, they were unhappy to learn, no special allocation of cash would be provided for the programme. So who would pay for the vaccines, the needles, the cold chain, the training? Another problem they foresaw was sustainability: how, after the campaign finished, could they maintain immunization at the new projected levels unless the government gave a higher priority to preventive medicine? And finally, within the Ministry were several divisions each with responsibility for various aspects of child welfare, whose duties overlapped with a corresponding wastage of manpower and resources; these activities would now have to be integrated and some bureaucrats would resist. But they were civil servants; the chain of command in Turkey is crystal clear: the political decision rules. So once the President and the Prime Minister had decided, the Minister of Health and his staff had to execute the plan.

Outsiders too, had reservations. Meeting Turkey's Minister of Health, Mr Mehmet Aydin, at an international conference, Halfdan Mahler observed that Turkey was to have a campaign, but afterwards, what then? The Minister, an economist, gave his reasons concisely: at a time of budgetary constraints prevention was the most cost-effective way to use what resources he had; and the objective of the campaign was not so much to immunize children, but to induce a permanent demand for health services that future governments would *have* to meet.

Now when UNICEF achieves one of its triumphs it is easy to overlook the fact that in any country involved the Ministry of Health above all bears the burden of responsibility for the ultimate success – or failure – of the child survival programmes. As all who work for UNICEF are at pains to insist, the agency acts only as the catalyst. Those involved in the Turkish saga emphasize that from the start – April 1985 – there were several elements already within Turkey that augured well both for a campaign and its eventual sustainability. A health system existed, manned by some 30,000 doctors, midwives and health aides. The Ministry of Health provided excellent planning that reached from the centre to the provinces under the leadership of the Minister himself, augmented by the skills of his charismatic and energetic Under-Secretary, Dr Yunus Muftu, who had been specially seconded from Hacettepe Hospital. However, a Turkish phrase captures the real situation: 'There was flour, fat, sugar and water, but no cook.' In other words, two elements were lacking, energy and commitment, and in the persons of Sarojini Abraham and Richard Reid, UNICEF provided both.

Sarojini has been with the agency for over twelve years, a dynamic Indian of great dignity, whose compassion and strength of will are her most immediately apparent features. Born in southeast India, in a small rural village without water or electricity, she graduated in sociology and economics at the London School of Economics, and remained in Britain for twelve years carrying out poverty surveys for the British Government. Two of her reports were printed by Her Majesty's Stationery Office, and when she finally left

Britain the *Observer* newspaper ruefully remarked that it took someone from a developing country to reveal precisely the extent of poverty in a developed one.

When she arrived in Ankara as UNICEF's Senior Programme Officer, Sarojini first found somewhere to live and then began to work in UNICEF'S tiny office on the top floor of a building that houses a number of United Nations agencies. Its one room soon expanded to three, all semi-divided, and each finally held six staff members, smothered by the noise of typewriters, telephones, word processors and discussions.

Once settled in, Sarojini took stock and began to work out what had to be done in the dauntingly short time available. The task was not simple. The difference in the quality of health services across the country was enormous; some were equivalent to the very best in the world, others were totally primitive. The disparities could be found even within a single city such as Istanbul, or Izmir on the Aegean coast, or Denizli in the mountains, five hours' drive inland, cities in which affluence and poverty co-exist in adjoining neighbourhoods. These cities have large migrant populations that flood in from the poorer eastern provinces, and finding out how many children there were, or keeping track of them once found, would not be easy. By contrast, in the small rural villages of the centre or west, within reach of the many traditional health clinics, with perhaps only three babies of immunizable age, achieving good immunization coverage would be simple.

However, the further east the health workers travelled, the more difficult their task. In the high mountains near the Syrian and Iraqi borders, the people are poor, isolated and neglected. Sarojini visited one settlement where no health personnel had ever been seen. One mother had delivered all her five babies herself, the first time using a knife blade to cut the cord, the second a sickle, the third a razor – whatever instrument came to hand, all of them unsterile. Though tetanus might have set in, she and all her children survived. But this was exceptional, for the infant mortality figures reflected the neglect and it was in these regions that the rates were close to those in Africa. Immunization coverage was as low as 0.5 per cent in parts of the southeast, and even in the west the highest figure was a mere 20 per cent of all children under the age of five.

One major difficulty, however, was widespread ignorance of the seriousness of the problem. That the infant mortality rate in Turkey was so high came as a great surprise not only to many Turks, but to most world health leaders. Thus one of the first jobs would be to build up an awareness among people of influence that despite their progress politically and economically, in investment for the future through the health of their children they lagged behind.

Since President Evren was fully committed, and awareness and political will thus ensured, there was no doubt that the Turkish population could be won over, and to do so Evren would use one compelling comparison. Turkey is Europe's major wool-producing country, livestock a vital element in the economy. 'Our country,' said Evren, 'understands clearly the need to vaccinate its animals, but neglects its children.' However, if children were to receive comparable protection there were major logistic problems of supply and psychological ones of demand to be faced. How many people were available to give vaccination, and would mothers want it? From the moment Sarojini arrived, she heard the same gloomy litany from every single person in the Ministry of Health: the constraints are severe; the obstacles are great; to achieve total immunization would take a miracle.

Their attitude not only demonstrated a healthy and totally justified scepticism – in the past, many global health campaigns had begun with loud explosions only to end in silence – but also reflected certain difficulties

unique to Turkey. To begin with, the health service was,
and is, mostly manned by newly graduated doctors doing
two years' compulsory service, a condition that does not
always make for enthusiastic work. Turkey is the only
developing country Sarojini knows – and she has worked
in many – where it is futile to pull rank or flaunt
influence. To say, 'My father is a government minister so
I'll do my service in Istanbul, rather than in a remote,
primitive place in the east' will get you nowhere.
Whoever you are, the number in the lottery determines
whether you end up in a cushy Istanbul billet or in a
settlement around Lake Van, where you won't understand the local dialect, where support systems don't exist,
where living can be so tough that you will need great
inner resources to survive.

Constant turnover was another obstacle. The directors
who supervise the health services in the sixty-seven
provinces spend on average only seven months in a
particular province and there are several reasons why.
Once the two years' service was mandatory for every
doctor. But now, if they gain admission to a medical
school for a specialist course, they can leave – and many
do; in addition, conditions are often as harsh as salaries
are low – one-tenth of what they can earn in private
practice – so when their service is completed most move
away at once. Lack of resources is a third constraint. In
1985, only 2.5 per cent of Turkey's national budget went
to the Ministry of Health; in the provinces this meant no
vehicles, no fuel, and low morale. With fierce personal
energy a doctor could overcome such difficulties. But so
pervasive are these that many struggle for one,
sometimes three years, then finally admit defeat.

The officials who intoned the litany of difficulty were
not deliberately erecting bureaucratic barriers – indeed
many saw the campaign as a unique opportunity for their
country and the very obstacles themselves as providing
the most compelling reason to undertake the campaign

and so change health care in Turkey for ever. But the facts were stark and if they did succeed it would indeed be a miracle. Yet, as Sarojini realized, everyone's perceptions were also coloured by an overwhelming multitude of petty details and niggling requirements. Thus the vision and energy necessary to surmount the obstacles were stifled. So one day she took a deep breath and said to herself, 'OK. Jim Grant has parachuted me in here, and in July he'll parachute in another colleague, and together we must make the impossible possible.'

Despite groups of dedicated workers – doctors, nurses, midwives and *saglik memuru*, the health paramedics – neither existing personnel nor facilities would be anywhere near sufficient to reach the target of tripling the country's present immunization coverage. At the very most, the people responsible – the staff of the Ministry of Health, the Director Generals in the provinces – had at their disposal 12,000 health staff working out of some 7,000 health outlets dotted unevenly around the country, many far away from the villages and settlements. Yet their calculations showed that to immunize over five million children they would have to provide 41 million doses of vaccine at 45,000 vaccination stations, injected through 17,500,000 hypodermic needles by 65,000 additional helpers, who would need training in techniques of the cold chain as would many of the 12,000 health personnel. One precious month had already gone and within the space of the remaining four all supplies had to be ordered and delivered, and training accomplished.

Were there other people who might vaccinate, and locations other than clinics where they could do so? Unlike Colombia, where schoolteachers and others were co-opted, the Turkish authorities insisted that no one except medical personnel could give injections – although finally they allowed paramedics to be seconded temporarily from hospitals. The Armed Forces Medical Corps volunteered their staff and the Army offered a full supporting panoply of aeroplanes, helicopters and jeeps. But given Turkey's immediate past the government wanted the campaign to be totally civilian, so refused these offers. The campaign's supply side was finally met by a diverse multitude – 220,000 primary schoolteachers, 54,000 Imams, many thousands of village leaders (*Muhtars*) and district leaders (*Kaymakans*) and 67 provincial governors (*Valis*) – all supporting the small group who actually gave the injections.

The *Valis* wielded the most power. As the President's representatives in the provinces, they could hire or fire, appropriate or refuse, initiate or block. Their co-operation was crucial, for the government stuck by their decision to grant no additional cash for the campaign over and above existing health budgets. The only extra resources available were $2.2 million from UNICEF to buy vaccines and cold chain equipment and the polio vaccines donated by Rotary International. Local resources – for cars, petrol, meals – would have to be tapped, whether from Rotary, or individuals in the private sector, or businesses, or through the edict of the *Valis*.

The next urgent task was to recruit staff. They would have to be Turkish nationals, of course – they knew the country, the customs and language – and this was their campaign, not UNICEF's. They would have to be flexible, be able quickly to switch directions whenever necessary. Sarojini looked, too, for people with analytical skills, able to admit the problems, analyse the options and then move forward. They should have neither territorial ambitions nor delusions of grandeur, since whatever the job everyone would have to pitch in: one moment a person might be dealing with a prickly provincial governor, the next licking envelopes. The posts were not advertised. Word passed along the grapevine that UNICEF was recruiting, and applications flooded in.

Once the Turkish staff was in place, UNICEF would revert to its traditional role as a catalyst. 'We are merely the *Hamals*,' says Sarojini, 'the porters who carry big loads on their backs.' By acting as planners, communicators and zealots, they won the co-operation of people who might normally have withheld it. From the President and Prime Minister down, through the Ministry of Health, and those of Interior and Education, who all joined in the planning and execution, to provincial leaders in education, religion and politics, the entire society of Turkey was mobilized, and the network created that ensured success.

By mid-June 1985, just six weeks after Sarojini arrived, the team consisted of four people, one in charge of administration, finance and personnel, one supply assistant and two secretaries. Then Incila Diker joined as Assistant Administrative Officer. She described her job as 'being responsible for everywhere and nowhere, at one and the same time . . .'.

Her prime responsibility was to bring in the vaccines and deliver them to the start of the cold chain, a term she had never heard before. But whatever it was they had just six weeks to set it up. Dr Peter Poore, Director of the EPI programme for Save the Children Fund in the UK, was called in to advise on the mechanics of the chain and how to store and handle vaccines. Then Incila had to order 41 million doses of vaccine from UNICEF's store in Copenhagen, receive them off aeroplanes by August, organize them into trucks to be sent many hundreds of miles further on, being kept cold all the way. A group in the Ministry of Health battled with the logistics, calculating the requirements of each province, district and village. This village has a refrigerator, this shop a deep freeze, this health centre will need twenty-five cold boxes for these twelve health workers who must walk or ride the seven miles to those six remote settlements. Once every single piece of equipment was properly in place, meetings were called in six separate regions for all health directors, immunization co-ordinators and cold chain supervisors from nearby provinces. Piece by piece the equipment, its use and maintenance, was demonstrated. Then all these people returned to their own provinces and began training their own people.

At the end of June, Nefise Basoglu joined the staff. A young social science graduate, she was responsible for analysing all the data as the immunization reports came in. She quickly became involved in the cause even though initially she had serious doubts about the likelihood of success. She simply could not believe that, in the time left, Turkey could be mobilized and a demand for immunization created. Yet once swept into the whirlpool of frenzied activity, with her analytical and demographic skills stretched to the full, she was soon too busy to question anything, let alone the campaign's feasibility.

With just two months to go Jim Grant sent in Richard Reid and the programme really moved into high gear. Sarojini and her staff describe the American Reid as 'the ignition that set the campaign alight'. He arrived with a mixed reputation – energetic and charismatic, brilliant and critical, difficult and at times intolerable. Incila's first reaction was despair. 'If he's really like that, I'll resign,' she said. Her relief when she finally met Richard Reid was tremendous, for she was infused with an immediate sense of excitement and quickly realized that the gossip was false. He had his own obsessions, of course, those of a workaholic, clever, determined, confident. But his sense of urgency was combined with the broadest vision, and Sarojini had recruited just the kind of people this perfectionist needed: he worked impossible hours but so did they, and if practical constraints did not allow the perfection he desired, Reid would compromise. His calculated use of flattery was keenly judged, advocacy he could use with finesse. He kept the staff constantly abreast of progress and opinion; he held brain-storming sessions at which they discussed tactics and strategies, for if failures occurred he would want to know how later to avoid them. Within days after Reid's arrival the staff would have given their lives for the campaign. 'We never ever considered the possibility of failure,' says Incila.

Reid knows Turkey well. He first went there in the early sixties, as a schoolteacher and then head of an American-sponsored secondary school in Istanbul. After six years he joined the United States Peace Corps and directed their programmes in Iran, then in Morocco. A job with the American branch of Save the Children Fund followed before he joined UNICEF in 1980, becoming their representative in Nigeria. Thus as he set out to co-ordinate those processes that would mobilize Turkey for peace rather than war, Reid possessed some very significant advantages.

The first step was to let everyone know that President Evren gave the campaign the highest priority. He had already called for weekly progress reports and the Minister of Health insisted on daily reports from his co-ordinating committee. Reid reinforced these actions by infiltrating the entire bureaucracy with statements and rumours, by placing an article on the campaign in the Official Gazette issued regularly from the Prime Minister's office.

Attention was next focused on the *Valis*, the provincial governors with the power of feudal barons. On 8 July 1985, the Prime Minister summoned all sixty-seven to Ankara – the first time in the history of Turkey they had ever met together – to discuss not economics or tourism, but how to save their children. To the moral obligation and the political imperatives with which Grant had influenced the President and Prime Minister, was now added competition as fierce as between football teams. Since each governor yearned for a major success in his province, political ambition became a powerful element in social mobilization. It was just as well, for if the *Valis* hadn't wanted to co-operate, no cars, funds or personnel would have been available. But from now on governors, too, began pestering their staff every day: 'What is our coverage? Why is the neighbouring province reaching more people than we are?'

Meanwhile the Minister of Health was mobilizing his provincial health directors. They were ordered to meet the key people in every village whose advocacy would be crucial in creating a demand for vaccination – the schoolteachers, the Imams and the *Muhtars*. Of them all the Imam is most powerful. Every Friday night he climbs into the *mihrab* in the mosque to deliver his sermon; whatever he says the people do. Together these three form a triad so powerful that, once convinced, the battle would be more than half over.

The final person in the entire chain, and the most important, was the mother. Compared to ensuring her demand, assuring supply was relatively simple – a matter of seeing that the local health system had potent vaccines in the fridge at clearly identified health posts with personnel standing by to give immunization on well-publicized vaccination days. But, Reid insisted, all this had to be set up in ways that would both attract the mother the first time, and encourage her to come twice more with her child. All promises made must be kept, everything must be ready at the advertised hour, and the process be rapid so that she did not have to queue under a blazing sun for five hours. Yet when the injection had been given she had to be moved out fast so that the next child in the five million could come in. She had to be made to feel good for travelling so great a distance, her reward being her child's future health. Such attention to her needs was revolutionary for, as Reid rightly says, health officials are notoriously autocratic and dour. So training sessions were arranged everywhere. 'Get that goddamned grimace off your face,' he would tease, 'because it's a plague. You have to vaccinate cheerfully and you must be real nice to the mother.'

Throughout August the complex process intensified.

National consciousness and stores of equipment expanded side by side. While the Ministry of Health co-ordinating committee planned, Incila travelled, Reid encouraged, Nefise analysed and Sarojini negotiated. To obtain 41 million doses of vaccine Sarojini had to tap supplies from over twenty-two countries, as far away as Japan, the Philippines and Canada. Each day she would place telephone calls to a dozen different countries, cajoling, pleading, insisting. 'You're the best thing that ever happened in this world'; 'If anybody can do this you can'; 'Now stop procrastinating. Produce the vaccine and fly it in, please.' Afterwards there was criticism that during the campaign vaccine was diverted from other countries where it was equally urgently needed. So it was, but Sarojini had done her calculations correctly: if Turkey had been left to follow its existing procedures for child immunization, universal coverage would not have been achieved until the year 2005.

The Turks had never met anyone like Sarojini. Bemused, they liked her immensely and found her irresistible. Dr Utku Unsal, Deputy Director for Primary Health Care at the Ministry of Health, recalls: 'I had never before seen anyone so enthusiastic on one subject. I cannot really express it . . . Oh, what a lady . . . always smiling. But underneath that smiling face you knew she was pushing you to do something, and you would do it! Two or three times a day she was phoning. "Dr Unsal, I have this problem. Can I come to your office to see you for a few minutes, please?" You could not refuse. We had organized various vaccination teams – young doctors from the Ministry and other staff, and she would say, "Dr Unsal, Team A needs some typewriters, please." So I'd be telephoning to Supplies asking for typewriters. Or, "Dr Unsal, did you know that Dr X has been moved from Y – this would likely be a remote village – and so there is no doctor in the Health Centre. What do you suppose can be done?" So I would be telephoning Personnel and asking

"What's happening in that village?" And she would go away happy. She was visiting all over the country; she was telling *us* about the situation; she knew everything.'

As the vaccines arrived, so too did Incila's headaches. She faced terrible problems, for August is the height of summer and in the hinterland the heat reaches insufferable heights, 30°C or more. She insisted that every consignment come directly to Ankara where she could exercise strict control over it. Her team had mobilized the entire cold storage facilities of Turkey's meat and fish industries and could monitor the vaccine closely. From these superb facilities the vaccines were shipped to every last province in refrigerated trucks, to be placed in local deep freezes until, on vaccination days, they would be packed into long-life cold boxes. Then they would be taken, on motorbikes, horses or carried by hand, to the immunization centres.

Things began to go splendidly wrong. The arrival in Ankara of the very first consignment was almost a total fiasco. As part of the effort to raise national consciousness, Incila had arranged press and television coverage of the moment when the Lufthansa flight, ferrying the vaccine from Copenhagen through Frankfurt to Ankara, taxied majestically into the unloading bay. As the packages came off Incila realized that it wasn't her vaccine at all; indeed the entire cargo had absolutely nothing whatsoever to do with UNICEF. By a combination of fast talking and extremely fast footwork, suitably ambiguous photographs were taken and until this day no one ever guessed what had happened.

On another occasion the Lufthansa plane in Frankfurt was overloaded, freight had to be taken off and the vaccines were shifted on to a Turkish airliner bound for Istanbul, where there were no storage facilities. The UNICEF staff in Ankara received the worrying telex only one and a half hours before the plane was due. Incila immediately asked a colleague – a timid man who had

never been in an aeroplane before – to fly to Istanbul to
receive the vaccine. Since he had no warning he was
without money for a ticket, so he borrowed from a
Customs officer. Although Incila had alerted the Health
Ministry in Istanbul, when he arrived nothing had been
done. But the imperatives of the campaign stoked his
courage and he acted with real nerve. Ignoring both the
dictates of protocol and the sensitivities of bureaucrats,
he telephoned the Governor of Istanbul at his home and
insisted on speaking to him personally. The consignment
was quickly moved to the refrigerators of a city hospital.

Sometimes refrigerated trucks carried the vaccine
from Denmark. UNICEF monitored their progress along
the route with telephones manned twenty-four hours a
day. Before leaving Copenhagen all drivers were
instructed to ring UNICEF when they reached the final
border checkpoint and someone would drive out and
meet them. Or they could wait at a certain motel outside
Ankara where one of UNICEF's 'pilots' – all women –
would escort them to Customs for clearance, and then on
to the storage depots.

One day, a truck driver was torn with indecision.
Should he go or not? His wife had just given birth to a
most beautiful baby daughter and he wanted to stay at
home. His wife had no doubts. 'All babies are beautiful,'
she said. 'Look at ours. You must go.' When they heard
this story the UNICEF staff planned to have his picture
taken by the press on arrival and generally make a great
fuss. During the next two days every truck driver arriving
from Copenhagen was accosted by the 'pilots' asking,
'Have you just had a baby daughter?' Since the drivers
thought they were going to get a prize, most invented
children or gave names of those who weren't their own.
Sadly the real driver was never found.

The people who really held the network together,
however, were the ordinary citizens of Turkey, and the
media provided a magnificent channel of communication

to reach them. If UNICEF's strategy for creating demand was exercised partly through the political hierarchy and leadership, the most direct way to the people was through radio, television and the newspapers. The message was simple: 'Get your kid vaccinated.' Since television is watched by 85 per cent of the population this was easily the most effective means of communication, and the equivalent of $5.5 million worth of free prime time was donated. Educational programmes, commercials, spot messages of where to go for vaccination, a video cassette distributed to ten thousand coffee houses throughout the country, a rallying speech by President Evren, were all part of the campaign. Turkey's best-known comedians produced immunization skits; a travelling children's theatre group toured around giving up to five performances of their immunization sketch a day; a rousing march, written by Yusuf Nalkesen, Turkey's leading composer, became the campaign's signature tune; thousands of posters were stuck on to thousands of billboards, thousands of leaflets thrust into thousands of hands or showered upon cities from helicopters. From August 1985, six major articles were run daily in the main national newspapers. All mail carried a franked immunization message.

The town of Manisa, sixty miles inland from Izmir on the west coast, faced a unique problem when private practitioners tried to get the campaign stopped. In the past whenever a baby was brought in for immunization the doctor would examine the child too and charge a fee; the campaign would undermine this practice. Soon a rumour was circulated claiming that not only were the vaccines ineffective but they might even cause infertility. The health authorities reacted vigorously with a video of the whole process, from vaccine production in the factory to delivery into the arm of a child, showing that the vaccine was pure and protected at every stage. The doctors' attack soon fizzled out.

Publicity varied from place to place. Izmir used a great variety of methods in an impressive array of public and private resources that when listed, covered eighteen typewritten pages: banners; newspapers in each district; presents for the kids – balloons, toys, flags, T-shirts and chocolates, all bearing the campaign logo. The milk company, Pinar, printed on its milk cartons, 'Have your child immunized; this is the date and this is the place in your district' – a mosque, a school, a coffee shop, a campsite, a shooting club. An ancient aeroplane flew over the city and dropped ten thousand leaflets. The Coca-Cola company gave two refrigerators; the main poultry company lent a cold truck. Three days before the campaign started was Izmir's Independence Day and the captive audience was saturated with details. The Ankara campaign march was modified for Izmir – the tune so lively and catchy that when kids heard it blazing forth from the loudspeakers, they poured out of their houses and danced after the cars which, like so many mechanical Pied Pipers, drew them into procession. The entire country was mobilized similarly, smothered with information; only 2.7 per cent of all mothers in Turkey would not hear any message, and these mostly lived in the isolated areas of the Central Anatolian plain.

By September, as the deadline drew nearer, every *Muhtar* had visited every family in his community, and urged parents to have their children vaccinated. They also arranged to transport mothers and their children from outlying areas so as to arrive at the vaccination posts in succession at specified times. Sometimes they went to fetch the children themselves, as did some village Imams too.

The Ministry of Education ordered the 220,000 primary schoolteachers to report before the start of the school year and assist with preparations. They would play a key role for they have strong credibility in the community. In a society that still regards education as a key to upward social mobility they are regarded with awe for their status. Often they are more successful than the police in settling disputes, whether verbal or physical; people use them as a second medical opinion to check on the value of a prescription or therapeutic regimen. Many come from a rural background and are poor themselves; they know the dialects and attitudes of ordinary people in a way that doctors – who seem distant – and government officials – who seem suspect – never do, and they have day-to-day contact with ordinary people. They would speak at training programmes, parents' meetings, at women's literacy classes, at evening sessions held in adult educational centres. Schoolchildren, too, were encouraged to act as educators of their families and friends.

The General Directorate of Highways undertook to keep all roads open, especially in remote mountainous regions. All Turkey's communication facilities were placed at UNICEF's disposal, as were those of the army. Rotary and Red Crescent gave their services free of charge, using cars to transport people to vaccination centres as enthusiastically as political parties use theirs to transport voters to the booths; they helped to compile checklists of children, fill in their record cards, give promotional help. Private companies paid for after-vaccination aspirins; an Istanbul-based pharmaceutical company, Dogu Ilac Fabrikasi, provided five million health passports, given to mothers to record a baby's vaccination, growth and other health milestones during the child's first five years.

By now Sarojini had noticed a profound change amongst the bureaucrats. People who otherwise would spend most of the day drinking tea were now working around the clock and staying late. Instead of writing the usual bland or frankly obstructionist letters, they battled to get things moving.

Many individuals made quiet, unrecognized contributions. On a farm of 1500 acres of cotton and tobacco,

near the town of Akhisar across the plain of Manisa, Mrs
Selmin Karaosmanoglu would talk to her migrant
Kurdish workers every day, urging them to take their
children for vaccination. But her aunt, aged well over
eighty, was the real heroine. After hearing about the
campaign she travelled for weeks on end to remote
villages in the mountains. While her niece recruited
workers, she sat in the coffee shops and drank
innumerable cups, politely waiting for the men to speak
to her. Then she told them that their children must be
protected. 'Are you a doctor? Why should this concern
you?' they questioned. 'For the future of Turkey's
children,' she would reply, and would then interrogate
them in turn, asking how many babies in the village had
died, which if vaccinated would have survived.

However hopeful and inspiring the preparations,
Sarojini Abraham and Richard Reid knew that parts of
the country would present special difficulties. The three
rounds of immunization were planned for September,
November and December. But by November the eastern
and southeastern provinces would be cut off by snow. So
it was decided that the first round for these areas should
take place in August, and be used as a trial run for the
rest of the national campaign. The second round for the
east would begin on 11 September, the day when the
national campaign proper was to be inaugurated by the
President. This first round in the east was to prove most
valuable in highlighting problems that would require
special attention. For there *was* resistance, arising quite
naturally from a mixture of ignorance and suspicion.
Some mothers were so worried about the side-effects of
vaccination that they hid their babies under the quilts.
They had no understanding of the process – why should
healthy children be injected? – and furthermore, they
were afraid of the mild fever that often followed; they
didn't need any complications in their busy lives. As this
trial run progressed, it was seen how difficult it could be

to persuade parents to bring their children, and in a few areas gendarmes had to be used to 'accompany' people to the vaccination posts.

The key figure in the east once again proved to be the schoolteacher, who in many villages was often a health worker as well. Many parents had to talk face to face either to him, or a *Muhtar*, before they were convinced of the need for vaccination.

The sprawling city of Istanbul whose boundaries, population and traffic seemed to expand as you watched was another potential problem. Because of sheer numbers, rising 5 million in 1985 – 10 per cent of Turkey's population – and inflated each day as migrants with large families poured in from the East – the key to the country's success or failure lay in the city. But Istanbul was branded 'hopeless' by some and written off even before the campaign started.

Some 'city fathers', especially the Rotarians, reacted strongly to the implied slur. Ali Muderrisoglu, their Governor, and Cetin Demirman, Chairman of the PolioPlus Committee, took a careful look at the plans of the Ministry of Health and UNICEF, and spotted a flaw. The government's network was brilliant: 654 vaccination posts, from sweet-shops to schools, dotted around the city and so placed that a mother and children would never have to walk more than two kilometres. The doctors and nurses, too, were already mobilized and knew where they had to go.

But the problems Rotary saw were, first, how would the health personnel, the mothers and the suppliers find these small posts; secondly, how could each post communicate with HQ when, say, more vaccines were required; thirdly, who was going to transport and feed the workers; fourthly, who would ensure that all posts and staff were without exception ready for action on the dot of 9.00 a.m. each day? With military precision they tackled them all. They placed signs on all posts and plastered a multitude of arrows in neighbouring streets pointing the way; they assembled an army of drivers with cars and on D-day minus three showed every doctor, paramedic and driver where their post was; for three days they made the chauffeurs drive their routes over and over, until they could have gone blindfolded; they arranged with the traffic police that those marked cars should be given priority during vaccination days – a wise precaution as Istanbul is one big traffic jam; they took care of everyone's creature comforts; they mobilized their wives to provide 12,000 packed lunches and also keep the workers supplied with refreshing drinks throughout vaccination hours; they handed out balloons to the kids, along with sweets and stick-on badges that boasted 'I've been vaccinated'; they would be curt with those doctors who, with typical casualness, turned up late on the first day; and they made it clear that there was no room for such cavalier attitudes on a national matter of such importance. People either came on time or not at all.

By the beginning of September, every conceivable section of Turkish society had been mobilized, somehow, somewhere. The final, poignant event came on the last holy day before the campaign, the Friday before Wednesday, 11 September. Fifty-four thousand Imams in fifty-four thousand mosques climbed fifty-four thousand pulpits and preached a sermon prepared, as usual, by the Chief Imam.

> Esteemed Muslims, the child is an important being in society: a guarantee of life and a hand stretched towards the future.
> With the aim of reducing the number of deaths in infants and providing our children with the means to grow more healthy, an intensified immunization campaign will be launched throughout the country, on Wednesday, 11 September 1985 . . .
> Every member of society who is aware of this fact must fulfil a religious and national duty and support this

expanded and intensified immunization campaign
because those who will be protected and vaccinated
against disease are our own children.

Let us not knowingly endanger our children who one
day will be the embodiment of our religious and national
values. Let us participate in this immunization campaign
through which our children will be fortified and
protected and not let any of our children down, lest we
grieve their memory for the rest of our days.

On the night of 10 September, the UNICEF staff
snatched some rest. Yet the nightmare that for many
weeks had disturbed Sarojini's sleep returned to haunt
her once more. Tomorrow 5.1 million children would
flood into the vaccination posts; but there would be no
needles, no syringes, no vaccine and no health workers.
So they would all go away again and never, ever, come
back.

Some events are so etched in people's consciousness that
afterwards they can always remember exactly what they
were doing on that day. Whether glorious, as the end of
the Second World War in August 1945, or tragic, as the
assassination of John F. Kennedy in November 1963, the
precise details are recalled in an instant. For the Turkish
people the first official day of the immunization
campaign was one such occasion. Ask people where they
were and what they were doing on 11 September 1985,
and proudly they will tell you.

That morning the entire UNICEF staff went to the
auditorium of the Hacettepe Hospital, Ankara, where
the campaign was to be inaugurated. The place was
packed. Squashed in a corner, Incila Diker was pinned
against a pillar by a crowd of doctors, medical students
and delegates from the Diplomatic Corps of many
countries. On stage were the dignitaries: besides
Turkey's President, Prime Minister, Chief Imam and the
Minister of Health, were Jim Grant and Richard Reid, all

of whom spoke in turn according to a well-defined protocol. President Evren spoke last, but he was only a few minutes into his speech when the curtains behind him moved gently, disturbed by a small breeze. Then a baby's cry punctuated his words, and this provoked another which was followed by chortles, squeals, squeaks and gurgles and all those little noises that for the next three months would provide a moving counterpoint throughout Turkey. Everyone started to laugh, and as the President finished, the curtains were drawn to reveal ten babies, dressed in their best, sitting on the laps of ten nurses, also dressed in their best. Covered by microphones and cameras, in a scene relayed all over Turkey, President Kenan Evren, followed in turn by each of the other dignitaries, dropped five drops of polio vaccine into a baby's mouth. In each province the ceremony was repeated, with the first vaccination being given by the Governor and the second by the Health Director.

From then on all was organized frenzy. There would be three rounds, each lasting ten days: 11–20 September; 18–27 October; and finally 25 November–4 December. Every city and every province was poised; each had its own particular problems. The co-ordinating committee worried about them all. In Ankara the vaccination posts were manned twenty-four hours a day for the first four days of the campaign. Once again the workers were fed thousands of sandwiches made by the wives of Rotary members. Istanbul's social mobilization had been almost too effective: people flooded into the vaccination centres, especially in the slums, and mothers had to be chased out of the posts and organized into queues. Against the counterpoint of crying babies, health personnel were confronted with an impatient mass of people. Where the health teams had already co-opted teachers to help, order was more or less quickly restored, but in other districts the police had to be called. Yet even they were unable to overcome the 'first-day syndrome'. Eventually

the teachers calmed everybody down, organized the
queues and, going from person to person, assured the
rest: each round would last ten days so there would be
plenty of time for them to bring in their children. Even
so, the headmaster in a working-class district whose
school was being used as a vaccination post worried that if
the crowd were sent away some would never return.
Quickly he assembled a second team of three teachers
and with two doctors and two nurses kept the assembly
line going non-stop for the next eight days.

Izmir, lying south of Istanbul, some five hours' drive
along the beautiful Aegean coastline, also had some
special problems. Once a quiet sea-port it is now a
thriving, bustling, overcrowded town whose population
has exploded, with slum areas invaded by migrants from
the east of the country. Of the two and a half million
people in Izmir, one and a half million live in the
metropolitan area and the remainder in the outlying
districts. One hundred and fifty thousand children in
Izmir were in the immunizable age group, five and
under, but the problem was to find them.

For thirty-nine years Dr Guzin Aksu had been
paediatrician of the Esrefpasa Health Centre in the
Konak district that lies up from the seafront. Above the
district the ramparts of the old citadel command a
magnificent view of the town and harbour. The health
centre serves a core population of 50,000 medium-
income people with 7000 known children to be
immunized. Their registration records, meticulously
accurate, go back to 1961 and show not only the numbers
of people in any one street, but where they live and how
many children there are of what ages. So, Dr Aksu
emphasized, they didn't really need a campaign in Konak
because they had been vaccinating children there for
years and knew them all.

There are thirty-six similar, excellent health centres in
the city of Izmir, but the problem lay in the periphery

around each core. It is believed that the Esrefpasa Health Centre actually serves a population four times greater than the registered fifty thousand, though this is only a guess. Some people live at the boundaries of two overlapping centres and fail to register in either, and a significant proportion of the population is migrant. Most come to the city unvaccinated, and if it were not for the campaign would have remained so, since they never register and are impossible to follow. House-to-house searches are impractical, as a walk up to the ramparts on the citadel will show.

Looking out from the top of the ramparts across the harbour, one's eye is first drawn to a slim minaret and then to the hills on the far side. The colours – the red tiles and the slate blue of dirty harbour water – are pale in comparison with the vivid red, blue and yellow materials spread over the ancient stones. Leaning against these, facing away from the town, the migrant women from Anatolia in brightly coloured clothes sit in line, suckling children, sewing and weaving. At their feet the wool warp is stretched out for some ten yards; hour after hour they stay under roughly built shelters, weaving cloth, rugs and bags. Their husbands are nowhere to be seen; they work down in the docks, or on the roads.

These migrants live in houses or shanties, packed tightly into narrow streets. Broken-down homes, concrete steps and large stones tumble sharply towards the area of the health centre, half a mile below. Amongst the stones, foraging goats mingle with playing children. A small boy clutching a brick and a piece of plastic smiles shyly, while a girl pinning down a rooster in a broken plastic bowl pays no attention to the stranger. But a gang of grinning street urchins happily show off as they slide dangerously fast down the steep streets on flat pieces of tin. The kids are glorious; their mothers shy but friendly; their fathers protective, cautious and suspicious.

No one quite knew how many children there were, yet

the campaign had to reach them all. Each health centre
was made responsible for immunization in its core area
and   surrounding   district.   With   the   registered
populations in the core areas, nurses merely told parents
where to take their children – to a school, a mosque, a
cafeteria or barber's shop. But in the unregistered areas
recent census figures gave only the roughest of estimates
and since these were unlikely to be accurate, the staff
allowed for a number of children far higher than likely
and hoped that things would average out.

A child's vaccination progress was recorded by colours
on its card: green marked shots given during the first
round, red the second, blue the third, and if a child
dropped out health workers would try to track him
down. Locating missing Arabic or Kurdish children was
extremely difficult. On one occasion, while checking
details, the staff realized that one household in a
particular street had been left out. When they asked the
Kurds why they hadn't mentioned this, they said,
'Because the people living there are Turks and don't
count.' Other problems arose when a child, father and
grandfather all had the same name and the team would
turn up to find that they were about to vaccinate
Grandpa. Such difficulties were predictable, for the
migrants were ignorant about immunization. Many
thought one dose of vaccine was enough; in spite of the
posters, television announcements and loudspeakers on
moving cars they didn't always know where to go; they
feared that a child might get sick from the vaccines; and
they didn't think a sick child should be vaccinated at all.
Some wanted the dates changed to fit work schedules;
others thought vaccination a sin; others were too busy
and no neighbours were available to help. So, where
necessary, the teams went to the children, working well
into the night and at weekends. Even after the campaign
was over, checks continued on a house-to-house basis.
The Izmir authorities finally reckoned that in their

metropolitan districts they probably caught all the children in the first round, and 97 per cent in the third within an error of 5 per cent.

One and a half hour's drive through the mountains directly east of Izmir is Manisa, where the Health Director in that new, prosperous, industrial town had similar worries over migrant groups. His province, the eighth largest in Turkey, has a population of only one million, and based on the well-established network of health centres, immunization coverage in the past had been about 50 per cent. But every summer 50,000 migrant workers arriving for the harvest spread over almost 14,000 square kilometres, some in settlements in remote countryside, and their children might never have been seen at all. And how could health workers reach children whose mothers, working in the fields, wouldn't bring them in because they didn't want to lose a day's pay? The health teams had to go to them. Through pressure on his Provincial Governor, the Health Director managed to get a further thirty-six trucks to supplement his existing thirty-four and when roads gave out, his workers would proceed on foot or horseback.

On 11 September the Director first went to a primary school and held the baby which the Governor vaccinated. The baby cried. The Director then visited every single centre thoughout Manisa province. The cold chain worried him greatly, for he believed that failures in the past had been entirely due to ignorance about this. The large Electrolux cold boxes used for taking vaccines from refrigerators to outlying posts were far too heavy to carry long distances, so he had had special, small packs designed. And as he travelled from centre to centre, checking and rechecking, the Director grimly remembered those doctors who had tried to undermine the campaign. He would not have the success of this or any future campaign prejudiced by ignorance; now no one may obtain vaccine from the central store in Manisa unless they can show that they are able to maintain a cold chain.

The Deputy Director stayed at headquarters in Manisa all day, responding to demands for supplies. In the evening, along with a hundred others throughout Turkey, he waited for the results, noted the percentage and numbers of children vaccinated, and then telephoned the figures to a room in the Ministry of Health in Ankara, manned twenty-four hours a day by a cheerful group of young doctors, who collated all the results.

Thirty miles away from Manisa, tucked among the granite hills on the south side of the plain, where the mountains form a rampart against the cooling effect of the Mediterranean Sea, the Karaoglanni Health Centre is just a small house in a beautiful garden, where staff and patients drink tea as they wait. The staff faced the day with equanimity: the married team of midwife and male nurse were responsible for no more than four villages, population 2500, with only 302 children to be vaccinated.

At the village of Gokkoy, fifteen miles away into the hills, thirty-four babies awaited them. Hidden in the hills above the ancient town of Sardis, the village is a mere twenty years old. The first fifteen families who settled cleared the hillside of stones, planted fruit trees and discovered the seven natural springs that provide gloriously pure water. As more people came those families who had first worked the earth were given title deeds to the land. Now they work fifty-six acres of figs, apples, pomegranates and other fruits.

There is a natural cohesion in this community of just over four hundred people totally missing in the migrant groups, whether on the Izmir citadel or in rural settlements. Their *Muhtar* is in his late fifties, though he looks much older. Their Imam, in his late twenties, whose wife was expecting their first child, had been so moved by the sermon prepared by the Chief Imam in Ankara, especially the part where the Koran speaks of the value of children, that he preached it several times.

On the day the vaccination team was due, he and the *Muhtar* assembled all the babies in the schoolroom. It was a beautiful day. The two-year-old toddlers began to cry before the needles ever appeared. But curiously, the Imam recalls, the nine-month-old babies were quiet, except when the hypodermic neatly shot the measles vaccine into their arms. The whole community was inspired by a campaign during which they came to understand very clearly why immunization protected against disease. They were aware then – and still are – that 11 September was a very important day. For once upon a time child after child had died of measles, or been disabled by polio. But now there was going to be 100 per cent coverage in Gokkoy for ever. So between each round the Imam and the *Muhtar* together visited and re-visited homes.

Five hours by car still further east from Manisa the large industrial town of Denizli lies in the bowl of hills near the tourist centre of Pammukale, where warm water gushing from springs among the rocks evaporates under the hot sun and leaves thick white deposits on the mountainside. The authorities here faced problems similar to those in Izmir – a large migrant population, widely dispersed and rural. Yet this province, with remote settlements in wild mountains many miles away from the capital, was one of the earliest to have an excellent national health service. There had still, however, been a high child mortality rate. Once again, the Health Director of Denizli believed this was due to an inadequate cold chain, simply because no one had ever been taught the necessity of keeping vaccine cold. So in Denizli 800 people were specially trained, who then fanned out across the province to instruct others.

Record-keeping had been another problem. Few parents would actually hide their children but most were indifferent. But the system was now so tightly organized that not a single child could slip through the records.

However, the authorities were absolutely confident that Suleymaniye, a small mountain village above the silk town of Buldan, in Denizli province, would meet its target. A ten-mile dirt road with hairpin turns climbs up to a high, flat basin of land with cedar trees and streams. In 1985, there were 204 inhabitants who worked mostly at weaving cloth and in agriculture; a few bred cattle. The school had twenty-three pupils – nine girls and fourteen boys. The teacher, Omer Kilic, has been there for seventeen years; his wife is the midwife for four villages – not an onerous position since there are only some four births a year in each village. The pair of them were the linchpins in this minuscule local campaign. Once they had listened to President Evren on the television the teacher began speaking with fathers in the coffee shops. Whomever he met – strangers or acquaintances – wherever he met them – on the roads, in the mountains – he described the campaign and invited questions. With an eye to the future he discussed vaccination with his pupils, most of whom were well above age, describing the diseases their brothers and sisters would catch if not protected. He and his wife anticipated no opposition, but to be doubly sure they visited every house in each of the four villages, made lists of the children of immunizable age, and checked to see that no one had been left out.

So, on the morning of 11 September, in the garden of the schoolhouse with the entire village looking on, the three babies of Suleymaniye were vaccinated. Not one cried. On the tally sheet provided by the Health Director at Denizli, the midwife solemnly recorded the details of their immunization. The sheet was rushed down the mountain to the health centre at Buldan, the collecting point for rural vaccination posts. All over Turkey the tally sheets flooded in; each evening the daily figures were telephoned to Ankara, but so heavy were the demands on the circuits that it was at times difficult to get through. Each morning the numbers in relation to the daily targets were announced on television and radio, and posted on a nationwide chart maintained by the Ministry of Health. Day by day they climbed.

During the first round it was too early for exultation or despair, but Sarojini remembers being deeply impressed by the interest shown by everyone. As the weeks had passed, many of her earlier worries had faded. She had been sure that, in a Muslim country, they would meet resistance from the men who wouldn't let their women go to the vaccination centres. So the health workers contacted the fathers in the coffee shops where only the men go. Yet in Kayseri and other remote parts in the east, it was the fathers, grandfathers and older brothers who brought in the children for vaccination. They stood in a circle monitoring every movement. The television had shown them that the syringes were disposable. So had this nurse, about to give their grandson a shot, really thrown the syringe into a disposable bag? Far from being resistant to change they were most open, and observed every stage of the procedure very carefully.

Such involvement sometimes had farcical consequences. The village of Bolu lies just outside Istanbul. During the first round a team vaccinated all the children but not, of course, any over five years old. On the second day the villagers went to the Governor of Istanbul to complain: the team hadn't vaccinated *all* the children. The outraged Governor telephoned the Health Director and ordered him to send another team out immediately. Shivering in his shoes, the Health Director of Istanbul province ordered out the emergency reserve team on permanent stand-by. The next day the village received the team in total silence and all the babies came in again to receive double doses in twenty-four hours without any apparent ill-effect.

*

The first round ended on 20 September and was followed by a breathing space of twenty-eight days. While vaccination workers rested, UNICEF and the provincial health staffs planned how to cover those who might drop out in the later rounds. The crucial test was yet to come, for all eligible children needed to return twice more. Clearly rural villages such as Gokkoy and Suleymaniye presented no problem, and even in Izmir, with all its difficulties, a whole variety of encouraging events had occurred. One five-year-old boy who had trotted in alone for his shots in the first round came in again, still alone, for rounds two and three. Ten-year-old children whose parents were busy brought along their little sisters and brothers and neighbours' children also. The only problem was that though they knew the names of their siblings they often didn't know the names of the others.

But in one rural area near Izmir resistance was expected and in the second round it finally came. So now the teams were accompanied by the military police. A local doctor who didn't approve of such 'coercion' insisted, 'Officially I don't want to know anything about what you're doing.' But their mere presence was enough, and the workers quietly rounded up the unvaccinated children. Another technique was to put pressure on the *Muhtar*. Lists of all the missing children were given to the *Muhtar*, along with full responsibility for finding them. Since he suspected penalties for failure, the *Muhtar* felt obliged to fetch the children and personally bring them to the posts. This, too, produced comical moments. One *Muhtar* went to find a child and was promptly hit by the landlord of the house. They had a good old fist-fight and the case ended in court. In another village a *Muhtar* promised to find the children but did not, so the *Kaymakan* – the Governor's deputy – sued him in the civil court for dereliction of duty. A fourth strategy exploited the fact that social life is governed by certain legal requirements. A rumour circulated that it was illegal –

which it was not – to fail to have one's child vaccinated.

In Denizli province another rumour circulated amongst the migrant community: parents who failed to produce their children would be fined 10,000 lira. In Denizli town, people who failed to bring their children in were publicly shamed as loudspeaker vans travelled round the city, blaring forth their names.

The second round also had its lighter moments. One vaccination post was in a mosque, but the Imam had gone off with the key and the team couldn't get in. A male nurse volunteering to open the door from the inside hauled himself through a small window and leapt into the inner courtyard, but landed in the tub where the dead bodies were washed. He had to be excused for the rest of the day.

Rumours of the miracle occurring in Turkey now began to reach the outside world, and representatives from the Health Ministries of ten countries, as far away as the People's Republic of China and Nigeria, came to watch. So over and above their jobs of monitoring, travelling, evaluating, encouraging, sustaining and planning for the third and final round, the staffs had to look after the visitors. All were seeking elements of Turkey's social mobilization which they could apply to their country: all vowed to do even better than Turkey.

Rapidly the days moved towards November and the final round. Morale was high, success within reach, for in rounds one and two their target had easily been surpassed. Hoping to reach at least 80 per cent of the 5.1 million eligible children, they had reached 83 per cent by round two. Now, with one final heave, they aimed to increase the coverage still further. Sarojini and Incila were determined to kick off round three in magnificent style.

'Her suggestion was at first very strange for us,' laughs Dr Unsal, still bemused. 'We would never have thought of doing this. Maybe Sarojini was really Oriental, we

decided. She has such a creative nature ... always
thinking, even dreaming. Oh, what a lady.'

For on Sunday, 24 November, two rival first-division
football teams faced each other in Ankara's famous
Nineteenth of May Stadium for the match of the year –
Ankaragucu, the home team, playing Malatyaspor, from
a southeastern province, and they had asked Ankaragucu
if UNICEF might place immunization banners around
the stadium. That was the easy part. Early on the Sunday
morning Incila and two drivers strung them up. The
messages: 'Have your children vaccinated'; 'Each must
receive three doses to be fully immunized'; 'This is the
date of the final round'; 'This is where you can go in
Ankara'; 'An immunized child is a healthy child', greeted
the crowds. Those with tickets were handed a leaflet on
admittance; other leaflets were scattered over Ankara
from an aeroplane. Since the match was being broadcast
nationally a series of television and radio 'spots' would be
relayed both to the crowd and the audiences. But
technicians failed to check the connections and the
microphones were dead. Incila was furious.

Jim Grant was there, along with Richard Reid, Sarojini
Abraham and many Turkish ministers, and soon the
crowd in the stadium started a huge chorus, chanting in
rhythm, 'Vaccinate your child.' The players jogged on to
the field carrying a banner so large that it took all the
players from each team to hold it. At half time the team
captains and staff members of UNICEF ran on, each
holding a baby in their arms, and urged parents to bring
their children for the final round. To everyone's huge
delight the spectators added their own contribution in
the second half with a slogan now frequently roared out
at Turkish football matches. Anyone playing badly
provoked the taunt: 'Mustafa, get vaccinated; Abdul,
you'd better be immunized.'

The next day, Monday 25 November, marked the start
of the final round. In the same auditorium where it had

all begun, under the lights of the television cameras, Turkish nationals and visiting UNICEF staff, now joined by visitors from Indonesia, Nigeria, Vietnam, Yemen, Bangladesh, Syria, Pakistan and the People's Republic of China, once again gave polio vaccine to ten small babies. As the country swung into the familiar routine all attention was focused in that small room at the Ministry of Health in Ankara.

Suddenly failure appeared imminent. Winter came early in many parts of the country, with torrential rains, landslides and blizzards. Most teams could not reach the villages. Even before any returns came in matters looked very serious. Daily, the twenty continuously manned telephone lines in the Ministry of Health took the same dismal message from all provincial health directors: the teams could not get out.

Despair, anxiety, sleepless nights were now their lot. They all prayed to their different gods that the snow would stop, the rain dry up, the mud cease moving, the roads open. Time was running out. If they were to cover the children the third round would have to be extended by one further week.

The President and Prime Minister offered to mobilize the Army to take in the teams by helicopters or special snow trucks. The details of the operation were formulated but the Ministry of Health stuck to their earlier resolve that the campaign should remain a purely civilian affair. While understanding the reluctance Reid and Sarojini took this decision hard. This was a major crisis: the campaign could founder.

But now the Governors turned up trumps and mobilized bulldozers from their construction departments to clear the way for the teams. National pride became an added goad as health directors urged the teams, 'We Turks can do it'; 'You *have* to go out', and the people responded, sometimes with their lives. The village *saglik memuru*, health assistant, from Kocacli, a small village in the east, set out on foot to take vaccine to an outlying settlement. When he didn't return, the village head and his vaccination team set out to find him. After two days' search the body was found: caught by a sudden blizzard, he had frozen in his tracks.

Not until the ninth day did the tide appear to turn. Late into that night Sarojini, Incila, Richard and Nefise waited in the UNICEF office, while Dr Unsal and the Ministry of Health officials waited equally anxiously in theirs. Then for the first time in the third round the numbers immunized each day began to climb. Even if the results were not going to be an overwhelming success, at least there would not be an appalling disgrace. The suspense was unnerving. There were moments of shocked surprise, even tears, when unexpectedly low figures came in. But a telephone call would invariably follow: apologies, someone had made an error. Correct numbers and normal heartbeats were restored together. When really magnificent results came in they would shout and hug each other. Slowly, day by day, the totals mounted.

Against all odds, and in a pattern never seen anywhere else in the world, before or since, the numbers of children coming in had increased with every round. The final tally – after, as Reid insisted, months of quite extraordinary effort, sacrifice and heroism on the part of the entire Turkish population – exceeded their goal: 84 per cent of the children had been reached. Had it not been for the appalling weather in the third round Turkey would have achieved exceptional results, reaching over 90 per cent of the susceptible children. Still in under three months 4.6 million Turkish children had been immunized. Had they not, over 1,376,000 of them would have caught measles, 873,000 whooping cough, and 9300 poliomyelitis.

From the sidelines members of the Task Force were quietly applauding, for a minor miracle had taken place.

But all reserved judgement, and rightly so, about long-term sustainability; others withheld any applause till the WHO evaluation of the campaigns came in, a year later; others still – not trusting campaigns – withheld it permanently. Turkey's infant mortality was reduced from near 100 deaths per 1000 before the campaign, to 87 deaths, and in 1988 was down to 65 per 1000. This may not appear much of an improvement, since respiratory and diarrhoeal infections wreak a greater havoc on young children than the immunizable diseases, but possibly statistics are not the sole point. Far more significant is the fact that the success did have several immediate and crucial consequences. Demand was indeed induced. Most Turkish mothers now expect immunization; moreover, since they now appreciate the benefits of such interventions – many for the first time – improvements in all aspects of child health are expected.

The status of the health service, too, was altered. Though as in all countries finance and defence take priority in the national budget, health and health staff did acquire a new respectability, and morale throughout the service began to rise. In 1986, the Health Director of Manisa interviewed 3000 applicants for 120 places in his service – an enormous jump over previous years. In addition, since households in the remotest areas were sought out, tens of thousands of families came on to the health rolls for the first time.

Yet a high infant mortality rate still remained in the poorest areas, as well as a high birth rate. So in 1986, President Evren launched a second programme, to tackle all problems. Under a newly-established organization the vaccination programme would be sustained, tetanus immunization in pregnant mothers accelerated, breast-feeding promoted, child and maternal nutrition improved and family planning vigorously tackled. In the cities the programmes are focused in Mother and Child Health Clinics (MCHC). On average fifty new mothers arrive each morning at the Esrefpasa Health Centre in Konak district, Izmir. But before their baby is even examined they must listen to a talk about vaccines, cleanliness, growth monitoring, nutrition and birth control.

Specialized units concentrating on family planning now work in conjunction with these clinics and, as before, other ministries have been co-opted. Ninety per cent of the population are aware of family planning though only 50 per cent practise contraception. But since Turkey is a secular society Muslim fundamentalists cannot, without breaking the law, actively fight the service; they merely avoid using it themselves. In the mosques the Imams preach about the effects too many children have on the health of mother and child, on the difficulty of providing adequate education and on jobs. Television still remains by far the most important medium for getting the message across and the Turks are now as optimistic about getting their birth rate down as they were their infant mortality.

Yet although Turkey started with enormous advantages – an excellent health infrastructure that can cope with the onslaught of concentrated campaigns – it will face for ever the problem of sustaining and expanding the system. In the months following the campaign immunization began to fall to as low as 45 per cent in the east. The reasons were multiple: flushed with success, many mistook the victory of battle for winning the war. Holidays postponed were taken; tasks set aside received attention, others were renewed, for tuberculosis and malaria control suffered for those three months in autumn 1985; the people in other ministries who had participated in the campaign returned to their own territories. But children continued to be born, one and a half million each year. So serious was the fall that soon the President was back on television appealing to all parents, urging all organizations to help and serving notice on the sixty-seven governors that by 1988 he expected annual coverage to be back at 80 per cent. They responded . . . they had no choice. Schoolteachers have been permanently co-opted into immunization campaigns, intense efforts have been made in areas of the east and southeast and once more the figures are climbing. These results are being watched closely, for whatever their individual beliefs about strategy everyone agrees: if we can't sustain immunization in Turkey, we can't sustain it anywhere.

The health problems that Turkey faces today are as challenging as any of those which provoked the campaign, and one ex-Minister of Health told me that the demands provoked by the campaign are definitely not being met. For the truth is that the health services in Turkey are still inadequate and unwieldy – as a recent report showed. Commissioned by the state planning organization, this uncovered serious deficiencies and inadequacies in spite of the fact that health education is spreading rapidly, many more midwives are coming on to the rolls, and malaria has not made a major comeback as it has in many other countries. But even by 1994 staffing levels will still be half those now existing in the member countries of the European Community that Turkey wishes to join.

Part of the continuing health problems also lies in poor sanitation and lack of water supplies – even in urban areas. The report notes that 'a greater proportion of households had colour television than a drainage system'. Industrial pollution is equally appalling. Those who knew Izmir and Istanbul thirty years ago can only weep.

Reforms are badly needed; many doctors doing their year's compulsory service spend more time studying for future specialities than tackling primary health care in rural settlements. Money for transport – drivers and fuel – is still short, preventive measures not sufficiently emphasized.

And what are the figures for infant mortality now? The report believes that it is still around 100 per 1000 – and in isolated places, where one in three births are not even reported, it could be double that.

Gloomy though all this may seem, one does sense a great desire on the part of many Turks to tackle the situation. Many organizations who worked together in the campaign are collaborating in a number of joint endeavours in the eastern and southeastern areas of the country where the health and economic situations are still bad. Seminars held in centres like Elazig, or Dyakabir, bring in *Muhtars*, Imams and teachers from outlying areas, who are taught about all aspects of preventive medicine – not only immunization. Education and literacy programmes are being emphasized. Indeed one *Muhtar* taught himself to read and write at one such seminar; his texts were vaccination schedules.

Thus the will, the commitment and the motivation are still present, and since the success of the whole campaign was ultimately due to the Turks themselves, it is appropriate that here the last word should be given to one who was part of it from the very beginning.

'You see, matters can't end here,' says Incila Diker. 'This whole action has to go on and on. For we are like athletes who have received a gold medal and if we don't build on our achievement, we shall feel betrayed and angry. The campaign became a very personal crusade: I think I'd murder anyone who got in the way of the next stage. We all feel the same. No one would dream of saying, "Well I'm tired now so I can't do any more." We've got to live with the fact of our success for ever and ever.'

7
More Important than War

'I have lost friends, some by death ... others through sheer inability to cross the street.'

Virginia Woolf, *The Waves*

In late September 1986, one year after the start of the Turkish campaign, a regional meeting of UNICEF was held in Istanbul. Jim Grant and Richard Reid both attended. By then Reid had moved to Amman to take charge of the UNICEF office responsible for eighteen countries throughout North Africa and the Middle East. Two years later Sarojini would join him as Deputy Director. At the meeting the discussion focused on the problem of those Arab states which had unacceptable immunization coverage. Of them, three countries – Sudan and the two Yemens – were visibly low and one, Lebanon, was a mystery.

UNICEF, whose regional office, staffed by nearly eighty people, was once situated in Beirut, has been in the Lebanon since the 1950s as have a number of other agencies – Save the Children Fund and those United Nations relief organizations that work in the Palestine refugee camps. All remained throughout the years of continuing and bloody civil strife. However, the UNICEF staff were aware that official Lebanese statistics claimed an immunization coverage of nearly 65 per cent but they knew this had to be a reflection of the past, when

Lebanon was a peaceful country with a model health system. Indeed, when they looked more closely, they saw that far from having a good vaccine coverage, Lebanon had a declining one. The rising infant mortality rate was attributable to several connected factors, the main one of which was war, leading to a paralysis of the health system and national immunization services, which in turn led to inadequate vaccination coverage. There were, certainly, 425 health centres operating in the country but supplies were unreliable, so a mother and child with an appointment might arrive only to find that there were no vaccines.

One evening at that meeting in Istanbul Raymond Naimy, the head of UNICEF in Lebanon, took Jim Grant aside and said, 'Look, our children are desperate.' 'Yes, we know. We are ready to help,' Grant replied. 'But whatever we do must prove to the world that something really *can* be achieved, countrywide, because everyone regards Lebanon as a snake pit and believes nothing can be done.'

In a very real sense the children of Lebanon, without constituency, friends or voice, are the unrecognized hostages. No governments intercede on their behalf, no media report their activities, no ransoms are paid for their freedom. They are hostages not only because their lives are of little account, but if they are lost, so too is the possibility of a future. So UNICEF's staff conceived an audacious and dangerous plan that would need to be kept highly secret.

It was dangerous because as a country Lebanon had, to all intents and purposes, almost ceased to exist; the rule of law had vanished. The state always was a coalition of feuding interests and religious factions, but nevertheless until recently these had managed to live in some semblance of harmony. The Lebanese are for the most part either Christians or Muslims, though each has its own sub-groups – the Sunnis and the Shiites on the

Muslim side; the Maronites and the Greek Orthodox on the Christian side. The Druze form an intermediate group. Each faction has its own very powerful and individualistic confessional entity, each its own political and religious ideology. To make the situation even more complex, political persuasions overlie the confessional boundaries so within all groups are people who belong to the extremes of the political spectrum. To complicate matters further, watchful, fearful neighbours, especially Israel, Syria and Iran, consider Lebanon to be vital to their security and within their sphere of influence. The great powers, too, have their own reasons for remaining deeply involved.

In the past the shifting mosaic was kept in an uneasy, fragile balance by the proportional legislative system that Lebanon managed to evolve. But by 1986 the encompassing framework had shattered and each piece of the mosaic was drifting apart. At least seventeen factions, each with its own warlords, operated within the country. Anyone who now wants to do anything must face some stark realities, on three levels: the international one of the great powers; the regional one – Syria, Iraq, Iran and Israel; and that of the local factions which employ their own hit teams swimming like sharks in the muddy waters. These hit teams must be paid for. In the past oil revenues provided substantial cash; now it comes from drugs and even sea piracy. The latest lucrative racket is 'losing' ships and cargo, claiming insurance, renaming the ships, retrieving the cargo and offering to sell this back to the insurers. Whoever is prepared to wield a gun will get money and food; whoever pays the most money to the gunmen will wield the most power, if only temporarily. Assassination settles many scores, personal as well as political, as does arms dealing. As Raymond Naimy once said to me, 'If only outsiders would stop giving us locals bullets, then everybody could quietly go home.'

Once the jewel of the Middle East, Lebanon certainly

had many problems and many injustices, but in the past
the small population was energetic, healthy, and sustained
a vibrant economy with a superb health structure. But by
September 1986 the situation was disastrous; the economy
had declined dramatically, and passivity and despair pre-
dominated. Garbage was piled high in the street; oil was so
expensive that power stations cut out twelve hours a day;
the water supply regularly failed. Trade plummeted
sharply; there was no external banking; agriculture was all
but destroyed. Five hundred and fifty Lebanese pounds
equalled one US dollar, and the rate of inflation was
enormous. Parents could not afford to send their children
to school, for all traditional sources of income had dried
up. The country imported 85 per cent of all its needs and
400,000 people lived in abject poverty. The militias of
each faction exploited even this situation, because a
gunman is far better off than even a bank manager. It is
said that whatever is offered to a gunman, one of the
competing outside countries will always top this by $100
per month more. In 1987 the minimum monthly wage of
$18 bought a paper, a sandwich, a drink or a bullet. Even
bullets were becoming expensive and finally people were
being forced to sell guns to buy butter. Parents went to
heroic lengths to protect their children and get them out
of the country, even selling them – which in Islam is
unthinkable. Kidnappings, the taking of hostages, mur-
ders were a daily occurrence. Lebanese are still held for
ransom day after day, though only Western hostages
make the headlines.

In 1984, as the chaos deepened, UNICEF decided that
their regional office would have to move; they went to
Amman. But though twelve of the Lebanese staff moved
to Jordan, sixty or so stayed behind. By 1986, the office in
Western Beirut, just across the Green Line, had a staff of
thirty-five men and women. These were the people who
would try to immunize at least 80 per cent of an estimated
380,000 children throughout the country.

*

Raymond Naimy, who became head of UNICEF in Lebanon, is a fifty-year-old Lebanese, with crinkled hair, short, genial and quiet. He graduated at Ankara University as a telecommunications and systems engineer, finishing with a sound practical and theoretical knowledge. By 1975, when the war between the political factions finally erupted, he had worked in North Africa, the Gulf and Saudi Arabia. There he met his future wife, a Saudi Arabian Muslim. For her to marry a Christian Lebanese was tantamount to a death sentence. The pair fled Saudi Arabia, were married in Switzerland and went to live in Beirut. Having that genuine Lebanese entrepreneurial flair, Raymond Naimy soon held a series of consulting and contracting jobs in engineering throughout Lebanon.

In 1978 a UNICEF programme officer asked him to take on part-time work as an engineering specialist. One day each week quickly became three and soon weekends were thrown in too, for UNICEF was helping the government with emergency programmes for the children, building schools, clinics and water supplies. By 1981 Raymond Naimy, as full-time head of UNICEF's Technical Section, was moving all over the country setting up the necessary engineering works.

One morning in June 1982, he was at the dentist's. As he lay back in the chair, staring out of the window and bracing himself for the pain of the drill, a jet trail crossed his line of vision. Urgently he turned to his dentist: 'Hurry and fix my tooth; the Israelis are attacking Beirut.' Quickly leaving the surgery, he wondered: 'What the hell can I do?' He knew one thing for sure: if the invaders cut off the power and water the whole of West and East Beirut might fall. Months beforehand he had located the positions of the many wells that lie beneath the city's buildings; all that was required to get at the water was drilling. So now he assembled his teams, called in a contractor and said, 'Go and make me a series of enormous water tanks. I've got no money to pay you. But don't worry because eventually I'll sell the operation to someone.' The tanks were then strategically placed all around the city. The next problem was power. Working equally fast he located all available generators, 243 of them, called in another contractor who had pick-up trucks and had the generators moved to the well-heads. Working round the clock his teams drilled 23 wells and set up emergency supplies of water and power. While shells rained on the city, young men delivered water at 85 centres for twenty-four hours a day to the half a million people living in Beirut, and using the generators, supplied power to nearby buildings. If they had not done this the city would have been out of water and power within three to four weeks and would have fallen.

Within a short space of time UNICEF had become Lebanon's national water corporation and main salvage operator. Gradually its five water crews of engineers and hydrogeologists extended the water network throughout the country, working often under fire. If a pipeline was blown up one day, UNICEF teams were repairing it the next. If that well needed fixing, that pumping station repairing, UNICEF crews crossed the lines and asked the local militia, 'Do you mind just holding off sniping this morning? We've got to fix the water.' Pumping stations, reservoirs, dams, large and small, are regularly hit by bombs, rockets and small arms fire, but nevertheless UNICEF makes repairs in a matter of hours and keeps the water flowing. Because they built and now maintain the water network, the range of their contacts is unique and throughout Lebanon they are seen as honest brokers, with no political axe to grind.

Their teams – one headed by Gloria Canaan, a remarkable woman who works mostly in the Beqaa Valley where the Iranian factions hold sway – run other programmes too. They started the peace playgrounds – areas, pathetic and fragile though they may seem, where children can play and experience some semblance of normal, carefree childhood if only for half an hour a day. They run homes for displaced persons, and education programmes in the Beirut schools.

From their headquarters in West Beirut Raymond Naimy sent his staff across the Green Line and out into the country every morning. He never returned home until he had counted them all back every evening. The courage and resilience of these young teams – the average age is about thirty-eight – is awesome. Two years ago Naimy received the UNICEF award for bravery. Nabila Breir, a Lebanese of Palestinian descent and a militant activist, was dragged from a car and shot down in 1987 while working, perhaps too visibly, in an area of great conflict and controversy, the Chatila refugee camp into which many Palestinians had been herded and subsequently massacred. Afterwards word filtered down the grapevine that her death was not to be considered as a gesture against UNICEF. Amal Dibo, who was to do most of the co-ordination for the immunization campaign, and Anna Mansour, who works with orphan children in schooling and redevelopment programmes, showed enormous bravery. Day after day everyone is at constant risk. There continue to be times when they cannot reach the office because they are pinned down in their homes by sniper fire. Though Raymond Naimy lives in a village not far from the centre of Beirut he often can't cross the Green Line and get into work. Crossing this line is a traumatic experience because anything can happen, from the indignity of being asked interminable and irritating questions for the thousandth time by young people who in normal circumstances would be expected to show respect, to being physically roughed up. Sometimes the staff become so frustrated by the long waits that they scamper along unauthorized routes only to be shot at by snipers.

*

For the people at the Istanbul meeting, whether
Lebanese or not, watching the politicians of the different
countries trapped within their own ideologies, their goals
detached from reality, the children mattered more than
anything else. Here, waiting in the wings, was a whole
generation; if they were not taken care of, what chance
did they, or the future, have? Richard Reid was imbued
not only with this imperative but also with the same
motive that had propelled Jim Grant and UNICEF into
the days of tranquillity in El Salvador. Might not the
possibility of peace itself be enhanced if the people
shooting each other in Lebanon could be persuaded to
stop on behalf of the children, if they could show that
even after the bitter years, there was still a reservoir of
decency and positive, constructive purpose? To demon-
strate this became a personal crusade for Reid.

So in March 1987, he flew to Beirut, the first of a
number of journeys he would make in the next few
months. His visits could be considered extraordinarily
foolhardy: one year after the TWA hijack, with many
Western hostages already taken, an articulate, high-
profile American was a prime target for kidnap. Extreme
precautions were taken to guarantee his safety. Only one
or two people within UNICEF knew of the plan, and no
one at all outside – not Foege, nor Mahler, nor Warren,
none of the Task Force staff and no one in the donor
agencies. Sometimes Reid drove overland from Damascus into Lebanon; sometimes he flew in. The road from
the airport into West Beirut is the most dangerous
highway in the world; one boundary fence of the
perimeter is controlled by the Iranian Hezbollah 'Party of
God'. Reid would later remark on the impeccably correct
behaviour of the Syrian soldiers who were to establish
very tight control, looking as innocent as a Californian
highway patrol. No one except Naimy was ever told when

Reid was coming, though everyone knows that all communications – whether telephone, telex or fax – are monitored, and that little can be kept secret. After press conferences or meetings Reid was immediately whisked out of West Beirut and across the Green Line to the east of the city where he was housed. Yet one day even their most stringent precautions were fruitless. Crossing a checkpoint on his way to visit a refugee camp the UNICEF car was stopped and they were all questioned. But this checkpoint was in a politically very sensitive area that the media were temporarily covering. On Lebanese television news that night the UNICEF car appeared with Reid sitting next to the driver plain as a pikestaff for all to see.

Reid was accompanied on these trips by André Roberfroid, an equally brave Belgian. In May 1968, Roberfroid was a student in Paris who firmly believed in the revolution to come, after which everyone would love each other and the whole world would change. Then he realized that the world would change only if he personally helped to make it change. He joined a French non-governmental organization working in a remote rural area of Niger and later moved to UNICEF. At this time he learnt that infant mortality is not merely someone else's statistic. His two-year-old daughter died in just a few hours from the dehydration that follows acute diarrhoea. As a student Roberfroid had glibly assumed – as many of us have been tempted to do – that 'they're used to death in Africa; so many children die that they don't feel it.' But when his infant girl died the neighbours came to share their grief. 'I, and we, and they, remember every second of that time – as they do when any one of their children dies.'

Roberfroid did not believe the proposed plan was possible, but one day, as they drove back to East Beirut after meeting the water engineers in the countryside, Reid convinced him. For as he travelled across Lebanon,

on his first visit to Beirut in March 1987, Reid had
unerringly picked out the two key elements that would be
vital to success. The first was Raymond Naimy and the
water network. 'With these water guys on the ground, with
their connections and knowledge of the country, it's a go.
If we didn't have them, no way.' The second was a consequence of the first for it gave Naimy access to those
'warlords' – the factional bosses – who alone really decided
what happened in Lebanon. They now trusted him.

Reid knew better than anyone that major national interventions for children cannot happen unless the people in
power are enthusiastic. For the most part this meant one
government and its Ministry of Health. But in Lebanon
the people in power made up one hundred and eighteen
factions, of which seventeen were dominant. Raymond
Naimy would have to talk to every one of these power
brokers. It took from March 1987 to July 1987 for Naimy
to put out feelers and get responses; only then did he
begin meeting the individual faction leaders face to face.
He saw them all. This time he didn't ask them to stop the
sniping for a few hours for a pipeline repair or a sick child.
He wanted the fighting to stop for several days.

But Naimy did not want just passive agreement, he
wanted enthusiastic support. 'We wanted them to own the
idea,' he said. But how to make them? 'By a combination of
pride and flattery.' If one side of pride is fear of humili-
ation and a desire to save face, the other is the wish to look
good – and in no respect was Lebanon looking good. A
totally fragmented breeding-ground for killing, it was a
country to spurn. Yet, Naimy argued, if all the power
brokers would support the campaign and agree to the
days of tranquillity (the word 'ceasefire' carried too many
humiliating overtones) the world would see that the
Lebanese could, even temporarily, recast their image to
one of decency, humanitarianism and national purpose.

So, on visit after visit, Raymond Naimy travelled from
the Shouf Mountains where the Druzes hold sway, to the

Beqaa Valley where the Iranian groups predominate, to the south where the Israelis and Christian Lebanese have power, and put the proposition to all. Nobody could be the loser, he argued; everyone a winner. The children would have the shield of vaccine protection; if the country collectively was seen in a somewhat more positive light, those participating might actually feel good about themselves; perhaps even a measure of national self-confidence might be restored. Logic told him that they should respond to the challenge and they did. What no one imagined was that the response would escalate in enthusiasm.

Richard Reid meanwhile was pondering another problem – the capacity of the Lebanese staff. They had been numbed, traumatized, some destroyed, by what they had been through during the past years. There was not one who hadn't lost a family member; not a week went by without a relative, friend or colleague being killed. He had no doubt of the staff's commitment to UNICEF's goals but they were being asked to make an enormous investment of emotion, time and energy for a project that carried a very real risk of failure. Did they have the strength? Divisions existed amongst them too, not along military or religious lines, but emotional ones, from the pressures that come when people have been shipwrecked for so long. Days went by with nothing to do except wait, and wait, and wait until the fighting stopped.

Swiftly in May 1987, the outlines of the campaign were drawn up in UNICEF's Beirut office. It is now believed that the two senior United Nations officials told of the plan were unhappy and forbade Reid to go in, but like Lord Nelson he just clapped his telescope to his blind eye and went. Jim Grant, however, encouraged the Lebanese UNICEF staff and during April and May 1987, the support of everyone who mattered was enlisted. Given this support a few people from UNICEF, WHO, the Lebanese Ministry of Health and some local and

international non-governmental organizations formed a
coalition for action. Rush procurement orders for
vaccines and equipment sped to UNIPAC in Copenhagen; the bills to WHO.

In September 1987, three weeks before the campaign
was to begin, UNICEF did a pre-vaccination survey
following a protocol designed by WHO. Throughout the
districts of Lebanon, 410 random clusters of twenty-five
children in each were surveyed for vaccination coverage.
Of these, 53 per cent had received shots for diphtheria,
whooping cough and tetanus, a figure higher than
expected. But only 39 per cent had received a measles
shot; this alone, they felt, confirmed that they were right
to try and do something.

Nothing was left to chance, no detail of tactics,
communication, transport or cold chain overlooked. The
energies of the Ministry of Health directors from the
twenty-four *kazas* – districts – of Lebanon were
reactivated. Meeting with mayors and *Muhtars*, Imams
and priests, elected official and local factional leaders,
Boy Scouts and Red Crescent workers, the members of
UNICEF's Beirut office, each responsible for the
planning and operations, fanned out through the
country. Seven hundred and sixty vaccination posts
were established in the districts. Most were in existing
health centres, a few were in mosques, a few in schools,
and others in houses of the rich. The usual social
mobilization seen in other countries was mounted, but
actually matters were easier because Lebanese parents
knew all about the value of vaccination. Still the mothers
had to be convinced that genuinely potent vaccines really
would be available, and that it would be safe for their
infants to come. Again, as in other countries, the Imams,
the Sheiks, the priests, teachers and political leaders, all
manned loudspeakers urging people to participate. A
campaign song became a familiar jingle, saturating the
air waves. For once all rural radio stations relayed the

same messages and the two-minute television spot – 'the Kalashnikov number' – was starkly unique to Lebanon. The camera cuts between three children walking hand in hand towards a hidden sniper, who tracks them in his gun sights. The children come on, the man cocks his gun; the children look at him, smiling trustingly; the man takes aim; closer and closer they come until they are looking down his gun barrel. As the camera cuts away the commentary says, 'Why not stand tall? Why not protect them?'

The building that houses the Lebanese Ministry of Health is situated right on the Green Line, between two checkpoints of West and East Beirut. Soldiers are everywhere. The destruction in the area is so great that the landscape is as desolate as the moon. Yet during the planning process, 400 Beirut Ministry of Health officials and district staff – Christians, Muslims and Druzes – who had not seen each other for years, came in from all over the country for two four-day orientation sessions, one on the east side, one on the west. Then every week, they would be driven into Beirut by UNICEF vehicles, assemble at the entrance to the Ministry of Health building, take the key, open the door, walk up the ruined staircase and along dusty, empty corridors, enter damaged rooms, wipe rubble off tables and chairs, sit down, discuss, take notes and decisions, then leave, locking the outer door of the Ministry as they departed.

The usual launching ceremony at which the major political leaders would speak was planned but at the last moment cancelled: it seemed too risky and they might not all attend. A national press conference was held instead.

And the peace held. In those days of tranquillity, as the fighting stopped, and military vehicles transported women, children and supplies, 380,000 infants were protected. Vaccines and syringes, not bullets and

mortars, crossed the lines. It was a remarkable time
which, the Lebanese insist, will never be forgotten by
those who took part. The UNICEF staff in West Beirut
worked from five o'clock in the morning to midnight,
co-ordinating activity in the districts, from the Beqaa
Valley to the Shouf Mountains, to Tripoli in the north, to
Sidon and Tyre in the south near the Israeli border. The
first day brought such a tumultuous rush of mothers,
especially in the Shiite sections of West Beirut, that the
harried vaccinators – doctors, nurses, schoolteachers –
were working in rooms jammed to the walls by the
crowds. Older children carried in younger siblings. Some
five-year-olds clutching vaccination cards, came alone.
Posts that were supposed to be open at 7.00 a.m. were so
overwhelmed that they couldn't start functioning until
8.30 and in Beirut most of the immunization services
were on the verge of collapse. At one post old men
queued up with the children. The television broadcasts
had said that vaccination prevented disease so they, too,
came in for shots. When told, 'This is not for the old,'
they were furious. 'You don't like me. You're a bad guy.'
It proved simpler to vaccinate them than to argue.

On the second day of the first round, the National
Workers' Union called a total strike and everything
ground to a halt. Then a coincidental technical fault put
all telephone services out of action for twenty-four hours.
Transport was always likely to be difficult because of the
permanent petrol shortage, but suddenly, just before the
campaign started, the price of fuel rose 100 per cent in
twenty-four hours, so the vehicles were unable to run.
Few budgets can cope with such sudden extras. So
UNICEF caught twelve taxi-drivers straight off the
Beirut streets, of whatever nationality or religious group
they happened to be, struck an immediate bargain and
used them as their shuttle communication system. Car
radios and walkie-talkies were mobilized as standard
equipment for all staff members, some of whom had to

climb on the rooftops so they could be heard in the control centres. Fleets of Toyotas, Datsuns and Land Cruisers dashed up and down the city streets and country roads. Everyone doubled up on jobs; staff members became drivers; secretaries and programme officers delivered and gave vaccines. Dr Mohammed Mohanna, the director of Lebanon's EPI programme, and Raymond Naimy, went everywhere. Very cool under stress, Naimy drove his beat-up Datsun between all the health posts throughout Lebanon, fielding several radio calls simultaneously, trading and exchanging vaccines, encouraging people, while keeping in touch with UNICEF's headquarters in West Beirut. During this first round there was the most beautiful Indian summer weather, with a stillness that was palpable. Like stalked animals, everyone was sensitive to the unusual silence. Apart from some scattered gunfire and the heavy crumps of two explosions that no one ever traced, the days passed as they were meant to, in complete peace.

Suha Majdalani, a Lebanese woman, recalls her exhilaration as she visited her country for the first time for years. She drove right across Lebanon, and as her car with its UNICEF logo pulled up, she was stopped by each militia in turn, at checkpoint after checkpoint, whose protective sandbags now carried vaccination posters. All she had to say was 'Vaccination,' and without exception soldiers broke into the campaign song, 'Vaccinate your child before it's too late. They are the hope; they are the future', and let her through.

Rivalry between the militia was finally being turned towards the most humanitarian of ends. One group who had opened seven posts heard that a neighbouring group a few blocks away had eight, so promptly opened two more. The Beqaa Valley, under Iranian control, boasted the most efficient immunization campaign of all, perfectly conducted.

As usual the UNICEF office combined the ambience of

a military command post in the middle of a battle and an election centre when the returns are coming in. Each evening eager local district co-ordinators radioed in the numbers and at headquarters the staff recorded the incoming reports, in a frenetic atmosphere that was both hilarious and exciting. The daily results were immediately fed into a computer, then telexed to Geneva and New York. André Roberfroid, in Lebanon with his wife, played a major role in the decision to extend the programme for a fourth day, for the early returns showed that the strike was affecting the coverage in a number of places. So the word went out to the militia, 'Please hold it for one more day,' and with every successive hour the coverage improved.

Richard Reid, who had flown in from Amman, covered the country, travelling north to Junie, Kessronan, Koura, Tripoli, the Shouf Mountains and all around East and West Beirut. He was accompanied throughout by Dr Unal Ural, an old campaigner from Turkey, representing Rotary International who once again were providing all the polio vaccine. Ural recalls the atmosphere as both bizarre and exhilarating. He flew into Beirut airport where his 'minders' were to pick him up in the VIP reception area. But he missed them, so blithely wandered out into the Arrivals forecourt wondering which of many armed bystanders were supposed to meet him. For four days he and Reid travelled together but from the very first night in West Beirut they were moved into a fresh hotel each day, being instructed never to check out in the morning – just walk out. Others would pay the bills later.

Then, on the evening of the fourth day, Reid and André Roberfroid, with some of the Amman Lebanese staff, drove out through Damascus. As they travelled across the desert, they relaxed in quiet exhilaration; on the most important point the dream was coming true. 'There was,' he says, 'joining of hands amongst groups that had not met ever before, and reconciliation amongst people who had not met for years. I think we got high marks on the spiritual side and the sense of shared national purpose.'

But at the nitty-gritty level of technique and organization, they knew they would have to do much better. There were too many queues of harassed mothers with tired kids, too many harassed vaccinators. The job had been done, but not with ease. Although by the fourth day most of the organizational problems were overcome, the distribution of personnel and supplies was not as good as it should have been. The cold chain, however, which had been thoroughly checked, worked perfectly and 80 per cent of the children were vaccinated.

The second round took place on 21, 22 and 23 October. This time Richard Reid did not come in: he was told by his Lebanese colleagues not to push his luck any further. But André Roberfroid went back, again with his wife. This, too, was a good round. But though the organization was much better and over two thousand additional social workers came in to help, there were also greater expectations from the people that had to be met. The weather – torrential rain and cold days, especially bad in the Beqaa Valley – didn't help and made the logistics of delivery very difficult, particularly in the isolated country villages. The UNICEF staff in the districts, keeping in touch by radio, lost contact with each other and their families. But this time special efforts were made in those southern suburbs of Beirut under Shiite Muslim control, for during round one the mothers had been reluctant to crawl from the safety of their homes. Now with the help of all the religious leaders, their fears were overcome. Though there was no fighting or gunfire, the situation remained very tense: it was election time, and in West Beirut some Syrian soldiers were kidnapped.

By the third round, 23–25 November, information and communication systems were working smoothly. This final round was to focus on measles, for it was essential to get that coverage high. So enthusiastic were the television people that they ran spots at every available moment, until finally the UNICEF staff had to beg them to stop because people's enthusiasm was peaking too soon. Then there was a new complication: some schoolteachers went on strike. Since the schools were being used as vaccination posts, it was feared that mothers would think they would be shut. So fresh messages had to be broadcast: even though there were no lessons, the schools would be opened for the children to come.

Because of the successes of the first two rounds much self-confidence had been generated. The capacity of the health system to respond to the increased demand was excellent and there was no doubt that Lebanon was going to do what UNICEF hoped it would. So the world was invited to watch. The Italians would come in to film; representatives of the media would be there. I and a colleague had been invited to go in with a Swiss photographer, to cover the final round for this book. Women, we were assured, had never been kidnapped – nor had they up to that time. Plans were made, visas obtained, tickets purchased. Keith Graves of the BBC advised us not to fly in but to take the boat from Cyprus to East Beirut. There the staff would pick us up and take us to a hotel in West Beirut, near UNICEF's headquarters, where we and the other press would remain for four days. But, like everyone else, we assumed that the contents of every telex or telephone call were known, and many had been exchanged. Then a few hours before we left two telexes arrived, from UNICEF in New York and in Amman. All facilities were withdrawn: our safety could not be guaranteed.

One month later André Roberfroid and Raymond Naimy were in London. Naimy explained that generally he would hear two weeks before anything happened and the warning had been quite explicit: 'Don't bring any foreigners in.' Something did happen. Hang-gliders had flown over the Israeli border and there had been a skirmish. Retaliation was expected. Then shortly before the final days of tranquillity of round three, two bombs exploded, both carried by women on suicide missions. One went off in the airport, the other at the American Hospital, when a woman walked into the lobby carrying a bomb disguised as a box of chocolates. Raymond said, 'We didn't have any time to think too much about all this because we were too busy setting up the last round. But in my country you dare not make a single mistake, nor should you ever be afraid to appear ridiculous for having been over-careful. So that's why we wouldn't bring you in.'

Yet the ceasefire was maintained once more and the children vaccinated for the third time. Those sheltering in the basements waiting for Israel's revenge had to be persuaded to come, and they scurried back home immediately afterwards. Two hours after the end of the round sporadic shelling started up again in Beirut and with only a few hours to go, Naimy, sensing that something was about to erupt, ordered everyone home.

Still, all 2,025 villages in Lebanon had been covered and on Sunday 29 November, a big party was held for the staff and volunteers to celebrate the achievement. In three months the coverage for DPT and measles for the under-fives had been raised from 30–40 per cent to 92 and 79 per cent. Public, private and non-governmental organizations had been pulled together for the first time, the morale of the health staff enhanced and their status restored. Regular vaccination days – Thursdays once a month – had now been established for all health centres, and UNICEF would ensure that vaccines and syringes were always there. They believed the campaign would have a lasting impact since the high-quality Lebanese media coverage had raised public awareness to new levels.

The positive public response had impressed many

political leaders, so UNICEF expected that 'children first' activities would thereafter receive greater political support. Lebanon's capacity to implement humanitarian projects had achieved renewed credibility, and this could be expected to influence those who funded other humanitarian projects in the country. Finally, and more difficult to measure, was the psychological impact of the initiative on various militiamen. Most people agreed, though cautiously, that their participation in a peaceful, positive and self-rewarding action could not but be a further stepping-stone on the way towards peace.

But all was not sweetness and light. For some other agencies who also had never left Beirut, it was all a bit too much, and I encountered marked anger at Save the Children Fund. This was just UNICEF skimming off the cream of media attention once again. Some claimed that the campaign had not even been necessary, for estimates from the American University showed an immunization coverage during the last four to five years of between 80 and 90 per cent. While conceding that the rich always obtained vaccines for their children through private medicine, they pointed to the fact that the Lebanese Red Cross, the Mouvement Social and various other local agencies and charities had maintained a high level of immunization throughout the past years. In Sidon, for instance, a mini-government headed by Mustapha Saad ran social programmes for Sunni Muslims with properly established cold chains and people could bring in their children for vaccination at any time. But the real reason for their irritation was that by getting all the publicity UNICEF could undermine these ongoing efforts and erode the morale of ordinary locals who, exposed to the dangers for twenty-four hours a day, had been beavering away for years.

Not unnaturally UNICEF disputes the claim that the campaign was unnecessary: it would have been foolhardy in the extreme to have exposed so many people to so many risks, and to have sought to pull the wool over the eyes of an extremely sceptical world media for an entirely superfluous action. Moreover if the campaign was not needed why, they ask, did the Lebanese Ministry of Health embrace it so wholeheartedly, be so ready to admit that a problem existed, that the health services actually couldn't deliver the coverage, that vaccine supplies were always intermittent, that only privately paid doctors could get them, that for some months the interruption of electrical supplies in West Beirut had compromised the cold chain, that the probability of a severe measles epidemic was high? This sniping between agencies – luckily nothing like so lethal as that which usually goes on in Lebanon – is in part explained by people being at the end of their tether, emotionally and physically exhausted from battling away day after day. But there is no doubt that UNICEF's capacity to capture the headlines, a tool they use quite openly for their campaigns, generates enormous resentment. Nevertheless, the Lebanese involved insist that what began as a suggestion to achieve the impossible metamorphosed into a remarkable event that seems likely to have made a lasting impression.

In the words of Suha Majdalani: 'It was a wonderful and a unique experience. I was enthusiastic about the possibility before we started, but I didn't really believe it would happen. I was rapidly giving up on Lebanon. In fact, I had decided never to return. But these days have made me think that at last, one day, things might change and finally reconciled me to my own country.'

Raymond Naimy said, 'I was down on the border with Israel not too long ago, at a small village whose name in Lebanese means "Good Gate". Along the whole border was the first electric fence, and then the second, with that area of earth between, which every day the Israelis sweep so clean that any footmark, even that of a bird, is immediately visible. The area is ringed with mines, electronic devices, rockets. On our side of the border, I saw an old grandfather of about seventy, ploughing the earth with his donkey and the ancient wooden plough that for generations has been used in the Middle East. I asked him, what did he think? He replied, "Sir, I have only got to throw a stone over that fence and they will unleash the whole lot at me, everything in the way of military power. You know, sir," this grandfather went on, "there's got to be a better way, otherwise there will be no peace." What we hoped we did was to introduce power of a different kind.

'Look,' he went on, 'so many people say to me, you stupid man, why are you wasting your time? And indeed, there are so many thousand reasons why I should take my children outside the country. But if I apply these excuses to my family, why should not everybody take their children and go? It doesn't matter whether it's Christianity, or Islam, or any religion. *All* say take thought for your neighbour; other people count; they, too, are human beings. So you can take Christ or Mohammed or Gandhi or anybody who really wanted to help humanity and, without exception, they all realized they cannot just preach. Practice is equally important. Preaching from behind a desk is very easy but to apply your beliefs practically is the most difficult thing of all, especially when everybody says how stupid or misconceived you are. Only the children can carry this torch forward in the future.

'So we went to everyone who has a parcel of the power in Lebanon and proposed something that could not possibly be debated, invited them to take an action about which they could not possibly be negative. Usually they are power brokers and tell us what's going to happen but finally they did something which *we asked*. So in the end we found ourselves having a real power of a very different nature – that comes from being fair, from being just, from asking yourself how much can you deliver to those in need, from being greater than you thought you were. We demonstrated power not only to talk but to act.

'Much of this is due to Jim Grant. He's a visionary who sees UNICEF as an instrument of peace. Some call him a flaming cowboy but he's an idealist who was looking for, and getting, a lot of political support. He is, of course, a pain in the neck. He never leaves us in peace twenty-four hours a day. Before he came we were a very small organization and most of us sat back and said because we are small we can't do much. Sure, the kids were there all right, but we took every weekend off. Well, in 1980, with Jim Grant, gears shifted dramatically and now I never look at Jim without seeing his vision for the future – a whole, complete child.'

Many will think that this talk of a different kind of power is being wildly naïve. But not Peter Coleridge, the Middle East co-ordinator of Oxfam, who with his Lebanese colleague, Omar Trabulsi, was kidnapped in 1988. Held by the extremist group of Abu Nidal, left blindfolded in a small dark room, questioned by people who believed none of his answers, he was threatened continuously. 'So when the knock on the door came the next evening,' he wrote later in the *Observer* newspaper, 'I put my blindfold on with trembling hands thinking it was the end. My legs were like water and I could hardly walk. "Are you ready?" they said. Dear God, I was not.'

But Peter Coleridge was released, and only then became aware of the vast network of support active on his behalf, inside and outside Lebanon. Thirty agencies working in the country – Oxfam, UNICEF, Save the Children Fund, the United Nations Relief Agency and many others – drew up an escalating series of measures they would put into effect had not both men been released. Coleridge wrote, 'All this was not just an expression of solidarity for us as individuals but for the work of this network itself, of which we and Oxfam are just a part. It was a spontaneous expression of people power and it was intoxicating. The last hope in Lebanon today lies in what such people are doing . . . In reality, the people running these projects are a dynamic network of individuals, groups and organizations committed to a process of finding an alternative to the violence and fragmentation as seen on TV. In the final tally of light and dark, perhaps [my going to Lebanon] was not a mistake but a prelude to a profound learning experience for many people, including Abu Nidal: that people power works.'

Raymond Naimy, asked if he had real reasons to be optimistic, replied: 'There are always all kinds of reasons to be optimistic, and this was but one. In a place where there is no more order, and no more lows to sink to, the worst that human beings can do to each other is actually being done, because nothing stops it. Now, when in that situation you go to people and offer them an opportunity to do something positive, you get a fantastic response. You can't *make* them do it. You're not even going to employ power, as they understand it, to *force* them to do it. Nothing forces them to help and nothing stops them from going on being bad. You merely offer them the opportunity, and you find they take it. For actually people like to be good.'

Several months later, in 1989, Bill Foege commented on the campaign. By then the situation in Lebanon had deteriorated even further; the army of General Michel Aoun, a Christian Lebanese, backed by the Iraqis, and the Syrians who back the Shiite Muslims, were shelling each other every day; the factions themselves were splitting. Then the Arab League organized a ceasefire, only for fierce ground fighting to erupt again and the bombardment to rise to its highest level in fifteen years. The country was on the verge of total anarchy; the photographs of small children crying, shattered, amongst the rubble, heart-rending. Once again feelings of the utter futility of any positive human action were overwhelming, cynicism an easy temptation.

*

Now during the years of civil war UNICEF and other NGOs had organized over one hundred Peace Camps where Lebanese children between five and twelve years of age of various religious groupings had periodically lived together. Over 23,000 had experience of these camps. The day after the latest ceasefire in September 1989, 10,000 of them were reunited in the West Beqaa Valley, in a mass gathering – another initiative for peace and solidarity. It is actions such as these that one must remember.

'We knew nothing about UNICEF's action until it was all over,' said Foege. 'But for a number of reasons, I think it was marvellous. First this is an area where it is difficult to do immunization and enhance child survival. So you have to come up with somewhat dramatic and different techniques to make it work at all. And I also like the idea of forcing on the consciousness of people in those areas the value of child survival, that every day can't be spent by fighting and hating and wondering how to get a political advantage. It *forces* you into thinking about the future. And, of course, I also like the idea that it gives a message to the rest of the world, that there are some things more important than war, even if they happen only for one day, or two, or three.'

8

Ambush in Maceió

'Let a man get up and say, "Behold, this is the truth", and instantly I perceive a sandy cat filching a piece of fish in the background. Look, you have forgotten the cat, I say.'

Virginia Woolf, *A Room of One's Own*

After the clean freshness of the Atlantic sky, the smog over Rio de Janeiro is murky, diminishing the beauty of the city's exquisite setting against mountains that rise sheer from the ocean. From the moment of arrival many such contrasts are hammered into the consciousness. If it is not rush hour, the taxi that speeds the traveller to the hedonism of Copocabana Beach can never travel fast enough to hide the poverty tucked behind the throughways. Swerving dangerously in and out of the tunnels, across the squares and around the headlands, the really wealthy will make for the most exclusively luxurious resorts of Ipanema and Leblon. The narcissistic bodies on the beaches – men twirling footballs, girls languorously swinging hips – the frenetic noise, the garish colours proclaim that for the privileged Brazil is a country where instant gratification is what really matters. So lie back; relax by the pool and let your eyes be drawn up to the green mountain summits where flocks of hang-gliders launch down through the mists to spiral earthward three thousand lazy feet on to the sand.

The beach chair will have been set to face south, not north, otherwise the browns and blacks of the *favelas* will spoil your view. Packed tightly, perched fragilely on the steep slopes, the overcrowded slums flow down towards the city. These are the shacks of the huge numbers of Brazil's urban poor. Here there is no fresh water; garbage and open sewers line the alleys; illiteracy and unemployment are as rife as disease, and many children regularly disappear into the streets below where they live in self-protective gangs, supported by their own wits and each other's friendships. What are they to make of Rio's famous statue of the Christ high on the mountain, His arms outstretched to embrace the humanity below – a place where, if the tourist is lucky, only money is taken? These children are a shocking testament to the indifference of the affluent, but from time to time the government take a note of their existence. For the people of the *favelas* may not have jobs or food or sanitation or education or a future, but they have always had disease, especially poliomyelitis – and now they have AIDS.

South America presents a bitter irony with regard to disease and poverty. For when it is decided to take measures against the first – rarely are any taken against the second – these can be energetic: the region was the first to eradicate smallpox; in the first few years of WHO's Expanded Programme on Immunization several countries made striking improvements in health personnel, training, the supply of vaccines and the cold chain. In the same period, the average coverage for DPT and measles of children under one year of age went from 25 per cent to 40 per cent by 1984; for polio, it rose to 70 per cent – a dramatic difference.

This came about because many countries adopted the same effective policy used in industrialized countries in the fifties and sixties – bi-annual, intensive national vaccination days. Cuba began in 1960, and the others in the region followed during the 1980s. The results were impressive: in 1976 there were 5,000 cases of polio in Brazil, in 1979, 2,500. But after their first nationwide campaigns in 1980, the numbers fell to 1,200; 1981 brought only 100 cases; 1983 a mere 43. By 1984, the year of the first Bellagio Conference, the fourteen countries of Central and South America were reporting only 542 cases; one year later this dropped to 470.

Similar statistics from all over the region captured people's imagination. So it was decided that the first objective of EPI in Central and South America should include the reduction of polio to zero. They would use the appropriate procedures not only to strengthen all EPI measures but also build surveillance systems into their operations to measure how effective they were in reducing disease. In May 1985, Dr Carlyle Guerra de Macedo of the Pan American Health Organization formally announced the proposal 'for the regional eradication of the indigenous transmission of wild polio virus from the Americas by December 1990'. The wording meant that eliminating the very last polio virus might be difficult but the chain of transmission between one human and the next would be cut. PAHO's decision, Dr Macedo now says, was as much political as scientific. Polio provided an opportunity both to target a specific disease and, with very effective measures, prevent it, and to reach the goals of the EPI target, too.

This ambition to eradicate polio became a driving force for Dr Ciro de Quadros, the Regional Officer for the EPI division at the headquarters of PAHO in Washington. A small, energetic, bearded Brazilian, de Quadros was a distinguished veteran of the smallpox campaign. In Ethiopia, a country totally devoid of any primary health care infrastructure, he had organized groups of young people into flying squads, who smothered outbreaks of the disease as they erupted, gave vaccination, and eradicated the virus. This successful strategy underlay his convictions about the best strategy to follow for EPI, especially polio, both in the Americas and indeed the world. Campaigns, he believes, strengthen, and sometimes help create, the primary health care infrastructure.

Paradoxically, however, this approach, using polio campaigns as a way of delivering all the EPI vaccines, brought PAHO into conflict with Jim Grant. They needed UNICEF's support, of course, since their staff would be involved and their money would be needed. But as Mahler had felt the goal of primary health care would be weakened by EPI, so Grant now felt that the goal of universal childhood immunization might be compromised by this emphasis on a single disease and single antigen.

But, PAHO argued, polio control leading to eradication, rather than the packet of six EPI vaccines, could really be the Trojan horse that would infiltrate the cycle of childhood disease. The call for polio control would first rally the people; then the mobilization and management involved in setting up polio control could be used immediately for the delivery of other vaccines.

The network would have to be extensive: for if polio was to be eradicated, coverage levels of nearly 90 per cent of the population would have to be maintained for years. Smallpox was easier: only a minor section of a population needed to be vaccinated before the virus was eliminated, for it cannot live long outside the human body and there is no animal reservoir that maintains it. But if PAHO took polio control as their goal a system would be set in place for delivering the other vaccines. Grant took some convincing but eventually agreed that UNICEF would co-operate on yet another fresh approach to the problem of childhood diseases. He promised $17 million, and a contract was signed between the two agencies.

The initiative was spearheaded and massively supported by several agencies: USAID and PAHO who together committed $40 million; the Inter American Development Bank chipped in with $5.5 million – the

first time a bank had given a grant rather than a loan;
Rotary International provided $26 million for vaccines
while local Rotarians worked long and arduously on the
ground to implement the immunization plans.

Rotary's PolioPlus campaign, that was soon famous and
greatly appreciated, had origins in Ohio more than
seventy years ago with a local society for crippled
children. Their major initiative to assist mass polio
immunization in 1978 started with $40 million provided
by USAID on condition they matched this. In just a few
years Rotary had further raised three times that sum in a
variety of ways, in a variety of countries: in England,
where carol singers from Rotary ring the doorbells at
Christmas to raise money; Lima, Peru, where once, a
street kid, washing the windscreens of cars captured by
traffic lights, spotted a sticker on the window. He cleaned
the screen, and then said, 'OK. PolioPlus. No charge.' By
1990 the initial appeal for $120 million made to more
than a million Rotarians worldwide had raised over $206
million with a further $24 million pledged.

Of all the control networks on which success would
depend, Brazil was the most extensive. For each national
campaign that ran on given days each year, one million
volunteers were recruited to help man 90,000 centres.
Soon, following the pattern established in Cuba in 1960,
routine polio immunization of all children under four
years was available on a twice-yearly basis, even in the
remotest regions. At these times Dr Milton Menezes, then
co-ordinator of Brazil's Technical Group for Polio, and
his teams might travel for thirty-five days up the
Amazon. Eating and sleeping on the boat, they would
search out the Indians on the borders with Paraguay,
who knew nothing about either Brazil or polio. They
would vaccinate the children, then return downstream.

Quickly Brazil turned social mobilization into a fine
art. Calling on the teachers, the armed forces, various
civil associations and syndicates, unions and students,

supervisory bodies and ministries, the campaigns were superb. Three two-day practical training sessions for all volunteers preceded each national vaccination day. The message was reinforced in the usual ways: press, posters and general advertisements, loudspeakers in the streets, articles in the newspapers; an immunization record with eight advertising spots for the campaign was distributed to twelve hundred radio stations. Since millions of people buy into the national lottery, every ticket carried a reminder – 'Bring your child for vaccine' – as did pay cheques and gas, water and telephone bills. Special television commercials, each running for thirty seconds, appeared frequently. Every day a different ministry of the federal government is allotted ten minutes' free air time; since this is not always taken up, during campaigns the Ministry of Health would request those ten minutes from other ministries. So the airways and television channels were flooded with the message. The campaigns were also tied into national events like the World Cup, or political elections. In 1983 vaccination occurred on 13 August, which became known as 'Hard Luck Day' – the slogan, 'Hard luck on your kid if he doesn't get his vaccination.'

Control of polio became the Ministry of Health's major priority. By 1985, there were only forty-five cases in the entire vastness of Brazil. Breaking the chain of infectious transmission was very close: with most of the children vaccinated, herd immunity could take over control – a process that operates when so many people are protected and unprotected individuals spread so far and wide, that the virus cannot reach them. The magic figure is 10 per cent of the population unvaccinated. So some people were almost euphoric: polio might be eradicated even before 1990.

Then one night, in June 1986, one thousand miles from Rio in a village in the northeast of Brazil, a small girl fell sick; a week later she died. Before long there

were signs of a major epidemic as children in increasing
numbers succumbed first to a fever and then the dreaded
paralysis. Within weeks there were 250 cases in the
country, 85 per cent of them concentrated in one area in
the northeast – not far from the coastal town of Maceió,
the capital of the state of Alagoas.

No one could understand how and why the campaign
had been ambushed, along with the possibility of failure
on the whole continent. Unravelling the mystery and
applying the lessons learnt would have consequences not
only for polio eradication, but for immunization in many
other countries besides Brazil.

When urgent enquiries began, health officials in
Alagoas claimed that over 90 per cent – sometimes up to
97 or 98 per cent – of the two million children under five
in their state had been properly protected by three full
courses of the oral vaccine, supplied by the famous
Oswaldo Cruz Laboratories in Rio. Its staff insisted that
there was nothing wrong with their vaccine, even though
the children with polio had received it. Shocked surprise
gave way to fear, then anger. Accusations flew back and
forwards between public health officials in the northeast,
bureaucrats in Brasilia and scientists in Rio de Janeiro.
Some said that the live virus vaccine could not have been
correctly attenuated, had reverted to its virulent form, as
it can and sometimes does, with known frequency:
instead of protecting against polio it had actually caused
it. Others charged the volunteers with gross incom-
petence in failing to cover all the children, or for allowing
breakdowns in the cold chain that made the oral vaccine
impotent – or both. Local officials and workers rallied to
each other's defence: both their coverage and the cold
chain were excellent. Polio is an unpredictable disease
with a variety of manifestations, they insisted, and since
many of the poor children of the northeast probably had
intestinal and respiratory infections, the failure ultimately lay, as always, in their poverty.

At the Ministry of Health in Brasilia two separate and practical actions were at once put in train. First, every single child under four in the northeastern state of Alagoas would be re-vaccinated immediately. In fact, everyone in the vicinity was already being re-vaccinated, but this did not end the epidemic. Secondly, every possible cause for the outbreak was to be systematically examined, whether vaccine failure, cold chain breakdown, missed children, or a mutation on the surface of live virus vaccine that had restored virulence and provoked disease.

From then on it was a matter of following classic detective procedures: identify all possible suspects, question and eliminate them one by one, until the culprit stands out. In order to understand the nature of the detection now involved it is necessary to understand the nature of both polio and our attempts to control it.

Though polio existed in ancient times, not until the eighteenth century did physicians realize that it was a distinct disease. Even then it took a wave of epidemics, first in Scandinavia and then the United States, before it was recognized as a serious medical problem, with social consequences grave enough to induce panic on a scale comparable to that induced by AIDS one hundred years later. For the virus can provoke paralysis overnight, even though a patient's first symptoms may be the mildest of fevers. Paradoxically, though polio existed everywhere, frightening epidemics were increasingly a feature of developed societies, though it was years before the reason was understood.

The clue lies in the way the virus is transmitted. Where standards of sanitation and personal hygiene are low, transmission is mostly through faecal contamination of food and water. As hygiene and sanitation are improved, the amount of polio virus in circulation is gradually reduced, along with the chances of meeting them. But it is these circulating wild viruses that, through a subclinical infection, can generate a natural immunity in young children. During this century, with increasingly good sanitation, more people in the West never met the wild virus, and were therefore highly susceptible. Many children in developed societies still grow up without ever having encountered it. But as so often happens, the older a person is when first infected, the more serious the complications. So when a polio epidemic did arrive, as after the Second World War, it caused great damage.

In the poor communities of the Third World, however, the disease is endemic and the virus circulates extensively. Most infants meet it early in life; some develop an immunity. As sanitation and health improve the level of the circulating polio virus in these countries will be greatly reduced; fewer people will be exposed and so if polio does erupt serious epidemics will follow. Thus it is vital to control polio *now*.

The virus was first isolated by Karl Landsteiner in 1908; in 1931, when two Australians, Frank Macfarlane Burnet and Jean McNamara, showed that it existed in more than one form. At the end of the Second World War, three strains had been discovered. Any control programme would have to protect against all of them.

In the thirties several events galvanized public opinion and scientific research. First, two different sets of trials – one using vaccines from a killed virus and the other from an attenuated, live virus – provoked such lethal outbreaks that immunization seemed a dead issue: it was far too dangerous. Polio was accepted as a highly contagious disease without a cure; anyone who happened to be in an epidemic area ran dreadful risks. But, in 1934, a serious epidemic in Los Angeles caused such paranoia, notably amongst hospital staff, that the demand for protection intensified once more. Secondly, Franklin D. Roosevelt, although severely paralysed by polio, became President of the United States in March 1933; on 30 January 1934, his first President's Birthday Ball took place, during which impassioned appeals were made for

Bellagio Conference 1984. Halfdan Mahler (WHO) makes a point to Jim Grant (UNICEF) in the grounds of the Villa Serbelloni.

Jim Grant (UNICEF) and Ralph Henderson (WHO) at the first Bellagio Conference.

Two hundred families have their homes at this rubbish dump in
Guatemala City.

Traditional healer, Maliyapattu, India.

Kiiza, an orphan, demonstrates oral rehydration in a
Kampala slum.

Rotary International's parade for immunization, Madras, India.

Outside the vaccination post, El Mathaba, Yemen.

Mothers and children in Zambia.

Mothers and children in the Yemen.

Health workers climb 3,000 feet to Mahango village in the
Ruwenzori Mountains, Uganda.

DPT vaccination, Adana, Turkey.

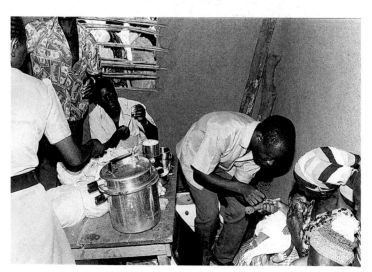

Rural vaccine post, Mahango, Uganda.

Polio vaccination, Salvador, Brazil.

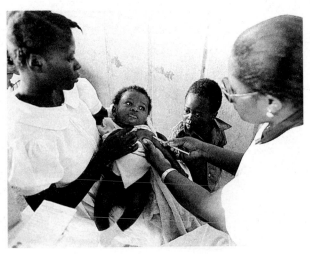

Measles vaccination, Port-Au-Prince, Haiti.

funds to sponsor research. This annual event was soon
given the macabre title of 'The Paralysis Dance'. Thirdly,
the National Foundation for Infantile Paralysis was
formed, whose director, Roosevelt's former law partner,
Basil O'Connor, knew brilliantly how to exploit the media,
using the image of the crippled president to whip up attention. He started the famous March of Dimes campaign,
one committed to finding an effective vaccine; the amount
of money raised each year was staggering. By the time
polio had been controlled in the United States some ten
years later, there were millions of dollars still in the bank.

Two men, Jonas Salk, the immunologist, and Albert
Sabin, a virologist, played a prominent role in the saga.
Both were deeply concerned to control the disease
globally, both had their own obsessive convictions. Each
developed different vaccines. The rift that developed
between them and their supporters caused a conflict
whose reverberations still plague the issue of global
poliomyelitis control.

The issue can be summed up in one simple question:
can one confer lasting immunity with a dead polio virus?
There was no argument about doing it with an
attenuated, live one. But from the outset Salk believed
that it should be possible to confer lifetime immunity
with one single shot of dead virus and therefore simply
inject it along with the standard injections for the other
childhood diseases.

In the spring of 1953 the National Foundation Vaccine
Advisory Committee decided to back Salk's inactivated
vaccine and Dr Thomas Francis, his army boss and
mentor, agreed to direct the first large-scale trials, but
only after he received a guarantee from the National
Foundation that it would not interfere. A total of 600,000
schoolchildren from three separate groups – first, second
and third grade – would receive either the killed vaccine
or a placebo.

Started in March 1954 the trials continued for three

months. In planning and execution they were meticulous. Public interest was intense, and the results were announced in a major media event. The spotlight was fixed on the brilliant scientist, Jonas Salk, the successful entrepreneur, Basil O'Connor, and the National Foundation. The results showed that 200,745 children had been given the vaccine without serious adverse effects; the incidence of poliomyelitis in this group had fallen by 50 per cent when compared to the control groups – a figure then considered a great success, so virulent was the disease.

Fifteen days later the sweet fruits of success abruptly turned sour. At the Center for Disease Control in Atlanta Dr Langmuir spotted a cluster of cases in places where the vaccine had been used. The problem was traced to the Cutter Laboratories at Berkeley, California, who had received live virus from the Connaught Laboratories, Toronto, to turn into inactivated vaccine. Seven of the batches they produced contained live polio virus. It didn't take long to correct the error in the manufacturing procedure, but the damage had been done. As many as 204 people contracted poliomyelitis; three-quarters of these were paralysed, eleven died. Of these 204, 79 had actually received the vaccine, 105 were family contacts, 20 community contacts. The strain used to make the vaccine had been particularly virulent, and only the sharp eyes of surveillance at CDC had averted a large-scale tragedy. Those who had resented the earlier media hype were the first to join in the recriminations.

The setback was deeply tragic for all – for the victims, for Salk, and for the reputation of killed injected polio vaccines. Nevertheless, the Salk vaccine has been successfully and widely used. In the late fifties Canada and Denmark began using it for mass immunization; France, Germany and South Africa followed soon after and a dramatic decline in the incidence of polio followed. As the incidence dropped so the disease spread more slowly. There were some disadvantages, however: in the beginning annual booster shots were required in order to achieve good levels of circulating antibody; the vaccine was expensive; some scientists continued to believe that polio would never be eradicated by a killed vaccine alone.

Meanwhile, spearheaded by Albert Sabin, work had already begun on a live vaccine. A classic study among Alaskan Eskimos reinforced his belief that this might have significant advantages over the killed vaccine. Polio was rare in the Arctic, but when an infection did occur, patients who survived – and not all did – appeared to have acquired lifelong immunity. So exposure to a live vaccine should have the same results.

By December 1957 Sabin's oral vaccine had been given to a quarter of a million people in the Congo. Between 1959 and 1960, 77.5 million people in the Soviet Union, 36.7 per cent of the population, were safely immunized. In March 1962 the three strains of Sabin's live virus vaccine were licensed in the United States.

Yet once again safety became a major concern as now this vaccine received a setback. The attenuated Type III virus was shown to revert to a virulent form with alarming frequency. Could its human recipients therefore get polio and paralysis merely from vaccination? The answer lay in the future and would be 'yes'. Embarrassment soon came – in 1958 62 cases of vaccine-associated polio occurred in Ireland.

As a measure for controlling poliomyelitis both vaccines have proved excellent. In Sweden, Finland and the Netherlands, where only killed vaccine has been used, paralytic polio has all but disappeared – but here the secret of success is, Salk emphasizes, to vaccinate 100 per cent of the population. Multiple doses may be needed, but wild virus circulation has been blocked. In the United States, which predominantly uses oral vaccine, among a population of 221 million on average there are ten cases per year, and here too circulation of the wild viruses has virtually disappeared. For the live virus vaccine is excreted from the gut and, if sufficient people are immunized, it gradually displaces the lethal wild polio virus in the environment.

But in tropical regions a fresh problem has surfaced in relation to the oral vaccine, the vaccine of choice for WHO, being cheaper than killed vaccine and easier to administer. The capacity to mount a good immune response appears to be less in children of the developing countries. No one knows why. Other intestinal infections may be one reason: like the virus, the route whereby the oral vaccine gets into the body is through the gut, and other agents may interfere with, even suppress, the localized infection that the vaccine induces. Next, as Sir Ian MacGregor always suspected, the problem may be due to the stew of viral, bacterial and parasitic diseases faced by small infants, and result in great distortions of their biochemical response. In addition, diseases like measles and malaria actually suppress the immune system, resulting in chronic imbalances in immune response.

Nevertheless many people argue for the use of killed virus vaccine in developing countries, arguing that injections of killed vaccine would complete protection in places where the immune response to the oral vaccine is not totally satisfactory. The vaccine's potency has been much improved, and mass-production is now underway both at the Mérieux Laboratories in France and the Connaught Laboratories in Canada. Preliminary results indicate that two doses – perhaps even one, as Salk always expected – may eventually provide the required levels of protection.

However, the Pan American Health Organization chose Sabin's oral vaccine for its control campaigns in Central and South America. Those responsible knew the difficulties: there would be a low conversion in many children; three doses spread over three months would place a heavy burden on the public health sector; a sound cold chain would be essential, for the vaccine is exceedingly heat and humidity sensitive, far more so than the killed vaccine. However it was cheap and easily administered. Moreover, starting in Cuba – which had been free of polio since 1973 following their systematic campaigns – the disease had already begun to recede. So Sabin now recommended similar, annual mass campaigns in all countries across the Americas, for the problems were, he insisted, not so much of science as of administration, funding and logistics. The ambush in Maceió, Brazil, would surprise him, too.

Yet those most closely concerned with polio control in the Americas were not entirely taken by surprise. They had been keeping a careful eye – not just on the numbers vaccinated but where polio still persisted and to what degree. For some weeks before June 1986, when the small girl died, there were disquieting indications from the figures. Ciro de Quadros and colleagues from PAHO, and the senior government official then responsible in Brazil, Dr Joao Risi, Jnr, met with others from the northeast, in Salvador, Bahia, to review the data and tried to work out what was going wrong. They suspected the vaccine.

The first major and persisting problem they faced lay in the fact that the office in the Brazilian Ministry of Health was a branch of the federal government. Whereas in Turkey lines of authority run directly from bureaucrats in the capital to administrators on the periphery, this is not so in Brazil. Here, as in the United States, the federal government has no executive control over the states. So the sole role for Dr Risi's office, Basic Health Actions, was to co-ordinate vaccination days nationwide, set technical standards for immunization, make funds available to the states to execute the campaigns, whose bureaucrats would then pass on responsibility to people at the county level. The

Ministry's influence is severely restricted; whatever the
area political goals at state level rarely reflect political
goals at the federal level.

A second difficulty was education – or rather the lack
of it. Though people in the National Immunization
Programme yearned to discover the best methods to
inform the people about polio, there was never any
money for research. All they could hope was that
continuing publicity might have a snowballing effect. But
though when the campaigns started it had been easy to
persuade people to bring in their children, in subsequent
years they became bored with it all. Apathy extended to
health bureaucrats as well: when a polio epidemic struck
matters were obviously serious, but when there were only
a few cases other problems – food, employment, housing
– seemed far more important. Who cared about a mere
fourteen victims? Since they did not appreciate how fast
polio can spread, Risi's group issued a video showing not
only how to distribute and administer vaccine and
mobilize people to deliver it, but also how quickly the
disease could get out of control and what a dent would be
made in a state's health budget when it did.

The administration was in truth facing a situation
compounded of tragedy, embarrassment, ignorance,
bewilderment and sheer numbers. In 1984 the figure of
only 45 polio cases in the whole of Brazil suggested that
nearly 85 per cent of the population had been vaccinated
and therefore herd immunity should have taken over.
Why hadn't it? There were at least two possible reasons.
First the returns might be suspect. Secondly, as Dr Milton
Menezes, Co-ordinator of the Technical Group of Polio
Eradication, pointed out, the concept of herd immunity
may look good on paper but it probably can never
operate in a country as huge as Brazil, for 10 per cent of
the child population unvaccinated means two million
unprotected children spread throughout the country.
Three-quarters of Brazil's population – 135 million – live

in the cities; the rest are dispersed over an area half the total land-mass of the South American continent. 'So,' commented Dr Menezes, 'if you think we're going to achieve control by immunizing 90 per cent of the country's kids and ignoring the other two million spread out over millions of square miles, you must be crazy.' They would need nearer 100 per cent coverage. But how?

Perhaps the outbreaks in the northeast were solely the consequences of a poverty-stricken, underfed population, with natural immunity destroyed. But Dr Risi questioned this, for a study in the *favelas* of Rio showed that the nutritional state of a child did not appear to affect immunity. He believed the cause lay in 'the lack of social structures' at the county level. There are 4,133 counties in Brazil, each with its own mayor and each with its fair share of graft and corruption. Forty per cent of all the latest polio cases were confined to nine of these, and 10 per cent were in one county alone. Dr Risi's 'lack of social structures in the northeast' meant that not only might the vaccine be ineffective but the cold chain could have broken down, the campaigns been badly conducted and the returns vastly inflated. So they would now examine each of these possibilities in turn.

The staff of the Oswaldo Cruz Foundation in Rio insisted that there was no question of the vaccine being ineffective. However, responsibility for transporting it from Rio to anywhere in the country lay with the Ministry of Health, which could if necessary move consignments in hours and even commandeer military aeroplanes to fly vaccines to the most remote areas. Certainly, from the moment the vaccine left their laboratories many things could go wrong, but if they did it was not their fault.

But was the vaccine really effective? The laboratories are set in a large, sprawling compound on the outskirts of Rio, guarded almost as closely as a nuclear establishment. In one sense the place is probably as dangerous, because it is full of live viruses of one sort or another. An enormous Gothic castle which dominates the modern laboratories is the spot where, eighty or so years ago, the scientist who discovered yellow fever vaccine did his work. So grateful was the government of the day that they set him up in this incongruous building of his choice, with turrets, minarets, slit windows and tiny porticoes – the perfect building to withstand a siege. Given the surroundings he requested, the authorities hoped he would repeat with other diseases his success with yellow fever. Sad to say, he did not.

The present policy in Brazil is to import vaccines only if they cannot be made at home, and although not a large company, Oswaldo Cruz is responsible for all vaccines produced in Brazil. But there is much friction between the bureaucrats in Brasilia and the scientists in Rio, who feel that the Ministry of Health doesn't really understand the realities of running a laboratory under the heel of people who seem neither to care about, nor understand, the problems of commercial development. These problems are not necessarily those of money, though in 1985 the laboratory was in so much financial trouble that it could do nothing except pay salaries: in 1986, after the polio epidemic in the northeast, the cash poured in. But the rules say that the laboratory cannot import electronics or glassware or any of the essentials required to manufacture and package vaccines. One example of such bureaucratic blindness concerned a digital counting machine. The appropriate papers were sent to Brasilia but the request was refused: a digital counting machine was an electronic device and electronic devices were barred. So, very politely they pointed out that the word 'digital' refers to fingers; thus, a digital counter is a mechanical device worked by the fingers. The bureaucrats didn't care: anything 'digital' was electronic and could not be imported. Dr Brogliato, head of the laboratory that produces the measles vaccine, spent a whole afternoon that he could ill afford writing another plea and explanation. Finally he received a telephone call from some nameless bureaucrat in the capital, who said he was personally very sorry but digital equipment was still barred.

Another source of friction is that the Ministry sets arbitrary targets for vaccine production without consulting the producer. In October 1986, the laboratory was told to double the next year's quota for polio vaccine from fifteen million to thirty million doses. 'How the hell are we supposed to do that?' snarled one of the staff, a question immediately echoed by Dr Fernando Lopez who, turning to Dr Brogliato, said, 'I'm going to have a breakdown. Brogliato, you must be a man of iron to keep going under this pressure.' 'No,' replied Brogliato. 'I'm not a man of iron. I'm merely a bachelor without problems.'

The experiences of this laboratory mirror what is likely to happen in any developing country intending to produce its own vaccine. Only 10 per cent of the polio vaccine used in Brazil is actually made here: the rest is imported and then tested. The raw materials for the 10 per cent manufactured are also imported, although by 1988 the Brazilians expected to produce these too. But in 1987 they were taking concentrated live polio virus from Holland and Belgium and making the vaccine. With only nine people who took three years to train, they produced ten million doses a year using a commercial process set up with the help of the Japanese government, who not only supervised installing the equipment for the production line, but also trained the key personnel for six months in Japan. Dr Akira Homma, a third generation Japanese in Brazil, was in charge of Biomanguinhos, the vaccine production arm of the Oswaldo Cruz Foundation. Occasionally the Japanese arrive for routine checks on output and quality, and, if anything appears wrong, track down the problem with typical meticulousness.

According to the resident staff, they are pernickety, difficult and a nuisance, but that's as it should be. Quality control is constant: I saw them throw out two huge consignments of vaccine that had just arrived from Switzerland: the validity date had expired. A contaminated shipment from Hungary was also destroyed. In 1982 alone, 41 million doses from Yugoslavia had to be thrown away.

Distributing polio vaccine poses severe problems, for the strains are very sensitive to temperature. Once taken out of the freezer and thawed the vaccine must be used within a day. After just twenty-four hours at average room temperature (37°C), the potency is reduced by 50 per cent. Thus the cold chain needs careful monitoring, and the key to success here is that only the minimum amount required should be delivered to the health posts. The Oswaldo Cruz Foundation sends written recommendations on all these points to the Ministry, the state secretaries and anyone else involved.

So did the vaccine mutate to a virulent strain and itself induce the outbreak? Dr Hermann Schatzmayr, a Brazilian immunologist at the Foundation, was told to investigate. There are now excellent tests for determining the strains of polio in blood samples from a patient, though ideally these should be done within twenty-one days of evidence of the disease. In the early years of immunization Brazil did see some vaccine-induced disease as any country that uses live polio vaccine always will. By October 1986, they had unearthed eleven possible cases of vaccine-induced polio, plus six suspicious ones, all of Type III virus. But as to whether Type III was indeed the cause of the outbreak in northeastern Brazil, Dr Schatzmayr still feels unable to say, because the data he was given were incomplete.

If all these possible causes were eliminated, the investigation had to shift to Alagoas in the northeast and the focus of the epidemic. What reasons did its health administrators advance for the outbreak; had they maintained the cold chain; had they vaccinated all the children in the area? They answered that the vaccine was good; they had maintained the cold chain impeccably; they had immunized practically every child under four. Before each campaign they would assess the numbers to be covered from the latest census figures. Then on the first day they would count the number vaccinated and express this as a percentage of the total child population under five. In 1980 they vaccinated 105 per cent of the population; in 1981, 98 per cent; in 1982, 96 per cent; in 1983, 110 per cent; in 1984, 96 per cent; and in 1985, 101 per cent. Given that more children in the age group 0–5 were being vaccinated than the census said existed, it was highly likely, suggested the present Secretary of Health in Maceió, that the census was wrong, and if children slipped through the net at census time it is hardly surprising that they also slipped through the net at vaccination time. Still, with figures like that, why was there any polio?

Dr Milton Menezes confirmed that the returns they received showed almost 100 per cent coverage. But when they checked doses used and other relevant information, they found that the coverage was actually as low as 70 per cent, and in some localities far far lower. There might be several reasons for this discrepancy: the data first goes into the regional offices before being sent to Brasilia; obtaining accurate information from rural areas is very difficult; no one knows who and where the missing children are, and there is no way of finding out; people who live in hovels ten miles along dirt roads through the forests of sugar cane never hear about the campaigns; there was no house-to-house searching, and although a federal law makes polio vaccination mandatory, it cannot be enforced because of lack of control over the states.

Granted that more trained people were needed and that access to the rural poor remained a problem, yet all

the requisite technology was to hand. So were the
campaigns failing in execution? Certainly, Dr Menezes
insisted, 'In order to control polio, let alone eradicate it,
we must work still harder – twenty-four hours a day,
seven days a week, every day and every night. We don't
have time to waste.' But the real villain was, he
emphasized, the system itself. 'We have too many: health
systems, information systems, systems run by professionals who don't see the importance of research.' (Shades of
D.A. Henderson.) 'Sometimes a health official will
report one case and then not bother about the next. They
do not understand just how accurate and systematic one
must be if the job is to be done properly. Few of the
27,000 health professionals in Brazil take any notice of
the central government and as the disease began to
disappear they no longer thought it important to report.'
So just as the scientists at the vaccine laboratories had
their problems with federal bureaucrats in Brasilia, those
in the country's Ministry of Health responsible for
eradicating polio had similar problems with state
bureaucrats.

After all, whose responsibility is it, ultimately? The
health officials in Maceió, who claimed that their only
mistake was not to conduct a major educational campaign
at all levels throughout the local population, were asked
that very question. In unison they replied, 'It's the
government's.' But when I asked which government,
state or federal, there was a dead silence. The Secretary
of Health finally spoke. 'I cannot answer this kind of
question. It's unwise to get involved, so I prefer not to
answer.'

Having systematically worked through all the possibilities, no one could truthfully point to the real root of the
problem. The epidemic might have been caused by one
of the various factors, or all of them, or for a reason as yet
unidentified. Help was needed, so Dr Ciro de Quadros
activated the international network and also raised the

problem with the Center for Disease Control in Atlanta, who assigned a thirty-year-old medical epidemiologist, Dr Peter Patriarca, to the case. Packing his shirts and his portable computer, Patriarca took the next plane south.

Patriarca's biggest problem was the language barrier, for he doesn't speak Portuguese very well. A physician escorting him served as interpreter and provided him with access to the people and information he needed. By the time he arrived blood tests had shown that whatever the cause, the epidemic was of Type III polio. He started by looking at the obvious things all over again. He, too, found nothing wrong with the Oswaldo Cruz vaccine; the antibody levels they provoked were low but acceptable. Since fresh vaccination campaigns had already begun in the northeast he travelled north with a team from Brasilia and visited twenty-five vaccination posts in Alagoas state at random and unannounced. Though not in the deep countryside these were miles from major population sites, but he didn't see any weak link in the procedures. With the exception of a few isolated centres, the cold chain was, in his opinion, properly maintained, though those lapses could, of course, have very serious consequences.

It did not take him long to agree that the census figures were not at all accurate and that therefore neither were the percentages of children covered. So although health workers had a very clear idea of how many doses of vaccine had been used, they had no idea how many children remained unvaccinated. Random surveys, however, conducted according to approved WHO methods, showed that the coverage was high: although certainly not as high as the 98 or 100 per cent claimed, at least 80–85 per cent of all children were thought to have received three doses.

Satisfied on these points Patriarca next began to sift through other available data. He was faced by a stack of papers and letters over three feet high because the mayor

of every municipality in the northeast had been asked to
write in whenever even one case was reported. They had.
As his analysis proceeded, he confirmed that the problem
lay with the Type III vaccine – the one that most easily
reverts to its original virulent form. This was totally
unexpected because in other developing countries Type
I vaccine – the one most temperature sensitive and most
quickly ruined by an inefficient cold chain – was the
culprit. Yet in Brazil this vaccine gave good protection
and the amount of Type I polio virus now circulating was
much reduced.

Patriarca learnt that Type III vaccine had been
introduced to Brazil several years after Type I, and for
some unknown reason 25 per cent of children were not
raising antibodies against it. He also suspected that the
one being used was only marginally potent. If, in
addition, a significant number of children had been
missed, the proportion of children in the state
unprotected against Type III polio would have begun to
rise; the amount of circulating wild virus would also rise
in parallel, quickly setting up conditions that would
inevitably lead to an epidemic.

Thus Patriarca concluded that the outbreak in the
northeast had been caused by a compounding of three
factors: a marginally potent Type III vaccine, a low rate
of antibody response to it, and many children still
unprotected against the Type III virus. His recommendation was that in all future campaigns both the potency
and quantity of Type III vaccine should be doubled. In
this way the level of antibody against Type III in the
general population would be quickly raised and the
circulating wild virus drop.

Meantime, Ciro de Quadros and his colleagues were
reviewing the entire scientific literature on polio control.
To their astonishment they found that Brazil in 1985 was
using a vaccine significantly less potent than one used in
the USA over thirty years earlier. Immediately PAHO

recommended a switch to a more potent Type III formulation. WHO up to 1990 was still analysing and designing new studies.

The first practical step was a directive from Brasilia to the Oswaldo Cruz Foundation to produce a trivalent polio vaccine containing twice the strength of Type III. The second was to mount throughout 1986 six more campaign days in northeastern Brazil using this new vaccine, and aim to reach every vulnerable infant once again. Two-day practical training sessions would be run three times before each vaccination day; indeed, the whole panoply of social mobilization would be in place two weeks in advance.

Dr Risi now made use of the information culled from previous campaigns. At the end of 1985 a letter had been sent to twelve thousand religious leaders in the country asking for information on their local polio and for suggestions. The answers and criticisms – of methods, of local officials, of the indifference of bureaucrats – flooded back by the thousand, and were carefully noted. This mail shot, besides producing information on other health matters such as malaria and measles, confirmed what everyone knew in their hearts: that local political problems – nepotism, corruption, indifference – were a major source of the difficulties. Dr Risi's group tried to implement every recommendation that came to hand, but once again were hampered by having no power at state level.

However, the fresh polio outbreaks had caused such a public outcry that the Ministry of Health in Brasilia was finally permitted to take direct action in state campaigns. Their staff could now actually go and see what was happening on the ground and assess how successful the campaign had been. So moving into an area unannounced and at random, they would run quality tests every day, checking samples of vaccine moments before it was given to a child. By 16 August 1986 this had been done and the new trivalent vaccine pronounced good.

*

October 11th would be the fifth — the penultimate — campaign day for 1986 — and I went to northeastern Brazil to follow it.

Rio may have terrible slums, but life in that city is one we recognize. Poor people exist, of course, but the rich have our health problems. They live well and along with all the good things of life get lung cancer and heart attacks. But four hours' flying time to the north is another world — the same country but with poverty on a scale hardly seen even in Africa. The official government figures acknowledge that twenty million people are starving: it's quite conceivable that there could be many more.

The state government is in Maceió, a coastal town stretching along the shores of a sandy beach with an estuarine swamp lying behind. By 8 October 1986, 480,000 doses of the vaccine had been already shipped to Maceió and the fourteen towns around, 16,000 to another country district, and 87,000 to the centre of the epidemic, the town of Arapiraca. The campaign there would be crucial because it was around Arapiraca that 39 confirmed cases of polio and 33 suspected ones had occurred. On Saturday 11 October, 68,456 children had to be vaccinated.

A training seminar in Arapiraca had already been held for three hundred people in the region — teachers, members of religious, health and the trade union groups. Two hundred and fifty clinics would be manned by 980 volunteers, some of whom would form mobile teams to drive deep into the countryside. Everyone was ready but, equally, everyone was reluctant to answer questions: their past failure weighed heavily, in a region where 56 per cent of all the people have nothing — neither land nor jobs nor education.

Arapiraca lies one hundred miles west of Maceió, in an area where acres of tropical forest were burned and replanted with sugar cane, a crop converted to ethanol and used for car fuel. It is a dreadful place. The town itself is superficially prosperous; one sees cars, some small industries, and a general air of commerce. But two related things are overpowering: the smell and the flies. The main industry is tobacco and stripping the plants is a cottage industry. Down the streets, round the corners, in country shacks, adults and children earn a few cruzeiros by pulling leaves from stalks. They do this on the doorsteps or pavements, or in their one-room homes. From October to January even ten-year-olds separate the leaves in the warehouses of the tobacco companies. They are paid miserably, by the weight they produce. The smell of the tobacco attracts the flies; they concentrate in piles of stalks for these provide an ideal place to lay their eggs. The flies and the smell penetrate everything. The locals felt that a few well-defined areas should be set aside, and only there should the stripping be done. The rubbish should be regularly collected, burnt and sprayed and the menace controlled. The companies that own the tobacco plantations are indifferent; the people and the health authorities angry but powerless.

Those responsible for the small hospital and community health centre run an exquisitely clean and efficient operation. The people and their town – an urban population of nearly 120,000, and 45,000 in the countryside – are the reality of which Dr Mahler so movingly spoke. Here were responsible, concerned, extremely hard-working men and women, doing their very best under difficult conditions to control the polio in spite of indifference, nepotism and corruption.

Dr Graca, the chief of the Technical Division of the Public Health office, looked like Tweedledum – for she was small, dark and friendly, and to keep cool wore dungarees cut off just short of the knees. She was very rotund, for her first child was due in a month. Her colleague, Dr Amelia Zelda, tall, elegant and briskly competent, was a supervisor in the Public Health clinic.

One other assistant and two supervising nurses made up the group of five ladies whose boss, a man, was away most of the time.

They were very distressed about their early failure but, unlike anyone else, admitted they didn't know *what* had happened. They had probably never seen Dr Patriarca's report. In contrast to the health bureaucrats in their state capital, Maceió, they believed only 75 per cent of their population had been covered with three doses of vaccine and had no idea why 25 per cent were missing. Any such figures were inevitably estimates, for there was no checking or attempts to trace parents who never come forward. On campaign day, this coming Saturday, the children vaccinated would be counted by marking lines on an appropriate form. A line along one side represents one child, so a completed square and diagonal equals five children vaccinated; the completed blocks are easy to count. But this is only a measure of the numbers covered, not those missed, and that number they could not even begin to guess. During the previous round, the fourth campaign day of 1986, they immunized 63,745 children of 0–4 years, and hoped to do so again this week. Nineteen other towns besides Arapiraca had to be covered. Every child had an immunization card; the vaccination posts would be schools, clinics, mothers' clubs, shops.

Twelve children with polio were still in the hospital; three others, all two years old, had died, possibly as much from other diseases and malnutrition as polio. But, they insisted, the root cause of problems is that neither the government nor the richer sections of society care about the rural poor. A major obstacle to progress are the *marajas*, those who accept personal political appointments in the government but do no work. Even the present governor of one particular province in the area was reputed to have one salary for that and a second just as a *maraja*. Most appointments in public health were, as in any other ministry, solely political. Some *marajas* not only had no qualifications but no understanding of health problems. Some indeed were illiterate.

Few at the grass roots level have any confidence that matters will improve. Politicians from Brasilia promise the earth, and after they have been elected return to the capital and quickly forget the northeast. Then someone starts a new campaign and a new programme but before long it stops. What is badly needed, said the two doctors, is strong and consistent support at both the state and the federal level for the Secretaries of Health, Culture, and Education. Indifference of families they find understandable. People are so poor, generally with six or seven children, and feel that life is hopeless, the deck stacked against them from the start.

They were worried about Saturday, though everything was in place – vaccines, supplies, cheerful campaign T-shirts. But the campaign might fail because there had been no publicity. Maceió hadn't sent enough support. One television spot was the only coverage, for the campaign conflicted with the elections so the loudspeaker cars that normally blared forth were offering not vaccination but politicians' promises. The state's agricultural department was giving help though, for the union has strong links with the rural communities; the Army, too, was lending a hand, young conscripts being trained to give the oral vaccine. Since there was serious vitamin A deficiency in the area every child receiving polio drops would also be given a vitamin A pill.

From the office, Dr Graca would co-ordinate the campaign in the towns, covering for emergencies, and rushing supplies of vaccine to the countryside where needed. Dr Zelda would commute between the countryside and headquarters. Volunteers – mostly women teachers – would be vaccinating. The day would be frantic with everyone working in top gear from seven in the morning until ten o'clock at night, when they would start counting the returns.

Meanwhile, at a local barracks an efficient lady from Brasilia was, with military precision, conducting a class. The recruits were taught how to administer vaccine; how to keep it cool; and not to waste any – it was very expensive. More importantly they would be personally responsible for the drops they gave to each and every infant; if they failed the baby could die.

One soldier was ordered to come up front and be mother. Another was chosen to be baby. Both were well over six feet, wearing heavy, olive green fatigues and large, black, clumpy boots. As 'baby' marched up the barracking began. A chorus of 'Sit, sit, sit' finally persuaded him to take his place on his 'mother's' lap but noise continued. 'Boy or girl. Boy or girl,' they shouted. 'I'm a boy,' he replied, blushing. 'You're not,' they roared. 'You're a girl, girl, girl.' Order was restored and the technique of vaccination demonstrated.

Then the sergeant in charge barked, as sergeants do everywhere, 'Any other questions?' Did they have to wear their uniforms on Saturday because their fatigues were terribly hot? The sergeant said they could wear jeans and a campaign T-shirt with its logo of eight small children in a row across the chest. But God help anyone he caught in Army trousers topped with the T-shirt.

The morning before vaccination day we toured some of the area's health centres, some superb, some very grim indeed. One, in a settlement some five miles from Arapiraca, consisted of just a room where vaccination, diagnosis, treatment – the whole lot – were done. Doctors from the city were supposed to come every day but being generally too busy earning money in private practice most don't bother. Food is handed out to the very poor – two kilos of beans, four of rice, two of manioc – a farinaceous powder that's ground up into the food – and one of sugar, once a month. Most people will never eat meat, and only a few vegetables sometimes and fruit rarely.

By contrast, however, at Limoeiro de Anadia, a beautiful small village in glorious countryside, with, everyone insisted, an incorruptible mayor, there is the only really decent health centre in the whole district. The staff who have run it for over five years take great pride in the fact that the maternity ward, the delivery and immunization rooms, and toilets were all spotless, fresh, and clean-smelling. Yet in this village the most tragic consequences of the earlier polio campaigns were to be found.

Down the hill at the end of the village next to the cemetery is a small side-street. Here Micheline Ribeiro Silva Santos lives. She caught polio at fifteen months and one year later was still a very sick and sad child indeed. Her eyes were filmed; she had a skin infection of some sort and, unlike a normal infant, was very quiet. Before polio she could say 'Ma' and 'Pa' but now doesn't speak at all. The tragic thing is that she did receive three doses of the polio vaccine; the first in November 1985, the second on 26 February 1986, and the third in May 1986. Shortly after the last drops she and two other children in the town developed the symptoms.

There are three other children in the family. Two had been vaccinated before but the seven-month-old baby, Cicero, never will be. His father will not now permit health workers near any of his children: the boy has not even been medically examined. Just recovering from diarrhoea he, too, was in a very bad way, neither eating nor drinking, though his mother did try to get him to take rice water. The house was a hovel – quite literally only eight short paces from the cemetery where both Cicero and Micheline are likely to go quite soon. Their mother is illiterate; the father a huge, simple, quiet but dignified, pained man, immensely hard-working when he can get work. Here in this hovel in this village, in the heart of northeastern Brazil, are the living expression of what Bill Foege meant when he said, 'Behind every one of our failures is a human face.'

Saturday, campaign day, was clear and hot; at eight we

were off on a tour of the vaccination posts, one next door
to the public health centre. Along came the children as if
going to a party. For campaign days are treated as feast
days, so scrubbed clean, their hair brushed, they wear
their best clothes, whatever these may be. Mothers bring
the children in their arms; if they can't the neighbours
do; failing that small children carry along even smaller
ones. One bawling toddler sitting furiously on the steps
of the centre was firmly admonished by her sister, who
must have been all of four, wagging a finger at her and
saying, 'Now, I don't want to hear any more from you.
You're going right in there to take your shots.' Those
who could walk stood with small faces upturned, mouths
open to receive five drops of polio vaccine and a vitamin
A pill. Those who were carried had their mouths tickled,
or gently prised open. Pacifiers were removed and
mothers told firmly not to replace them for at least half
an hour: the vaccine *has* to go down. Parents waited
patiently; children restlessly, amused, giggling, or crying.

By 10.00 a.m. it was clear that the campaign was not as
well organized as earlier ones. Some people were
vociferous, the complaints most forceful in a slum area of
Arapiraca, Escorrego da Catita – 'the slide of the lizards'.
The centres should have opened at eight o'clock but the
workers didn't turn up until 9.00 or 9.15. The people
waiting at a small shack of a shop were angry. But before
long, amongst a crowd of customers and onlookers
surrounded by beer bottles and Coke cans, with goods
being sold over the counter, oral polio vaccine was being
dropped into upturned mouths.

Into the countryside, Dr Graca's chief, Dr J.D.A.
Fernandez da Lima, was checking the procedures.
'Brazil is changing,' he said. 'Many many more women
than men work. They're studying hard and they want to
change things. They will.' He said that the reason why 25
per cent of his population is regularly missed is due to
poor communication. There had been lots of publicity

for the first and second rounds. But the government assumed incorrectly, that the women would automatically bring their child in for a third dose yet in fact only 30 per cent had – a serious failure. And since today was the fifth out of six vaccination days this year in the area people were bored; some sceptical. Finally he admitted that the only way in which they would ever find those missing 25 per cent was to go from house to house, using the half a million volunteers all over the country. Here perhaps lay the past failure and the key to future success.

By the middle of the day a row had erupted. One dominating bureaucrat from Brasilia had been bawling out the other doctors, saying the campaign was going badly and they hadn't done things right. For the women who, for a whole year now, had been working to exhaustion on behalf of polio control this was the last straw. They had the returns to tally; they had their everyday jobs as wives and mothers, and such crashing insensitivity was just one more example of the gap between those at the organizational centre and those working at the grassroots – the level that really mattered.

At noon Dr Milton Menezes from Brasilia arrived. His people had been out taking random samples of the vaccine across the whole district. He would stay on for three further days to collate the results and interview a cross-section of the people to see whether they had brought their children in, and if not, why not. When the figures came the final tally was just as before: 98 per cent of the children had been vaccinated. But how many had not?

Meanwhile back in the Oswaldo Cruz Foundation, Dr Schatzmayr had said that the new, double strength Type III, trivalent vaccine, notwithstanding, the northeast of Brazil would always pose a problem. Twenty-five per cent of children there would probably never raise antibodies against polio and if coverage ever dropped down from the high rates that the biannual vaccination days produced, the numbers of children not protected against Type III virus would accumulate and the same pattern of epidemics recur. Indeed Dr Peter Patriarca had said that five to six doses of oral vaccine might be needed for control in Brazil; others agreed. A recent study in India had come to a similar conclusion for that country. But seeing the organizational problems encountered by those two remarkable women, Drs Graca and Zelda, trying to administer three doses of polio to a huge, poor population, six seemed quite out of the question! Even so most children in the Americas do indeed receive many doses. Given twice-yearly vaccination days of a form here described, a Brazilian baby receiving its first drops aged three months might well have received eight or even thirteen courses by the time it is five years old.

Another alternative would be to use the killed polio vaccine in tandem. Some scientists were already recommending that although Sabin's vaccine might be appropriate at the beginning of a mass campaign, maintenance of protection may best be accomplished with the dead injectible vaccine. Indeed oral vaccine should be given in the first days of life when, even though a child's immune system is not fully functioning, at least a memory can be registered. Then dead, injectible polio could be given later, at the same time, and in the same syringe as the other standard injections of EPI.

Whatever happens in future the blanket coverage presently employed in Brazil was bound to lead to sustained polio control. And while Dr Patriarca and his Brazilian colleagues admit that the balance of the various strains in the vaccines may still not be right – and intestinal interference between them might explain why some children are not protected against one strain or another – they conclude that if polio does occur again the most likely cause would be failure to vaccinate rather than vaccine failure.

But at the moment polio was not occurring again. After the ambush in Maceió its incidence in northeastern Brazil dropped back to levels even lower than before. Gradually, Dr Ciro de Quadros and the multitude of his colleagues on the South American continent placed a stranglehold upon polio. Whereas in 1986, 1000 cases would be reported in Central and South America – half in northeast Brazil – by 1988 there were only 340 and by the end of 1989 a mere 17. These were spread over three areas: northeastern Brazil; in Andean villages on the borders between Colombia and Venezuela where, due to insurrections and clashes between the forces of drug barons and government authorities, security is difficult; and in Mexico. Ten cases, however, appeared in October 1989, along the American Highway in Mexico, nine in one state, one in a neighbouring one. A check of the vaccine – the first procedure – revealed that far from giving the new formulation as claimed, some old stocks from years back were being used up. Who was responsible? Who at state level was concealing this? No one knows.

Nevertheless by the spring of 1990, Ciro de Quadros could be confident that PAHO's campaign was in its final, mopping-up stages, that the transmission of the virus had been broken and polio all but eradicated in the Caribbean, Central America, the southern half of Brazil, and the Southern Cone countries – Paraguay, Argentina, Chile and Uruguay. In Brazil the young soldiers were now assigned to house-to-house searches seeking out the children. As in the last days of the smallpox campaign, rewards were being offered for the detection of cases – $100 to be given both to the first person to find, and the first health worker to identify, a case of polio genuinely caused by the wild virus, not a vaccine-associated case. So far there have been no takers.

There is a strong possibility that the reward may never be claimed, for other indications suggest that the spread of the wild virus of polio has been greatly diminished. It is excreted from the intestines of patients as is the oral viral vaccine from those of vaccinated people, and its presence can be detected by stool examinations. By September 1989, over 1600 stool examinations had yielded a mere 8 specimens of the wild virus and possibly this explains why PAHO felt so confident about offering the reward!

If by September 1990, on the occasion of the annual meeting of their nations' delegates, five months have gone by without a single detection of wild polio virus, PAHO may announce that the goal they set in May 1985 has been reached, and 'the regional eradication of wild polio virus from the Americas' has been achieved, several months before their target date. Making such an announcement involves some risk, of course, and Ciro de Quadros will be anxious to avoid the kind of embarrassment that occurred in 1975 when the *New York Times* ran an article under the headline: 'SMALLPOX IS ERADICATED . . . again!'

All signs are, however, that there will be no such débâcle, so what remains? So far as PAHO is concerned, control of the other EPI diseases to the point at which they, too, will disappear. In these countries the position with regard to measles is the same as with polio in 1982. 'We are at a moment of genuine "methodological switch",' says de Quadros. 'Using similar strategies, measles could be eradicated too.'

But what about the eradication of polio globally? De Quadros is equally convinced that if only other regions will faithfully follow the methods used in the Americas for over a decade now, polio will quickly go the way of smallpox. 'No longer is it a question of how to do it,' he says, 'but will it be done.'

But not all share his confidence. Some question whether the blanket strategy that works so well in his corner of the globe can be equally applied in regions such as India or Africa – indeed, whether it is even feasible? As the end of 1990 approached the debate would intensify.

Meantime the consequences of the ambush in Maceió remain: a small, crippled girl in a poor family in Limoeiro de Anadia; a new Type III vaccine of enhanced potency giving greater protection to thousands more children. Yet if it hadn't been for the ambush, says Ciro de Quadros with rueful sadness, 'We would never have realized that the weakness was the low potency of our vaccine.'

Perhaps another weakness lies in the dynamics of scientific research. Most scientists have little time for the history of their subjects: publications more than ten years old are regarded as irrelevant and old hat. Maybe they should go back to reading their literature.

9

Against All Odds

'Hope is the power of being cheerful in circumstances which we know to be desperate.'

G.K. Chesterton, *Heretics*

The aeroplane's final approach is over the largest lake in
Africa, Victoria. The conflict between the heat of the
land and the cold of the water generates great
cumulo-nimbus rain clouds above and a constant haze
below. The runway is visible only after a plane has nearly
completed its descent, so pilots overfly, frequently climb
and go round again. Until recently, night landings were
out of the question, for the electricity supply was
unreliable. As the plane makes its pass, the airport's
name can be seen cut out of elephant grass on the steep
bank of the perimeter: ENTEBBE.

In the winter of 1987, Dr Peter Poore, Head of the
Immunization Programme for Britain's Save the Children Fund, was making one of his regular trips to Uganda,
where his agency has maintained a strong presence
throughout the past seventeen years of civil conflict. This
visit, however, was special, for it would coincide with the
relaunch of UNEPI – Uganda's National Expanded
Programme on Immunization. Since the Save the
Children Fund's immunization programme shares similar goals, Dr Poore maintains close working contacts with
colleagues at WHO and UNICEF, for whom he often acts

202

as a consultant. Many other organizations besides WHO and UNICEF are immunizing children, not only Save the Children Fund but missionary bodies, private charities and refugee organizations. Though there is a degree of competition between the agencies there is now a great deal of co-operation too. From time to time they consult each other, evaluate each other's programmes on request, work together on joint programmes.

In approach to health, however, Poore and Save the Children Fund have always strongly sided with Mahler and WHO, even though many parallels exist between Save the Children Fund and UNICEF. Lady Eglantyne Jebb, who once said she had no enemies below the age of eleven, founded the Fund to succour the children of Europe after the First World War, as UNICEF was to do after the Second. The focus of the Fund's work is maternal and child health, and although they have a vigorous immunization programme this is offered only as an integral part of primary family health. Thus many of its staff, including Peter Poore, are deeply critical of UNICEF's approach. In turn the Fund itself has been strongly criticized by others for taking far too low a profile with regard to the problems of over-population, for concentrating on saving children's lives with too little attention to the quality of life thereafter.

The President of Save the Children Fund is HRH The Princess Anne, recently designated The Princess Royal as a mark of her outstanding work for children, on whose behalf she has travelled widely and exhaustively to some of the worst areas in the world. As a result of her patronage and the publicity that came through Bob Geldof's Band Aid and Live Aid programmes, the Fund's income quadrupled in the years 1985 and 1986. Like UNICEF much of the Fund's income has to be raised by public subscriptions. Yet what UNICEF is to WHO, so Save the Children is to UNICEF. The ratio of their sizes and budgets is similar. But Peter Poore argues that too much money can actually be a burden for a poor country. Having been convinced that solar refrigerators were best for Africa, UNICEF bought 100 for Uganda alone, even though at the time Save the Children Fund said they could use only ten.

However many times he takes this flight Peter Poore always feels twinges of anxiety. The memories that haunt Entebbe cause shivers even in those who have never set foot in Uganda. The air terminal building, once very smart, is now run down – peeling paint, a jungle of cobwebs in the roof and twenty defunct automatic opening doors. The crowds waiting for arriving friends lean over rickety balconies, gazing down on whirlpools of activity where health, immigration and customs officials provide those bureaucratic obstacles faced by all incoming passengers.

Cliff Webster was waiting: a fifty-year-old Jamaican, one of the Fund's most senior and experienced people, he had been in Uganda for many years. As Webster led him across to the one functioning exit door, Peter Poore looked for the children. When Poore visited Uganda in 1986, shortly after President Museveni's National Resistance Movement took control of Kampala on 26 January, the first child he saw was just one of many posted at the airport. All of six and a half years old and in full army uniform, he was enchanting – but the Kalashnikov rifle slung across his shoulder was not. Now, just one year later, they were again stopped outside the airport by a twelve-year-old boy, armed with a machine gun, manning a road block. These youngsters are all victims of the earlier fighting. As the waves of killing crashed upon the country-side and Obote's soldiers fled in lawless disarray, whole families were massacred. The children who managed to escape fled into the bush, where they were discovered and adopted by Museveni's men. Almost as mascots, the orphans lived with the guerrillas, became part of their movement, and lost their innocence and childhood.

Peter Poore wound down the car window, smiled at the 'soldier' and said, 'Jambo. Good morning. How are you?' The boy, not certain quite what he should do, spoke in Bugandan to Cliff Webster. They always assume that Webster is Ugandan and thus ripe for close interrogation. He takes it all patiently – he has no alternative. He shook his head and replied, 'Ministry of Health – UNEPI.' The boy frowned, hesitated, then waved them on.

Even during the short drive from the airport to Entebbe town, along the main road that gently climbs the peninsula with views of Lake Victoria on both sides, Poore saw reminders everywhere that the four horsemen of the Apocalypse have ridden through Uganda not once but many times. Once called 'the Pearl of Africa', the beautiful, fertile country had plenty of food, an excellent system of roads, a properly functioning civil service, a sound infrastructure, good education and a health care delivery that reached even into remote rural areas. The Wellcome Virus Research Unit at Entebbe was outstanding. Mulago Hospital at Makerere University was the finest medical teaching hospital on the African continent, with a paediatric department supported by UNICEF that spearheaded health care delivery throughout Central Africa, whose specialists were international names in tropical medicine. By January 1987 the British Medical Association, literally and professionally, no longer recognized the school. For between them, Milton Obote, then Idi Amin, then Obote again, presided over a steady destruction of Uganda, in a process that systematically tore out the heart of this once beautiful land. The British colonized the territory during the last century with a dual policy – divide and rule in the south, neglect in the north – and the moment the British left, on 9 October 1962, the loose federation disintegrated. The territory always had been a mass of warring tribal factions, so perhaps it was inevitable that tensions should explode once the country became independent. This happened in many African countries, of course, but the Ugandan regimes provoked genocide and destruction on a scale unmatched elsewhere.

But, as Poore could also see, stability was creeping back. The shooting and fighting in the capital had died away, the rubbish was being cleared off the streets. A few buildings were under construction, while the rubble of others was being reclaimed by the jungle. Throughout the seventeen years of strife some remained half-built; one crane still sits where it was first stationed all those years ago. But very slowly normal life is being resumed.

Reconstruction is going on in other towns, too: Bali, Nabingora, Fort Portal. But the small towns to the north and west Nile district and in the Lowero Triangle remain the most comprehensively destroyed and looted places imaginable. The Lowero Triangle, a mere thirty miles from Kampala and once the luxuriant agricultural heartland of Uganda, was the victim of the worst atrocities of all. Thriving towns were reduced to skeletons. Houses no longer have window frames or doors, and only small pieces of tin for roofs. Here ghosts abound, for here Obote's government destroyed entire communities, herding people into guarded camps and killing everything outside that moved. Those who survived the massacres disappeared into the bush. So even the deep countryside is haunted. Though plant and animal life abound, there is little evidence of humans until one stumbles on piles of skulls stacked on rough trestle tables alongside the murram dirt track. Every settlement has a similar macabre memorial – a pile of bones of murdered Ugandans.

Most of Peter Poore's staff lost a family member. One of his colleagues was simply taken out and shot, his body never found. The macabre conjunction between war and disease was dramatically highlighted when, in some destroyed settlement in the Triangle, Peter Poore came face to face with a four-year-old orphan, paralysed with fear and polio. When the Army came through everyone fled, but she couldn't run as fast as her mother and was abandoned.

The first flush of hope after Museveni took over is now tempered with a harsh realism that the government carefully, even severely, maintains, even although Uganda is now a 'fashionable' country and the recipient of much aid. But the economy is still in tatters, the problems of foreign exchange and logistics are immense. Just before Poore's visit in January 1987, food prices had doubled – but salaries had not. Monthly government wages were enough for only two weeks' supply of food. To survive people had to grow what they could – mostly matoke and cassava – a time-consuming task – and could not properly attend to everyday jobs. The situation was exacerbated in the Lowero Triangle because traders were reluctant to go to that haunted area; whereas in Kampala a kilo of rice cost four hundred shillings, in Semuto in the Lowero Triangle it cost five thousand.

Uganda is still on a war footing, the situation far from secure. During 1986, the transfer of power across the whole country, from Obote to Museveni, took several months to complete as the northern tribes, such as the Acholi, retreated into southern Sudan. Eighteen months later their presence in the northern districts around Kitgum and Gulu was still troublesome. Yet on this visit, Peter Poore could sense the palpable relief. True, as a white man he would seldom be hassled, but the Ugandans too were more confident that they would not be robbed, raped or killed. Museveni's troops were more controlled, more courteous and less often drunk than either Amin's or Obote's. There were also fewer road blocks and fewer soldiers manning them.

But such relief may be transitory, for the fourth horseman has returned to Uganda yet again, with weapons more frightening than ever. The plague is

AIDS, and causes 'the slim disease'. When soldiers on a
rampage surge across a country disease always follows;
AIDS happens to be the worst ever. True, as a local
surgeon recently observed, so destructive in the past have
been the visits of the horsemen that maybe a little virus
isn't going to bother the Ugandans, and of the many
governments in Central Africa, Uganda has been the
most honest in admitting the problem, allowing press
coverage, and facing the stark reality: that other than
education, no solution exists. Most African governments
have behaved like ostriches with regard to AIDS, but
Uganda has garnered both admiration and help from the
world's health agencies for its openness on the subject.
But an added worry was the possibility that the spread of
AIDS could be accelerated by the use of unsterile
hypodermic needles. And worse – might immunizing a
child with a live virus vaccine, such as polio, even trigger
a dormant AIDS virus? The government faces a situation
of unprecedented difficulty, for AIDS could be as
physically and psychologically devastating as war.

Kampala is a long, long way from Nettlebed, England.
This delightful small village in the Oxfordshire
countryside, where Peter Poore was living at that time, is
among the most privileged communities in the world.
The medical practice he joined had the enlightened
philosophy of allowing sabbatical leave. Peter Poore took
his in Ghana on a visit that was to change his life, for soon
afterwards he began to wonder whether he was making
the right use of his medical skills. Sympathetic to the
problems of affluence as to those of poverty, he
nevertheless felt that though his life might be comforta-
ble it wasn't particularly fulfilling.
  So he resigned, and he and his family spent the next
two years in Tanzania, where Poore quickly learnt that
medicine in Africa was a very different art form from
that in Oxfordshire. Preventive medicine was the best --

perhaps the only – answer to Africa's health problems. But Poore felt sadly disadvantaged, for his training had been orientated towards aggressive therapy: the more dramatic the cure, the better it was. So he returned for postgraduate work at the Liverpool School of Tropical Medicine and then did research at the Middlesex Hospital. After this he took his family to Papua New Guinea for four years, returning to England only when his eldest son was ready for secondary school.

But now Peter Poore didn't have a job, so he called Professor David Morley, a close friend and giant in tropical medicine, and gave his ideal job specification – to work, travel, teach and practise in tropical paediatrics. Morley said no such job existed. Two weeks later he telephoned: one did after all. Dr Nick Ward, well known for brilliant work on smallpox eradication in Bangladesh, was leaving Save the Children Fund, and his position, Head of their Immunization Programme, fitted Poore's specification exactly.

For half the year Peter Poore is in England working at the Fund's headquarters in the London suburb of Camberwell and though he enjoys travelling he is equally happy working with his London colleagues. However, the field staff are the prime reason for the Fund's outstanding reputation, he insists. 'They're amazing, interesting people, with a great sense of humour.' If hope is what keeps one going when things are desperate, humour is the capacity to laugh even when seventy-five people are dying of starvation every day. 'On one level it sounds sick. But it isn't. It's absolutely essential. Otherwise it is too easy to get disheartened and to think, oh, what the hell?'

The Fund's direct involvement with Uganda's revived immunization programme goes back six years. One night in 1983, their field director was sharing a beer with the UNICEF programme officer, Mark Stirling, who mentioned that his agency, also, wanted to support immunization in Uganda. Would the Fund help? The two men began touring the country to judge what facilities still existed. Everything had broken down; there were no delivery systems, no cold chains, no equipment. But matters were not entirely hopeless, for several factors were operating in their favour – of which the first and most important was enthusiastic people at the top. Secondly, since Uganda once had the most sophisticated health system in Africa – in 1965 the vaccination coverage for polio was 66 per cent – the population understood, and wanted, the benefits of immunization. Thirdly, the restorable remnants of the extensive health care infrastructure, whether buildings or trained staff, were also there, as were good roads, so the most distant place was only two days' drive from Entebbe. Delivering vaccines to the children should be relatively simple. There was also a devoted cadre of high-quality, local health workers who had kept going under appalling circumstances. On that first tour in 1984, Peter Poore and Mark Stirling travelled to an insecure area in the West Nile district, turning up at a small health post in the middle of nowhere quite unannounced, having walked in under a blazing sun with the temperature in the forties. Poore never forgot that place. Wearing jackets and ties, the health assistant and his team were beavering away in a centre which had absolutely nothing in the way of supplies – not so much as one ball of cotton wool. Yet they were doing the job for which they had been trained as best they could: delivering services in the prescribed manner, scrupulously keeping careful records on any old scrap of paper to hand. Thus, despite the desperate circumstances, the two men were optimistic that an immunization programme could be successfully mounted.

So in 1984, UNICEF, Save the Children Fund and the Ugandan Ministry of Health signed a trilateral

agreement for a three-year, renewable programme and
UNEPI, Uganda's National Expanded Programme on
Immunization, was formally established. UNICEF would
raise the money, underwrite the budget and act as the
conduit for massive donations both from Rotary
International for polio vaccine and those that the Italian
government had targeted to sub-Saharan Africa, for
vehicles, vaccines, hypodermics and Italian solar
refrigerators. Since they already had a strong, permanent presence in Uganda, Save the Children Fund
would provide specialist staff. Two senior advisers would
work with their Ugandan counterparts and train them to
displace the foreigners as soon as possible. The Ugandan
government would pay for local staff and costs such as
petrol and kerosene. By the end of that year the vehicles
were in and the cold chain re-established. Though
somewhat embarrassed by an excess of solar refrigerators, UNEPI was ready to begin.

The local staff had estimated that probably two and a
half million children under five were somewhere in
Uganda. Of these, 520,000 were under one year old, and
it was vital to reach this group in particular. So, one
district at a time, they would first determine what
equipment and supplies were needed, then train
workers, and only then would look for the children.
Gradually, region by region, the same process would be
extended across the country. By January 1985, progress
was good.

Then suddenly, almost overnight, everything ground
to a halt. As the battle for political control raged and
Museveni's National Resistance Army slowly fought its
way north, most of the Fund's supplies and its vehicles
vanished from the depots. First looted in July 1985 by
Obote's soldiers, these were appropriated in January
1986 by Museveni's. It was, and still is, very galling for
the staff to see their Land Rovers romping around
Kampala, with camouflage paint barely concealing the

Save the Children logo. However, matters could have
been much worse. Once Kampala was retaken, government control established and the country more or less
secure, an inventory revealed that at least the cold chain
equipment was rescuable and there was no reason why
UNEPI's phased programme could not continue. By
then immunization coverage in Uganda had dropped to
amongst the six lowest in Africa, but given reasonable
security and unstinting effort, the target for 1990 still
appeared achievable.

Security continuously worries Peter Poore. In
Mozambique his people have been beaten up and shot. In
Kampala, in 1987, a British worker was killed while
trying to foil the theft of a Land Rover. Since most of us
have a strong self-preserving reluctance to risk our lives,
what astonishes Peter Poore is the degree to which the
Fund's staff are prepared to do so. Although anyone who
chooses to join the relief agencies knows that they will be
walking towards, not away from, the sound of the guns, it
is still a heavy responsibility to send someone to a war
zone. The uncertainty is nerve-racking: a district is
considered safe until a bus is blown up; then it is unsafe
and remains so until a few hardy souls go through and
don't get blown up, when it is pronounced safe again.

But now help came from another quarter. Once the
country had been secured, President Museveni, faced
with the problems of a brutalized national psyche and a
shattered economy, realized that his first priority must be
to reunite tribal factions. Where cohesion and national
pride do not exist, unity must somehow be created. So
Museveni deliberately promoted non-sectarian issues in
order to encourage a more peaceful society. Seeing the
children's health programmes as one powerful instrument, he gave UNEPI top priority. He calls himself a
health worker, for years of guerrilla warfare have taught
him the unique value of preventive medicine and
primary health care. The adoption of the orphans by his

soldiers was probably another experience that led him to believe that the country could be rebuilt around its children, who were now ordered to relinquish their Kalashnikovs, take up their textbooks and go to school.

The celebrations in January 1987, the occasion for Peter Poore's visit, were to mark not only the relaunching of UNEPI but also the first year of power for Museveni's government. Several events were planned. The exhumed remains of Dr Lule, the progenitor of the National Resistance Movement, would be flown in for an honoured burial. Friday 24 January would be graduation day for all students. On Sunday the 26th, the date Museveni's guerrillas had taken the capital the year before, there would be a great party in honour of UNEPI, with ceremonies attended by the President and his dynamic Minister of Health, Dr Ruhukana Rugunda. Representatives from WHO, UNICEF, Save the Children Fund, Rotary International and the Italian government would all attend.

Peter Poore had decided to fly in before the celebrations began. He had several tasks to complete, new appointments to be made, decisions about management to be taken. He had to discuss the renewal of the Fund's three-year contract with the Minister of Health and the Director of Medical Services. This renewal would, in part, depend on the first full review of the Fund's programme that would shortly be conducted by experts from WHO. Then there was also the question of who would succeed Cliff Webster, who was ready to retire. Was John Barensi, the Ugandan whom Webster had been grooming for sole management, ready to take over, or should yet another foreign adviser come in? The matter raised a number of sensitive issues. After spending three arduous years rebuilding the programme, Webster might be ready to quit Uganda, yet he might also feel he was being rejected just as things were taking off. And what degree of authority should be

exerted upon local people by external experts in
scientific management? Should Poore propose appoint-
ing another British doctor for the position of senior
epidemiologist with UNEPI, or was this unwarranted?

But there was a far more serious problem. After years
during which Save the Children Fund had developed
solid relationships in Uganda, receiving praise from all
sides for their quiet devotion and solid progress in
establishing a sound primary health structure within
which – and only within which – immunization was being
applied, Poore had learnt there was a real possibility that
their quiet programme would be forcibly accelerated,
and subsumed under a major campaign involving
UNICEF and the Task Force for Child Survival. This was
potentially disastrous. Both Poore and his expatriate staff
in Uganda, indeed all those at the London headquarters
of the Fund, shared the worries aroused by any
accelerated campaign in countries whose political,
economic and social structures were delicate. Unless
applied carefully, such a plan might destroy the weak
health structure that existed by diverting resources and
people. No one, least of all Peter Poore, wanted to
discourage or reject enthusiasm for the massive global
commitment to universal immunization for children. But
in the glamour and excitement of reaching targets there
were very real risks, particularly in Uganda, that could
easily be overlooked.

Poore points out that for a country like Turkey there
was no problem because, as experience had already
shown, the existing strong infrastructure could both
withstand and support intense acceleration. But where a
fledgling and fragile infrastructure is suddenly burdened
with great pressures, it can topple under the weight. In
the face of humanitarian concerns such as childhood
immunization, Peter Poore dislikes being labelled a 'wet
blanket' – as does Mahler – but equally he is aware of the
dangers of over-enthusiasm. He uses the example of

Burkino Faso, once Upper Volta, to support his contention. This is often quoted by many in UNICEF as a prime example of a very poor country that undertook an accelerated campaign which actually did strengthen a very fragile health service, thus forming the basis for sustainable primary health care. From Poore's limited experience in the region, and that of his colleagues, he says this conclusion is rubbish. In the long term, the fruits of the campaign will not be maintained, and one reason amongst others he gives is that in the enthusiasm to immunize so many children, too little attention was paid to training people in simple matters, such as sterilizing the needles. Perhaps a few cases of measles were prevented, but how many cases of hepatitis B or AIDS were transmitted? Twelve months later Jim Grant was heard vigorously to repudiate any suggestion that the Burkino Faso campaign was not successful or sustainable. Time will judge.

Peter Poore often finds himself feeling very uneasy about taking this cautious stance, for there is something about immunization that makes it almost above criticism. Measurable, inexpensive, the EPI programmes are extraordinarily appealing, whether to donors, politicians, health workers or just ordinary people in a society. An immunized child is a protected child and this is, in one sense, such an achievement that it doesn't matter how it is done. If it were simply a question of throwing money at the problem — providing sufficient vehicles, fuels, vaccines and equipment and urging everyone to rush around immunizing every infant — it would not be difficult to reach any target. Even driving a bus across the Sahara, vaccinating any child one meets, will do some good. But the real point, Poore insists, is not how many are immunized today, but how to protect the largest number of children, not only tomorrow but next year and for ever. Vulnerable children are being born every day, and unless an ongoing routine is developed, with immunization carried out regularly on at least a twice-yearly basis, a country will always be left with diseased babies and aggrieved parents. So attention must simultaneously be paid to the questions of long-term commitment, long-term funds, and long-term relationships with a people and their medical needs.

Like Halfdan Mahler, Poore admits that the strongest – perhaps the only – argument for an intensive campaign is that it can establish the initial contact with mothers and children. But once this is made the agencies must offer everything they can – treatment, family planning, essential drugs and other disease control measures as well and the next steps must equally be taken by the communities themselves: they must reach out towards the health workers. This is difficult to provoke, but crucial to success. Equally Poore is painfully aware that giving things to others carries an enormous and continuing responsibility and one that must be reviewed constantly, for it is a most dangerous illusion to believe that all that is necessary is to do good. He thinks that, paradoxically, the successful smallpox campaign may inadvertently have done a disservice to primary health care. On that occasion vaccination was imposed on people over a limited period of time. But the imperatives of sustained protection are quite different, and anyone who is a serious professional would surely recognize the hazards of imposing a course of action without thought for a country's ability to continue. This is why Poore was so perturbed to learn that an accelerated campaign might be mounted in Uganda. For if the health services couldn't then sustain the increased coverage, either Uganda would be left with a vacuum, or the outside agencies would have to remain, immunizing for ever. Both consequences would be equally unsatisfactory.

If such considerations mean that the goal of 1990 has to be delayed, so be it. Targets are right and proper but, says Poore, 'it doesn't seem to me that it would be catastrophic if the target of 1990 was not met. Getting there by a given date is not the point; it's getting there and staying there which is crucial.' When challenged with the fact that some children will therefore die, he admits the pain, but adds, 'Health care is a tough business.'

At that time Peter Poore was not aware that the first impetus for an accelerated initiative in Uganda came not from UNICEF but from Ken Warren of the Rockefeller Foundation. The Foundation as a whole had become very interested in development programmes in Africa; Warren argued that one fruitful activity they could foster was the rebuilding of primary health care in Uganda and that immunization was one of the best points to start. The Foundation's senior officers debated whether such an initiative was premature; perhaps they should wait to see how Museveni's government was doing? But the clinching factor was a visit to New York by Uganda's Minister of Health, Dr Ruhukana Rugunda.

There was to be a meeting of the Task Force for Child Survival on health in Africa, so the Rockefeller Foundation flew Dr Rugunda first to Atlanta and then up to New York to meet Foundation officials. He made a tremendous impression with his energy, honesty and grasp of the problems, and as a result the Foundation decided to donate half a million dollars to Uganda's health services; the Task Force staff suggested that this money be used to co-ordinate all the immunization efforts – and this would include those of Save the Children and UNICEF.

Warren now admits that the two agencies were upset at this encroachment on their territory. Moreover the Foundation's initiative was followed by a visit of two people sent by the Task Force whose initial impact was not altogether favourable: their suggestion that they should help to mount an accelerated immunization programme had been, perhaps, too direct. Since a programme had been progressing well, though quietly, for two to three years, some people in the Ugandan Ministry of Health found offensive an attitude that implied, 'We'll come in and do this for you.' Dr Rugunda faced a difficult choice: should Uganda go with an accelerated programme under a new banner, or should it continue to rely on the low profile approach of Save the Children Fund which had served Uganda well through the turmoil of the last years?

How Rugunda would choose was preoccupying Peter Poore as the Land Rover drove up the slope, past the President's residence and the famous old Lake Victoria Hotel, towards the Fund's administrative headquarters. Preparations for the launch party were well advanced: lorries were being unloaded, the framework of a wooden grandstand being erected. A banner strung across two tall poles marked the dirt track that led down to the field where the party would be held. 'UNEPI welcomes President Museveni to the Launch of the Accelerated Programme of Immunization', he read, and wondered: had the critical decision already been taken?

In the compound, now more or less secure, Poore jettisoned his bags and then went over to the office. On the way he looked in at the storage depot for drugs and vaccines, a new warehouse completed in 1986. One side was stacked high, boxes of solar panels, crates of sterilizers, cartons of hypodermics lining the ante-chamber of the huge room that could house sufficient vaccine for the next ten years. At that moment two million doses each of measles, tetanus toxoid, DPT, BCG and polio vaccine were stored there, enough for two months. The warehouse managers told him that the electricity supply was still erratic and the emergency generator, too, caused some anxious moments, but so far power had always returned before any vaccine had been spoilt.

That evening, Peter Poore reviewed progress with his

staff. Though the northern part of Uganda was still closed to immunization teams, 540 immunization units had so far been established across the country. The sites had been selected and the buildings built, or rebuilt, in 1986. Two were hospitals, others just mud huts, but all were health posts where people knew they could get vaccination. More posts were urgently needed. When all were fully equipped the network would be in place to be fed by a steady stream of materials – vaccines, needles, swabs – from the new UNEPI warehouse. Refrigerators and the insulated cold boxes, sterilizers, pedal bikes, motorbikes and Land Rovers had already been distributed. From the established posts the staff fanned out, holding monthly clinics at twelve hundred outreach points that might be no more than a table under a tree, deep in the bush.

The cold chain was working well. Uganda has the largest solar-powered cold chain in the world. After their first survey, Peter Poore and Mark Stirling recommended that the cold chain should be maintained by solar power, for other fuel supplies were unreliable. Representatives of the Italian government who had provided the money, were also in Uganda for the party, awaiting progress reports on the project before they would release a second-stage payment. Money is not the only help the Italians provided. Simon, the Ugandan who was in charge of the cold chain together with three other colleagues, was trained in Rome. When the solar units arrived their installation was supervised by engineers sent out by the Italian manufacturers, Italsolar. Now, once the panels have been unloaded, it is a mere two hours before a solar fridge is quietly humming.

That night Peter Poore slept in the compound on the outskirts of Kampala, the main accommodation for his expatriate staff and the depot for its cars and Land Rovers. The roads are so pot-holed and ribbed that at any one time several vehicles are out of service, so the two mechanics are occupied full-time. Car thefts are common, but if the odds on a vehicle being stolen are high, those on it being cannibalised are even higher. When, if the car is recovered, anything valuable – tyres, battery, plugs – will have been removed. Thus huge iron gates and steel doors protect the entrance to the sleeping quarters, and the entire compound is guarded by an armed Askari. Along with music, the noise of gunshots is still a regular feature of the night.

That evening they all watched television. An hour of educational broadcasting was devoted exclusively to UNEPI and the importance of immunization. Several UNEPI and UNICEF staff were interviewed. UNICEF received thirty mentions, Save the Children Fund three. Peter Poore was quite unmoved by the discrepancy. His agency prefers to assume a low profile. Its objective is to foster self-confidence and technical skill so that, sooner rather than later, the Ugandans can take over completely.

The next day Poore called on Sally Fagan, the local Field Director for UNICEF. Even though Save the Children's annual budget in Uganda was a mere $400,000, in contrast to UNICEF's millions, as the sole agency to provide technical advisers, it has effectively controlled the health care operation. From time to time its staff have wondered whether UNICEF covets their monopoly. Yet now Peter Poore learnt that UNICEF, too, was worried about the Task Force moving in and 'taking over'. Without this intervention, renewal of the three-year agreement would be a formality, but Poore suspected that he would not quickly get a definitive decision because everyone was so preoccupied with the launch.

Unconfirmed gossip provided a counterpoint to the serious discussions: the Italian Minister of Health had called UNICEF, and asked them to try to get the event postponed for two days since otherwise he couldn't attend, a piece of news greeted with laughter tinged with anxiety; the Italians had wined and dined the Minister prodigiously; still more money had been promised from America; a host of epidemiological experts would be flown in from the Center for Disease Control to straighten out the entire operation. But while the men from Atlanta might have prestigious reputations, the Fund's staff had stayed in Uganda through years of bloody civil war, and the possibility that their programmes would be turned over to others just when things were starting to get back to normal was galling, to say the least.

The following days were hectic. A quick courtesy call on the Minister came first. Since making appointments is no guarantee that they will be kept, Poore just trusted to luck and, with Cliff Webster, drove the two hundred yards to the two-tiered building that housed the Ministry of Health. Officials, secretaries and visiting civil servants thronged the ante-chamber. While they waited, Webster told him that the Minister's private secretary had telephoned that morning asking for a loan of a million Uganda shillings so UNEPI could print invitations for the launch and provide soft drinks for the VIP's enclosure. The Fund would probably be repaid eventually, but if not it didn't really matter, since they too had an interest in ensuring a smoothly running party. As Poore and Webster were ushered into the Minister's office the Italian Ambassador was ushered out. They had a brief, non-committal conversation with Dr Ruhukana Rugunda, a great bear of a man whose craggy eyebrows that jut out from a sloping forehead are set off by a striking nose and a bushy beard.

On Saturday 25 January, Peter Poore and Margaret Kakumba, the Ugandan Operations Manager for UNEPI, flew up for a day's visit to Arua, near Murchison Falls, the main town of the West Nile district bordering Zaire and southern Sudan. The radio in the local hospital had been out of service for six weeks, and since there are neither telephones nor postal services, they had radioed the Church of Uganda in the town, hoping that someone would go over to the hospital to say they were coming. Though the West Nile district is secure, only a few ferries and one bridge connect it to the rest of the country so most medical supplies must come in by air. Vaccines are the exception, for Uganda Airlines refuses to take responsibility for unaccompanied medical supplies. Paying a special courier would be beyond the Fund's meagre budget and the journey by road takes an unacceptable, hot, thirty-six hours. So if they now decided to reopen the Fund's base in the district, they had somehow to establish the cold chain and regular vaccine deliveries.

The crucial people in the regions are the District Administrators – important members of the National Resistance Army and the President's most trusted administrators. So they called on him first. The National Resistance Movement has its own local council in every province and to get anything done it is sensible to go first to its members. Intelligent, co-operative and progressive, they have effective lines of communication. More importantly, they control transport and fuel supplies. Watered-down paraffin is a common commodity in this area, for there is neither petrol nor containers.

The District Administrator, a man in his mid-thirties, listened carefully as they explained their difficulties. They had tried without success to bring in vaccines from supplies based nearer, at Kitgum or Gulu. But since these two towns are major bases for the government's anti-rebel campaign, all medical supplies arriving there are automatically appropriated for the front line. The District Administrator agreed that the Fund could not possibly be expected to allocate a personal courier to travel with the vaccines. He had a direct line to the President's office and perhaps someone there could persuade Ugandan Airlines to co-operate. He also promised to look into fuel allocations, though there was still no sign of the next consignment. As for staff pay – another problem – the best he could offer was promissory notes for last month's wages. His district must raise revenue by taxes, but few people locally have any income, so what could he do?

They asked when he planned to form a district health committee – the basic local structure from which all immunization activities are organized. If, when, and only then, one was formed the Fund would send in an operations manager from headquarters, to survey the district and give money for local wages and fuel supplies. He agreed to set a date for a first meeting.

Driving out of the town to the airstrip their car was held up by a convoy of lorries from Zaire carrying three hundred Ugandans to refugee camps. During the civil war at least thirty thousand Ugandans are estimated to have fled to Zaire, but the true number is probably much higher. By now some people have homes in both countries, and move back and forth at will. As security improved, a massive return of refugees was predicted, so the agencies geared up to receive thousands. Though those three hundred would have been picked up in Zaire, driven over the border and just dumped, this was not a compulsory migration; anyone who had asked to return was being helped.

At four in the morning on Sunday 26 January, a tremendous electric storm struck Kampala, with howling gales, crashing thunder and torrential rain. Although by daybreak the air had cleared, the grandstand and the enclosure had been blown down. Men were hurriedly conscripted to rebuild them. The formal opening ceremony, by the President, of the new Essential Drugs Programme warehouse, was due to begin in a few hours. A white banner with red lettering had been stretched above the blue metal entrance doors the day before. 'UNEPI Well-Comes His Excellency the President of Uganda'. But when, first thing on Sunday morning, John Barensi, the Ugandan National Programme Manager, arrived, this banner had vanished and another was in its place. White, beautifully printed, with the logos of UNICEF on one side and UNEPI on the other, it proclaimed: 'UNICEF, United Nations Children's Fund, welcomes President Museveni, giving Uganda's children a chance'. Barensi was furious. 'Who put that up? Take it down immediately and put back our banner.' So up went the first sign again, now attached somewhat lopsidedly. Then a Nigerian and a Dutchman from UNICEF arrived and there was a replay. 'Who took down our banner? Put ours back up.' When, an hour later than planned, President Museveni and Dr Rugunda arrived, the UNICEF banner had been relegated to two trees in the field.

Soldiers and small boys in jungle camouflage, in turn serious and grinning, worried and frivolous, but all with Kalashnikovs, mingled with the guests who waited for Museveni to come and cut the ribbon. By now another two banners had gone up. The Danish Red Cross and the Uganda Essential Drugs Management Programme also welcomed the President. Wearing his best suit, Peter Poore stood with others at the entrance to the warehouse. The cars swept through the gates; the cameramen squinted through their lenses; all those lined in order of importance stiffened, ready to be introduced. But President Museveni started at the 'wrong' end, shaking all appropriate hands in his own good time, under the watchful gaze of his bodyguard, a large forty-year-old man wearing thick-lensed spectacles, who seemed to have come straight out of a Cuban school of guerrilla warfare. He was just one of a number of very serious looking people accompanying the President. Ceremoniously the white ribbon was cut; the entourage swept into the depot for a quick tour, talked to the staff and swept out again and into cars for the drive down to the grassy fields on the banks of Lake Victoria. Here a series of exhibits, on cold chain technology and other aspects of health, awaited them. Pressmen, television crews and everyone else quickly followed behind along an avenue of boy and girl scouts shaking little banners that read: 'UNEPI. Be wise, immunize.'

Now the sun blazed down. The obligatory brass band played the obligatory military music as Museveni started a leisurely stroll around the exhibits. Schoolchildren and nurses sang immunization songs. A troop of twelve Busoga musicians from Iganga provided an ethnic counterpoint, three blowing down Ugandan equivalents of the pipes of Pan, others tapping a series of stones, and one, the veins bursting out on his forehead from effort, alternately with one hand and an ivory stick, striking a large wooden xylophone placed on the ground.

Museveni took the displays very seriously and asked many questions. His interest in health was apparent, and for a Head of State he is disarmingly approachable. Anyone could walk up, question him and receive an answer. A solar panel, looking like a diminutive New York skyscraper thrown on its side, captured his attention and he was given a full account of how it worked. In another booth the story of the cold chain held him for several minutes, as did disposable and self-destruct hypodermic syringes. But at the final booth his questions were drowned by the noise of protesting children being ostentatiously vaccinated by health staff.

Then the speeches began; representatives from UNICEF, WHO, the Italian government and Rotary International spoke first. Peter Poore spoke on behalf of Save the Children Fund. Finally, the President and his Minister of Health in turn went to the podium and emphasized the government's commitment to the Expanded Programme on Immunization. Both were

clearly well versed in the rationale for primary care, and
Rugunda's account of the Ugandan health service was
disarming in its honesty about the problems the country
faced.

Seated on the platform in the first row of distinguished
visitors, Peter Poore enjoyed the proceedings. Only two
seats away from him was the chubby-cheeked infant
chosen to be the honoured recipient of oral polio vaccine
from the President. Poore had to be careful to avert his
eyes, for every time he tried to smile at the baby her face
puckered with the first signs of tears.

On Tuesday, Poore's last day in Uganda, the staff
threw a party, and later that night a suitably sedated
Peter Poore happily reflected on the fruits of his visit.
The tri-partite agreement would be continued. The
Minister of Health was happy to accept Poore's
recommendation of a British epidemiologist, and the
government planned to retain Cliff Webster as Senior
Adviser, although Poore had argued strongly that more
authority should be handed over to a Ugandan. While at
times being a big thorn in collective flesh, Webster had
been an honest broker and a strong mediating force
between the Ministry and the external agencies. Perhaps,
Poore had admitted, it was after all one stage too soon for
John Barensi to assume control.

Mellowed by the warmth of the African night, the
friendship, the beer and the progress, Poore was also
more relaxed about the future: firstly because his survey
during this visit led him to expect a successful review
from WHO later in 1987, as indeed happened. For the
health care infrastructure was rapidly being consolidated
and as delivery services were increased, immunization
levels could be expected to rise; the central vaccine store
was in place; good progress had been made in training
more health workers; a unit for the surveillance of
disease had been established; the Virus Research Unit at
Entebbe was at last being properly restored and this was

vital in the light of the AIDS epidemic. On the down side they still faced several problems: poor security in the north and the east; more Ugandan staff were needed, probably another epidemiologist and two more project officers; they must now concentrate heavily on training, so that needles were used only once or adequately sterilized, otherwise AIDS would nullify all the hard-won gains in child survival; a larger budget was therefore necessary. He would recommend to London that Save the Children Fund channel more money into improving the facilities for blood sampling and testing.

Secondly he had held a brief meeting with the two consultants from the Task Force for Child Survival who had now arrived. One, a young and well-heeled Ugandan, had been trained at CDC. The other, Harry Godfrey, a mellow man in his fifties, Poore thought quite outstanding. So he had raised directly with Godfrey his main concern: the Task Force was obviously keen to be extremely active so as to be seen to be extremely effective, but he was worried about the consolidation of Uganda's health infrastructure for it would not withstand gross distortions. Godfrey had agreed and replied, 'Look, tell me if we're a pain in the arse, and I'll go back and tell them so in Atlanta.' Without saying that they were, Poore implied only that they could be. If the fragile Ugandan system was to survive intact further support would have to be sensitively targeted, and his main worry was about the expected flood of yet more expatriates, 'whizz kids', as they were quickly dubbed. Staff from agencies who had been in Uganda for years had all agreed: sooner rather than later the Ugandans should run the whole show, and dependence on outsiders must gradually be diminished.

Yet it would appear that the initiative behind the appearance of the two consultants had stemmed in part from President Museveni. Uganda's development was almost totally dependent on foreign aid, and he and the major donor agencies were concerned that the country made the most effective use of the money. So Kwamogi Anywar, from the Task Force for Child Survival, spent several months in the country studying the health projects and found that the major donors rarely shared resources, rarely revealed their budgets to the appropriate ministry and were often unaware of what other donors were doing. Amongst numerous practical suggestions, he recommended the formation of an Advisory Council to co-ordinate such activities, drawing in people from the various relevant ministries from Finance, Health to Foreign Affairs. A Donor Co-ordination Office would 'provide visibility, accountability and effective use of available resources'. If it proves not to be just another bureaucracy, it might.

However, as Peter Poore would later admit, his worst fears were never realized. 'We did at least manage to contain the wilder calls for mass campaigns. Another whizz kid from CDC, seconded by the Task Force, finally turned up in 1988, a very bright man, who never stopped working or thinking. When he actually arrived at the airport there was no one to meet him and no accommodation had been arranged. Save the Children Fund lent him a car for the first four months. He had enormous resources, for the Rockefeller Foundation had given the Ugandan Ministry of Health half a million dollars to promote co-ordination amongst the agencies on all aspects of the immunization. But he and our epidemiologist didn't hit it off and eventually he was replaced by Mark Weeks, who is superb.'

Seconded by the Task Force and paid for by the Rockefeller Foundation grant, Mark Weeks was taken on by the Ugandan Ministry of Health as an across-the-board epidemiologist. However, 80 per cent of his time is now spent on AIDS. He made such an excellent impression though, that when Bill Foege visited Uganda in 1988, Sally Fagan of UNICEF made a point of thanking him, admitting, as she did so, that she too had at first been highly sceptical of the value of yet another expatriate coming in.

Over the long term, however, Poore is nothing like so sanguine. Since the relaunch of UNEPI in 1987 progress, though steady, has continued to be slow and still some 30 per cent of the country cannot be reached. The approach is also too vertical – not sufficiently integrated into a primary health care system. What is needed, he insists, is an immediate investment in people and training leading to a slow steady growth of the health infrastructure. Such an investment was once negotiated and government funds promised but cash has now dried up; not being glamorous, the need for recurrent long-term costs is generally overlooked in the razzmataz of campaigns and targets. Recently the Canadian Public Health Association, critically aware of this problem, gave Uganda $2 million specifically for two years of such costs. But when these are finished, who, Poore wonders, will foot the bill?

Certainly not Uganda, for the demands on the country continue to be overwhelming: relations between Uganda and Kenya are not good and skirmishes regularly erupt; the nation itself is still not united.

This is a country where anyone up to middle age knows nothing of the law, for they have never experienced the power of the judicial process, only the power of the gun. The fighting in the north and east still festers, the control of Gulu still not established, even after the defeat of Alice Lakwena who for months led a lethal rag-taggle group up and down the borders. Like some medieval rabble her 'army' of men, women and children moved through the land as the terrified villagers watched. Camping in the fields, they would slaughter some cows, eat, sleep, then move on, press-ganging people into their movement as they went. Talking to the wives of the rebels, whose husbands have voluntarily gone off, one realizes even now how damaging is the legacy of Britain's earlier divide-and-rule policy. As the journalist Mary Anne Fitzgerald reports, they say: 'We don't care how long it takes; if we have to die, we have to die. But we won't let the southerners dominate us.' The country is not yet under Museveni's control; the psychological divide between the northern tribes and those of the south, from where Museveni comes, is so great that it will take at least a generation to bridge, the children of Uganda notwithstanding.

And then there is AIDS, a joker in the pack that could hardly have appeared at a worse time, for it drains Uganda's resources both in terms of finance and people. Uganda was the first African country to report AIDS, not because the first case on the continent occurred there, but because they were the first to be honest about the problem. Although by now the Congo and Burundi are worse affected, Uganda, along with Rwanda and Zambia, has severe epidemics.

But Museveni is an energetic and courageous man of great resource. Generally agreed to be honest, he is 'big' in many senses of the word. Though socialist in inclinations he is not a radical and distances himself from the hardline Marxist-Leninist stances of those in power in Angola and Mozambique. While more at ease in military fatigues talking about battles than in a lounge-suit discussing economics, he is practical and realistic. When Foege visited Uganda in 1988 he was deeply impressed with Museveni's knowledge of health issues.

Like most people who have acquired power in Africa, and are keen to retain it, he announced in April 1989 that a return to civilian rule would shortly take place through elections. Possibly he will keep his pledge, although he has recently also announced that the country needs two further years before it will be ready to return to democracy. All in all, he and Uganda will need all the courage, help and luck possible. Poore, who prays that these will come their way, was once heard to murmur: 'I can't imagine how one could ever wake up in the morning and think, "My God, I'm President of Uganda. What *am* I going to do?" '

10

A Fitting Gift

'The earlier half of this century foresaw a scientific
solution to all problems; they dehumanized their
imagined descendants who were to live in a sterile
automation, whereas the happy actuality is that
technology, despite its dangers and aberrations, has
enlarged our compassion.'

Quentin Crewe, *In the Realms of Gold*

Some time in the middle of the twelfth century, a group
of monks built a priory at Talloires, on the shores of Lake
Annecy, France. At that time the village had many
characteristics of Third World villages today: the people
were poor, the children uneducated. Eight hundred
years later, another group of people met in the very same
priory for the third Bellagio Conference. Their hostess,
an energetic Frenchwoman in her eighties, welcomed
them with a mixture of pride and bemused affection.
'The place speaks to you all,' she said, 'because this was a
place where visions were born. The monks settled here
and helped the village with education, health and
everything. So it is most fitting that you have chosen to
come here, and if you insist on calling your conference
Bellagio, *tant mieux*. Bellagio, too, is a beautiful lake.'

For three days in March 1988, old friends would come
together, some for the last time. Not only were there just
twenty months before the target date of 1990 but the

wheel of life was turning and many who had conceived and led the planned miracle would soon disappear from the scene. Within three months Halfdan Mahler would relinquish his post as Director-General of the World Health Organization and one year later become Secretary-General of the International Planned Parenthood Federation. Though Jim Grant had several more years at UNICEF the agency was already identifying fresh problems to tackle. Ken Warren, too, was leaving the Rockefeller Foundation where he had served with distinction for ten years; its directions and philosophy were in flux so he would move into a fresh field, as Director for Science in the Maxwell Communications Corporation. The Task Force for Child Survival too, was taking on fresh challenges, such as a campaign to eradicate guinea-worm. In any case, new faces had once again replaced old ones: each Bellagio Conference had welcomed a different President of the World Bank – first Bob McNamara, then A. W. Clausen, and now Barber Conabel; others coming for the first time included Dr Ruhukana Ruganda, no longer Uganda's Minister of Health but now Minister of Transport.

A few of the world's press corps had been invited as well as our camera crew, for the first occasion of filming. So this was an opportunity to assess both achievements and whether earlier tensions had been resolved. At the Harvard Club in New York, a mere four years back, the group had spoken of a 'rare event' in the history of men, and as time had gone by others began calling the saga 'a miracle in the making'. Indeed, the Canadian International Development Agency (CIDA) was actually using that phrase as the title for its latest progress report. Thus everyone was imbued with a strong sense of occasion. At times the ambience was emotional, at others critically sensitive as to what still remained in order to sustain the initial successes. Though on occasions the meeting threatened to become a 'love-in', amongst the waves of pride were acerbic exchanges which served to remind us that while miracles are achieved by saints, this triumph had been achieved by human beings – extraordinary ones, no doubt, but mere human beings.

Halfdan Mahler was the focus of attention. Though one could not miss the affectionate respect beaming towards Bill Foege and Jim Grant, yet it was feelings for Mahler that dominated – awe for his stature, gratitude for his vision – combined with nostalgia, for a unique period was coming to an end. Not only were these people part of history; they had actually created the history, and no one wanted to sever the ties. So, throwing an arm around Ken Warren's shoulder Mahler was heard to say, 'Look, my friend, you and I will never retire. We'll go on being subversive terrorists for health for ever.'

One thing was certain. Though in this saga there had been heroes, heroines and ordinary people, and some who acted out of self-interest and others self-sacrifice, some who had fought competitively while others just quietly got on with the job – there were in it neither villains nor venality. Indeed there was only one knave, and that was poverty. The cause that united these different people was rooted in their belief that health is a fundamental human right; their ambition was to remedy a great disparity and ensure that all the children of the world had a healthy headstart in life by offering them the best of science and medicine. But as always, the successful application of the necessary technologies depended on a host of factors quite outside science itself – tradition, politics, history, culture, mores. As a consequence, the arguments that had arisen were reminiscent of those that in the 1950s had brought the scientist C. P. Snow into bitter conflict with the humanist F. R. Leavis.

As far back as the 1950s Snow had already foreseen the serious tensions that arise when one small section of the world lives in affluence, while the greater lives in want – tensions that this group had sought to defuse. Snow prophesied that as populations increased that want would deepen, and on a globe whose boundaries were, through communication, shrinking by the minute, such tensions would become intolerable. He had even predicted the famines, saying, 'We will sit comfortably in our sitting-rooms and watch people die on our television screens' – as indeed, in 1985, we did.

Yet Snow believed that science and technology could dramatically reduce the burden of poverty that afflicted the peoples of the world. The great divide was not, in truth, between the literary and scientific cultures so much as between the rich and the poor. But F. R. Leavis reacted savagely, arguing that the technical – he said cold-blooded – solutions that the scientific revolution offered were at the best inadequate and at the worst patronizing. No one should dare to presume to tell other societies what their people should do, or impose operational solutions from above, and certainly not without experiencing for themselves the lives that others live.

Watching the developing minuets of the three Bellagio Conferences it had been tempting to cast Jim Grant and Halfdan Mahler, or Richard Reid and Peter Poore, in the roles of C. P. Snow and F. R. Leavis. Whereas one group emphasized those eminently practical *programmes* that could make an immediate impact, the others focused on the gradual evolution of a *process*, with health care emerging out of a community by *their* collective decision, as part of evolving development. The facile interpretation was that the vertical immunization programmes provided the quick technical fix while the slower process of community participation and self-reliance on primary health care their humanistic counterpoint. But this time, rather than adhering rigidly to entrenched ideological positions, the two men most closely involved had deliberately sought reconciliation. Their subordinates might still be angry and defensive but Grant and Mahler had moved close together, and what each was now to say in 1988 at Bellagio III was different from what they had said in 1984, at Bellagio I. The common enemy was still poverty, but both men regarded the various health initiatives as Trojan horses in which to infiltrate its battlements.

Yet how far had they truly penetrated? Without the sustainability of the programmes, hardly at all, and this crucial issue was at the forefront of the agenda at Talloires. Every delegate held firm opinions that would be reflected in their practical actions. Both Ambassador Alan Woods of USAID and President Margaret Catley-Carlson of CIDA emphasized – as indeed did representatives from every other agency – that although they would continue their financial support they now expected recipient countries to make equal efforts to maintain the health programmes. However, a representative from Britain's Overseas Development Administration (ODA) [who works there one day a week and with Save the Children Fund for the other four] announced that although ODA's contributions would continue, they would be applied only to developing health services and building the infrastructure. Privately he spoke in vitriolic terms of his mistrust of Jim Grant and the directions taken by UNICEF.

Thus when delegates from countries as far apart as China, India, Morocco and Peru gave accounts of their immunization progress, they did so against the counterpoint of sustainability. Of them all Dr Ruganda of Uganda, humorous and telling, stood out. No longer was it a situation, he said, in which 'You were the donors and we were the beggars. Together we did the job. But remember the job goes beyond immunization. In Uganda, 27 per cent of my people still live beyond five kilometres of a health clinic; 57 per cent of them beyond ten. Our infrastructure was weak or destroyed and so we are trying to use these programmes as entry points for breaking the vicious circle of instability and poverty. Indeed, our remaining problems are poverty, political stability and war.'

Yet the message from the diminutive but distinguished Dr Fred Sai, Senior Population Adviser at the World Bank, commenting on the panel discussion he was chairing, showed that echoes of the old debate could well reverberate for a long time. Even though the existing state of affairs was a matter for congratulation, there was still, Sai insisted, a major polarity within the group.

'Clearly all programmes are alive and well and squarely in the hands of developing countries. We at the agencies are no longer the main movers and we are delighted. Once individual governments find that a good health service really helps, then all the components come together – the mother and the child relationship along with the science too.' Yet, echoing the words of Sir Ian MacGregor, he continued: 'But it would be both unscientific and amoral for anyone to say that they would not take advantage of an existing technology until a total system had been developed. So we can't say to those countries remaining, "Don't do anything until the infrastructure is in place." ' And with a trace of anger in his voice he finished, 'I tell you. I was born in West Africa, and if we had said that in the past, if we had waited, *nothing at all* would have been done. Any entry point can do – but something must be started.'

Nevertheless, as Foege reminded the delegates, despite the dissensions their achievements were both real and substantial. When the programmes began in 1984, immunization services reached less than 5 per cent of children in the developing world. By March 1988, only four years later, 50 per cent were being reached with three doses of either polio or DPT vaccines. By August 1989, WHO would claim that over two-thirds of all children in the world were receiving the three doses. However, the target had been to cover 80 per cent of all

children by 1990, and even with vigorous efforts during
the twenty months remaining it would be difficult to
surpass 70 per cent. Though the goal remained
tantalizingly close, there were pockets of difficulty in the
numerically largest countries of the developing world.
Forty per cent of all vulnerable children remaining were
in China, India, Indonesia and Nigeria. Over 20 per cent
were in India alone.

The problems posed by India seemed at first
surprising. The lowest figures for the third round of
immunization came from Africa, probably because it had
the least developed health infrastructure – and here
populations were still rising faster than anywhere else. So
surely the problem was there? Nevertheless in sheer
numbers remaining to be protected, India faced the
greatest challenge. Yet, Foege insisted, the Task Force
was not at all daunted by the low coverage of those four
countries for three reasons: a strong coalition for global
immunization already existed; all had a high degree of
political commitment to the goal; three had strong health
infrastructures which should, in theory, allow this to be
both reached and sustained, and the fourth, Nigeria,
where the Minister of Health, Dr O. Ransome-Kuti, was
an outspoken supporter of primary health care, and
eschewed campaigns, was now the focus for a major
programme run by USAID. Foege and Ralph Henderson
both predicted that by the end of 1990, all four countries
would have increased their coverage by 20 per cent – by
which time just over 70 per cent of the target would have
been reached and the majority of children in the world
finally protected. Theirs was the first promissory note to
be issued at Bellagio III.

Foege showed also that globally, the average infant
mortality rate had already dropped from 127 per 1000 in
1960 to 72 in 1986: if the programmes continued as they
were now going, this would be down to 55 per 1000 by
the year 2000. Thus by the end of the millennium, over

forty-five countries should have rates lower than 25 per 1000 and only in a few countries would rates be above 100 per 1000 live births. This was the second promissory note.

He also claimed that a dramatic association had appeared; one that showed decreased infant mortality was indeed followed by decreased birth rates as many had long believed. So coincidentally, the number of births in the world would peak, for crude *birth* rates also were falling. From 35 per 1000 in the year 1960 and 26 in 1986, these would drop to 23 in the year 2000. However, the drops were greatest only in those countries well advanced with their immunization programmes. Poor countries with high infant mortality would continue to show the smallest reductions in child survival and crude birth rates. So the sobering message he wished to drive home was this: great though their achievements to date, some infants in the poorest sections of the poorest populations in the world would still not benefit from twentieth-century science, even by the new millennium. They will be found not in the countryside but in the slums of the large urban areas, in the big cities of Africa such as Kinshasa or Lagos.

However even as Bellagio III took place, millions of children were not dying who otherwise might have. In 1960, one in three children died before the first year; in 1988, the figure was one in four. More people were now living than had ever lived before. So, he said, in a charming aside, 'the study of history is now a minority subject.' But if the infant mortality rate was a crude predictor of birth rates, when, Foege asked, could we expect the actual number of births to start dropping? He then issued the third promissory note: as family planning and child survival continued to reduce the crude birth rate this moment would occur in the next twelve years – a momentous occasion in human history.

There was, however, Foege continued, a joker in the

pack – AIDS. Since childhood deaths from AIDS do not occur before the second year, these were not (and still are not) used in calculations of infant mortality rates. But the moment the number of all infant deaths caused by AIDS nears 20 per cent, the epidemic would neutralize every success that has so far been achieved in child survival.

Others besides Foege were happy to offer hostages to fortune. Ciro de Quadros reported that following the ambush in Maceió and the multiple campaigns of 1986, cases of polio in Brazil had fallen to below the one-thousand mark for two successive years. A major national surveillance system, with a network of supporting laboratories, had been set up throughout Central and South America as a prelude to polio eradication by the year 2000, an achievable goal that meeting collectively endorsed, as a fitting gift from the twentieth century to the twenty-first. De Quadros predicted that though many factors – political and social will, managerial constraints, the adequacy of disease surveillance, vaccine efficacy, the capacity to control outbreaks rapidly – could still impede eradication, nevertheless it would be achieved. The problem of the efficacy and stability of the oral vaccine – still their vaccine of choice – remained a worry, but he believed that the new formulation developed in Brazil would overcome this problem and that new, specially designed polio vaccines would surmount the difficulty of low immunity in some children. However, others, such as Dr V. Ramalingaswami, past Director of India's Medical Research Council, remained highly sceptical: experience in his country suggested that the problem of mounting an antibody response would remain severe, and doses of both killed and live vaccines would be necessary.

The 'general' who had brilliantly led the earlier smallpox campaign conceded with amused deprecation that he was now known as 'the other Henderson'. At times relaxed, at others frustrated, D. A. Henderson agreed something tremendous had been achieved over and above immunization, for the agencies had co-operated as never before.

The real achievement however was that they had brought about a revolution in global public health, one that had garnered wide political support and thus well and truly laid the foundations for community-based primary health care. The cost had been minuscule. Prevention was the route everyone was taking, for medicine in the West was now so expensive that even the richest countries were turning to it, and the poorest had no other way to go. A major challenge to traditional health systems had been mounted everywhere, and that was why he was using the word 'revolution'. 'We have witnessed a remarkable advance in international caring,' he concluded. 'Now war is the only enemy of sustainability.'

But the three criticisms he had made at Bellagio II still held: the absence of any quantitative measure of success – neither the impact of the programme on disease nor the numbers of children *not* vaccinated were known; secondly, Maceió apart, there was insufficient analysis of programme failures; thirdly, new and better vaccines, preferably administered as one scratch, were urgently required.

But, as the end of the campaign approached, how did the two generals, Grant and Mahler, view the battle?

'The issue is now, of course,' said Jim Grant, 'not just one dose of vaccine but how frequently are the services available. Once a year is no good; it must be once a week or a month. The demand is there and we have to encourage it, for mothers are anxious to protect their children and they'll come and search us out. Given that, we realize our targets are achievable' – and he suspected Ralph Henderson's estimate of just over 70 per cent coverage by 1990 was too conservative – 'the question is how can we help countries reach them? The Arab world looks like doubling its coverage in ten years; Latin

America in twelve to thirteen. But in Africa where the per capita income is falling, there really is a problem.'

Their joint venture had achieved success on the three fronts of demand, supply and placing children's health so squarely on the agenda that it was now an important political issue. Grant was not disturbed by the fall-off that without exception always followed campaigns, for wherever this had occurred major political problems for governments had followed.

Grant went on, 'At Cartagena and Bellagio II, I spoke of the flood tide in the affairs of men that was shifting the course of history. All shared that feeling with respect to our ability to make significant changes in the world. It's even more apt now, especially as we put it into the context of a new momentum in development.

'Certainly there are negative features. The expenditure on the arms race has soared to such an extent that even the superpowers are facing a crisis. The global economic and debt crisis is worse than the most pessimistic of us anticipated and this continues to affect the poorest countries, and the poorest people in those countries, worst of all.

'On the positive side, though, perhaps we *are* beginning to see the dawn of an end to the arms race and a lowering of East–West tensions. And we really are seeing a very special willingness to work together for children with do-able, cost-effective programmes that political leaders can support. These campaigns are being turned into tools of social mobilization of whole societies. For example, when we analysed the cost in Turkey it came to $17 per immunized child. Of that, $2.50 was the actual cost of the vaccine; the remaining $14.50 came from free TV time, the Rotarians' work, and from the existing infrastructure – that maintained health clinics, paid the salaries, and provided transport. So for those countries like Burkina Faso that have neither organizations, nor communication networks, nor infrastructure, it is bound to be difficult.

'Take two examples. Last year (1987) Colombia suffered a major volcano, a disabling drug scene, a change of government with a new political party in charge. Yet they kept their immunization programmes going throughout, and spread the process into the remaking of the educational system. Every Catholic priest must learn about immunization and primary health care in his training; by law immunization is now one element in the primary school curriculum. Secondly, India has now 25 per cent more children than they had when Bellagio I took place – a time when one would never believe that the five countries with the largest populations would achieve anything. But now we can predict that they may possibly complete their target on time.

'Most important of all, behind all this momentum we see a new morality, one that says that instant death in the twentieth century is as unconscionable a fact as was slavery in the nineteenth.'

Finally, Mahler rose to give the peroration. 'As I come to leave the scene, I feel the world has become ice cold, at the temperature of a nuclear weapon. And if I ask myself, what is the difference in the development climate in 1988, from that in the early sixties when I first started, it is this. If, in 1960, I had said that we needed to export capital from the north to all of Africa south of the Sahara and the Sahel, I would have been called a liar, or people would have started crying. Now they simply shrug their shoulders and say, "Well, you know, that's the way it is." So I tell you – economic recession is a monumental excuse for doing *nothing*. Immorality is okay. It's amorality, the cynical and the indifferent, that gets me very worried. I believe that unless we break out of a climate of amorality, development doesn't have anything like a chance of winning.

'Yet in our recent business at Bellagio there are elements of truth and morality – elements that have run like a red thread through all Jim Grant's work. We have managed to convince ourselves the world can be a better place; we now have confidence in ourselves; we are neither too romantic nor too cynical; we can finally afford to tell the truth and it's important that we tell not only what we know, but what we don't know. Now one of the best tests of truth is how it can be accepted in the market place, which for us, is the developing world. In spite of malaria – our earlier mistake, of course – we do not now shy away from talking about polio eradication, or measles eradication, or whatever. And in the way we have been evolving together, we no longer run the risk of not facing up to the truth, for we are a very different crowd from when we came together at the first Bellagio. I think the bonds and ties inside the family have developed tremendously – a beautiful harmony has developed. My brother Jim and I have had many tactical arguments but we have *never* had any doubt about the strategy.

'Once the dreams have been realized one catches a glimmer of greatness and hope. So as these are my last words to you – and I hope to see you somewhere up there or down there – what I think has happened is that we've come as close to the truth as is possible in our human predicament. The human predicament is such that if one part pulls on our global blanket, the rest are left naked. And I do not believe that it should be impossible to convince the north to let go a little. But, on the other hand, development cannot be done by proxy. So equally there is an important moral lesson here – of self-reliance: those in the developing world can pull their own destiny together. And if *their* self-reliance is the ultimate issue, actually it doesn't really matter whether we, on the outside, are arguing about vertical or horizontal programmes.'

Towards the end of the last day, after the final session had broken up and those whose job it was were putting the last touches to 'The Declaration of Talloires', Grant and

Mahler, Foege and Warren, came before the cameras. The producer, like a patient sheepdog, was waiting to round up his quarry and shepherd them to the sitting-room of the priory where they would look over photographs of the first Bellagio Conference and reminisce informally. But there was a long delay, for they were debating fiercely. Some from WHO, reluctant as ever to offer hostages to fortune, were stalling, arguing that they should eliminate from the Declaration any reference to a target date for the eradication of polio, but wait until there was indisputable evidence that PAHO's strategy was working. An irritated Grant was saying, 'That's the very way to ensure that we won't meet the target. You'd be setting up a self-fulfilling prophecy.' An equally irritated Mahler, demonstrating that they were indeed a very different crowd from when they first came together, was emphatic: 'Either we are going to do it, or we're not. If we are, then we say so.' The discussion was heated: the date stayed in.

The four men trooped in. The cameraman juggled to get them all into one frame for the establishment shot, for Foege towered over the others. The photographs were handed out, and in an atmosphere of teasing and seriousness were passed from hand to hand, while the microphones picked up every word. Then Mahler held up a print, caught everyone's attention and said, 'Just look at us four years ago. How old we look. Our faces are less worried now. If from Bellagio I to II to III, you could have communicated with our faces, there would be no doubt: it would really be a happy ending.'

PART III

11
Promissory Notes and Banana Skins

'The wealth of nations has come to be predominantly the acquired abilities of people – their
education, experience, skills and health ... The
future productivity of the economy is not foreor-
dained by space, energy, and cropland. It will be
determined by the abilities of human beings. It has
been so in the past and there are no compelling
reasons why it will not be so in years to come.'

Theodore Schultz

One day during the Bellagio III conference in March
1988, Halfdan Mahler was heard to observe that there
were at least fifty different ways of slipping on banana
skins. 'Keep your eyes open for them.' As further
encouraging statistics continued to emerge and 1990
approached, this warning took on more force. Would
present promissory notes of Bellagio become future
banana skins?

When EPI was formally established in 1974, fewer than
7 per cent of the world's children were receiving
immunization against measles, or that crucial third dose
of polio or DPT. By 1984, the year of Bellagio I, this had
increased to around 20 per cent, by 1988 to 50, by 1990
to nearly 70. Universal immunization – the level of
coverage required to stop the transmission of the six EPI

diseases – once perceived as a Utopian dream now seemed
an achievable target. China, identified in 1988 as facing
special difficulties since one-sixth of the world's children
live there, claimed to have reached universal coverage
just twelve months later, when the Ministry of Health
announced that all thirty provinces had surpassed the
goal: immunization was a staggering 95 per cent for both
DPT and measles. This was not at all accurate. Where
children were registered coverage was indeed high, but in
many places the parents were not bringing them forward
for registration – and, it is said, feared to do so – possibly
because they had more children than China's government permitted.

But some countries – those in the Middle East,
Botswana, the Gambia, Rwanda, Tanzania in Africa –
really were converging on to the target and others –
Algeria, Kenya, Mexico, Morocco and Pakistan – would
arrive there within two years.

True, there were some areas where prospects were
nothing like so bright – Bangladesh, Sudan, Somalia, the
Yemen. Surprisingly, Brazil was also one. Polio vaccination, given on National Vaccination Days, was
supposed to provide the launching pad for an onslaught
on the five other diseases. But though this occurred in
most Latin American countries, in Brazil it had not – a
lamentable state of affairs that would ruin the global
target. So following vigorous representations from
UNICEF, on 22 September, the second National
Vaccination Day of 1990, all antigens were somehow to
be offered.

The logistics were formidable. There are 22 million
children under five in Brazil. The Oswaldo Cruz vaccine
laboratory could not possibly meet the sudden demand
for millions of doses, so these had to be imported from
Europe, requiring the equivalent of three jumbo jets to
fly them in. The Brazilian Air Force was asked to go to
Copenhagen and get them.

Another difficulty was tetanus immunization, which, worldwide, was still lagging way behind.

But on the whole the programmes were apparently surging onwards to fresh successes. But how reliable are the figures; are they alone an index of success? Might they prove to be just one of fifty possible banana skins? As happened time and again in the early days of the smallpox campaign, the desire to reach a target may prove overwhelming for stretched paramedics, whose promotion may depend on being seen to do the job – that is, producing the figures. Working in isolation, on low, irregular pay, without incentives or status or back-up facilities, temptations become both seductive and legion. One Indian doctor said: 'I wish targets were never mentioned. My people will always meet them; especially those who must carry vaccines ten miles alone, in overpowering heat. Even if they never arrive at a health centre they'll meet the targets.'

Other pressures too, may offer the same guarantee. In some countries, that WHO refuses to name, both the health worker and the parents are fined if the full course of immunization is not completed. So, of course, it mostly is. A second pressure – one which the agencies know they must guard against – comes from wanting to please the people who are giving money. On one occasion, a health worker in Haraghe, Ethiopia, was being congratulated on the remarkable immunization coverage his country recently reached, with a reported increase from 10 to nearly 60 per cent. He shrugged his shoulders: 'UNICEF gives us the dollars so we give them the figures.'

This is an extreme of cynicism, but so strong are such temptations that one must insist: given the announcement in 1989 that nearly two-thirds of all the world's children were receiving DPT and polio shots, how does WHO know?

When EPI began in 1974 there were no information systems at all, let alone reliable ones. So these had to be created, capable of providing a regular flow of data from all over the world and during the last fifteen years WHO's reporting system has evolved along with the vaccines, the cold chain and training. Now, Dr Ralph Henderson says 'It isn't bad.'

The system developed relies first of all on routine reporting of data. If that is not available sample surveys are accepted. The process involves clusters of children drawn from various communities across the country. A certain percentage of this population is monitored: households visited, mothers interviewed, vaccination records checked. From this local data an extrapolation is made to the country's entire childhood population and then globally. But of course people like to produce figures from communities selected just because they have wonderful coverage; there are very few totally random surveys. Indeed figures coming out of Africa – once considered notoriously speculative – are generally only to be trusted when taken from limited, specific surveys that may be done very well in some places but badly in others. So, overall, how much reliance can be placed on them?

Now, if the claims for global immunization turn out to be misleading, Dr Ralph Henderson, who has directed and managed WHO's EPI programme from the beginning, will shoulder most of the blame. A man who combines wide professional expertise and superb managerial skills with realistic caution, he has always been most reluctant to specify targets, whether of dates or numbers. But equally Henderson has willingly allowed public pronouncements of the percentage of children covered.

'We make a big issue of this,' he says, 'and probably these figures are true within 10 per cent accuracy. But the question is not so much are they accurate within a fine percentage but are they giving us a reliable index that allows us to make announcements? Are we trying to put something over on the public? We certainly don't believe we are.'

Yet why doesn't WHO use the drop in disease as their index? This would be even more complicated because, polio in Latin America apart, not all existing surveillance systems function properly. True: in some countries there are limited areas where hospitals report disease reliably, and here the immunization coverage can be shown to be having a genuine impact on disease. But reliable reporting systems and good immunization go hand in hand. So once again, as with smallpox, if assessors go to areas when disease has *not* been reported and seriously start looking, they will find disease no one knew was there.

Yet Henderson *is* confident about the overall global coverage, and because he knows all about banana skins, his attitude inspires confidence in his confidence. He insists: 'I want to be careful about saying "Yes, we have done this and now we can document these dramatic decreases in disease." Polio apart, I feel very uncomfortable about citing disease incidence figures, because most of the disease is not being reported at all and is anyway occurring in countries with lousy reporting systems.'

The second promissory note issued at all of the Bellagio Conferences was that these interventions would make an impact on infant mortality. A dramatic one could not have been expected since the mortality caused by the six EPI diseases is not as significant as that caused by diseases like malaria or respiratory infections. However, some specific studies have recently been undertaken in Africa to assess the value of *all* preventive interventions, whether delivered by primary health care or campaigns.

For a start it has been extremely difficult to get preventive measures adopted at all. Attempts to switch African health policies from expensive, urban, hospital-based systems to cheap, community-based preventive ones have often been frustrated by finance, the debt crisis, low morale amongst health workers and lack of both political will and supplies. Nigeria used its oil riches on several Western-style hospitals at a cost of 40 million dollars each, to serve the needs of the few, instead of simple, cheap health care serving those of the many. There is a huge gap between the rhetoric and the reality, and everyone who has ever worked in Africa has their own favourite horror stories of inflexible bureaucrats, reactionary physicians and poverty-stricken health departments strangling the very best efforts in prevention. Yet even where these have been successfully applied the impact has not been all that remarkable, and this drives us back to the beginning of this story and what happened in England, in the city of Birmingham, during the eighty years of this century (see page 9). The moral: poverty is still the most lethal of diseases.

On the one hand, since Alma Ata nearly forty countries have made primary health care a major component of their health policies and this genuinely shows. Although the exact figures are hard to establish, probably up to twenty million people in rural areas now do have fresh water supplies; eighty countries have an essential drug programme whereby health centres can – in theory – obtain pilfer-proof and cheap kits of standard therapies; the global demand for vaccine has increased fourfold.

On the other hand, if we look specifically at two African countries representing opposite ends of the spectrum – Kenya, large and reasonably well off, the Gambia, small and very poor – we see a revealing picture. Since the late 1970s Kenya has more than doubled its health centres: these are now nearly 2000. Even in 1984 a quarter of the infant population was regularly visiting welfare clinics; by now immunization coverage is in many places near 70 per cent. Across the country numerous non-governmental organizations (NGOs) promote clean water and sanitation, oral rehydration, breast feeding, family planning and good weaning practices. And providing the actions of the bureaucracy can be accelerated or circumvented, kits of essential drugs are available with many village shops marketing simple health remedies.

There have been comparable improvements in the Gambia: pump wells have been constructed in 800 of the 2000 villages; all settlements with more than 400 people have access to trained health workers; 70 per cent of the children have been immunized, at a cost of no more than $1.50 per person, mostly paid for by overseas health agencies.

Yet in neither country has the impact on child mortality been dramatic, as a major ten-year study by the British Medical Research Council in the Gambia reveals. Fourteen villages with comprehensive primary health care schemes are being compared with others which have access only to vaccination. Every month for four years field workers performed a whole range of physiological tests on the children. The first results showed that while there were indeed fewer deaths amongst small babies there was no overall change in the infant mortality. The Gambia still has some of the worst figures in Africa, with 150 deaths for every 1000 live births as malaria, pneumonia, diarrhoea and childbirth continue to take out the children. The Gambia is still a very poor country.

Sir Ian MacGregor's village of Keneba is the one exception – a focal point of success where the infant mortality has been reduced to 24 per 1000. This is hardly surprising, since Keneba has six qualified doctors and four midwives, all from the University of Newcastle, in attendance. Indeed some people argue that, if they will go, and it is a big 'if', it is more cost-effective to send fully trained health care workers into rural areas on a temporary basis than to train local village workers for permanent duty.

By contrast, Kenya, which in 1970 embraced the concept of primary health care, certainly has achieved a reduction in infant mortality. But this is in part undoubtedly a direct result of improved economic status: between 1960 and 1980, Kenya's GNP grew on average 5.8 per cent a year. Yet though the money spent on health doubled too, once again most went for urban hospitals. So while Kenya's infant mortality rates may be far lower than those of the Gambia, they are still five times as high as in Europe. Then in the 1980s, Kenya's GNP began dropping by nearly 3 per cent a year. The population is increasing while the people are becoming poorer. This situation is occurring all over Africa with important implications for the outcome of this story.

What does one conclude? That primary health care, which clearly has not fully worked yet, will never work? Or that its costs – both financial and political – are still too great for most poor countries to bear? That regular, targeted health campaigns are not only necessary but more effective? What is clear is that WHO's initial calculations about the costs were as underestimated as their confidence in the willingness of governments to provide them was over-estimated – and no one could have predicted the dire extent of the debt crisis.

More importantly, however, did the campaign initiatives of UNICEF help the process of building WHO's systems of primary health care? And, in applying their philosophy of providing immunization only when part of a primary health infrastructure, did WHO improve health care in developing countries?

The questions may be simple but the answers are not. In certain countries, Egypt for example, EPI did indeed enhance primary health care for children who, in theory, already had access to health services. Egypt had long before invested heavily in the health-care infrastructure, but it was not until the child survival programmes began that preventive measures were actually delivered.

Equally, in countries like Sudan, EPI has made a second contribution – taking services to people who never had them in the first place. By using mobile clinics and driving into remote regions, EPI has helped build the infrastructure and gradually more services are being added.

EPI has also been a major factor contributing to other improvements. Once the vaccines and cold chain were in place the services of EPI could be – and often were – extended to cover measures like the provision of essential drugs and nutritional surveillance of children. Pakistan, a large country with a population pushing 80 million, had a rural health care which was appalling. An energetic EPI programme raised immunization coverage to 70 per cent, and now extends even into remote tribal border territories where delivering health is a hazardous business, first because parents need constant education and reassurance. Remembering smallpox and cholera, they associate injections with epidemics and are puzzled by the regular appearance of EPI staff doing things to healthy children. Secondly, the workers are also regularly shot at. Still everywhere in Pakistan all primary health services are improving by leaps and bounds, not only in quantity but in quality. The cold chain is well maintained; the records assiduously kept; other interventions besides immunization – remedies for diarrhoeal diseases, information about family planning – are being delivered.

Now to the outsider primary health care programmes of the WHO style in Pakistan may seem very similar to a UNICEF immunization campaign. But though these did start in a rush of extraordinary activities, as doctors who normally did not visit remote areas suddenly began to do so, what really is happening is that a regular sustainable health service is finally being established.

These are the bright spots, however: and it would be dishonest not to admit that, globally, not only has the establishment of primary health care services been slow

and somewhat disappointing but, used alone as a
strategic method, it will never eradicate disease except in
limited localities. And in the last few years we have seen a
total collapse of state health services in most of
sub-Saharan Africa. There *is* no primary health care; 40
per cent of what care exists is provided by non-
government agencies.

But we must *not* conclude that since present efforts
have not made dramatic impacts, future ones are
doomed. Of all the morals to be drawn from the present
story one stands out, one Halfdan Mahler constantly
emphasized: the concept works only if it is part of a total
development package which includes self-reliant action
on the part of governments and their local communities.
Far from abandoning primary health care, efforts should
be intensified, but with the focus first on areas where
prospects for progress are genuine.

Where the concept exists but has not worked well,
problems with demand are often the main cause. Most
preventive measures – whether nutrition, hygiene or
immunization – depend on the mothers' active participation, and women were confidently expected to be the
main agents for building and continuing this health care
system. What was greatly underestimated was the extent
of their available time: they are grossly over-burdened.
Even if health facilities are supplied many are often
under-utilized as the demands made on the mothers'
time simply cannot be met.

Equally, wherever primary health care has worked
well, as it has in Kerala State in India, or Sri Lanka, and
where infant mortality and birth rates have both gone
down, it has always been preceded by an increase in
women's literacy, education and status.

Thus at Bellagio III, no one disagreed with Dr
Ruganda of Uganda, when he forcefully stated: 'Women
are the most exploited people on the African continent –
the ones who really suffer. Disadvantaged from the

beginning – by biology, tradition and political domination – they are entitled to emancipation, to education, and we must allow them fundamental rights.'

So, in an effort to consolidate their present successes, all the agencies involved in this story are now targeting their next efforts on women, aiming to reduce the risks of pregnancy, to provide better health and better education, all of which are as potent factors in child survival as immunization. In the past, women were largely ignored by all sectors of aid and development; whatever status they were accorded derived solely from their capacity to bear children. There are at last small signs that this may be beginning to change, but certainly not fast and not everywhere.

The next promissory note, or potential banana skin, was population. Many were convinced that only when parents know their children will survive are they able to contemplate reducing their numbers. Paradoxical as it may sound, saving children's lives would not provoke a permanent population surge, but be a potent factor in limiting fertility.

There are two aspects to this problem: will the present initiatives themselves have a major impact on demography; what really is the influence of increasing child survival on reducing fertility? Fifty years ago the crucial factors controlling human numbers were deaths, famine and war. But, although still shocking, child mortality presently does not provide adequate control, nor does famine or war and there is plenty of both. So far as population growth is concerned, that particular cat was already out of the bag long before the immunization programmes appeared. Moreover, since the six childhood diseases cause only a minor fraction of childhood deaths, these interventions will have little direct effect in reshaping demographics.

But to what extent does the knowledge that children will survive act as a direct spur to having fewer?

Sometimes, it would appear, not at all. On the one hand
the island of Lamu, on the east coast of Kenya,
congratulates itself, rightly, on having the highest
coverage for fully immunized children of any district in
the whole of Kenya. But they are also world champions in
population growth: at 6.5 per cent a year it is the highest
anywhere in the world, and occurs in a country that also
has one of the highest rates. By the turn of the century
the twenty million people of Kenya will have become
forty million; by the year 2100, 116.4 million people.

Conversely, and against received wisdom, Bangladesh
still has one of the highest infant mortality rates in the
world, yet the population growth rate has been falling
rapidly thanks to vigorous local efforts.

So though in the past a declining birth rate has *always*
been preceded by fewer childhood deaths, the present
evidence is inconclusive. Reducing infant mortality is
vital but by itself would now appear to be neither a
necessary nor sufficient condition for reducing family
size.

So it was not surprising that, from the very beginning
of this saga, the warning was given: unless an equal
commitment was made to both family planning and
health interventions, many countries would run hard but
still stand in the same place. This has indeed happened.
Along with malaria and AIDS, Africa's increasing
population seriously threatens progress. Over the last
twenty-five years the population growth rate of
sub-Saharan Africa has risen over 30 per cent; by 2000
the numbers in that region are estimated to be 700
million, reflecting an increase far greater than the
economies of those countries ever can be.

All over Africa and in the Gulf States of the Middle
East, too, the pressures – for health services, schools, jobs
– are intensifying. The demographic momentum is
gathering pace. In absolute terms the numbers will not
only go on rising but the greatest increase lies ahead with

the present 200 million young adolescents living in the poorer parts of the world, set to become 600 million. Not even the most optimistic economist believes that the countries' GNPs can keep pace with their needs. Accordingly some people are still indignant that birth spacing and fertility control were never made an integral part of the programmes from the start. Bill Foege said they should have been at Bellagio I; Fred Sai repeated it at every conference. But it was not until March 1988 that one sensed the beginnings of an equal commitment on the part of the agencies. Commenting on this perceived change, Sai said: 'I was about to get *really* angry, but perhaps I'm not now.'

Outsiders offered several reasons why agencies had either played down, even ignored, this problem. One reason offered to explain UNICEF's attitudes, neither substantiated nor denied, was that both financial contributions and moral support for the child survival programmes came from the Vatican and the Gulf States; another, that the agency still carried the scars of the bitter and divisive political controversy that nearly destroyed it in 1961, when their Swedish delegate first proposed birth control as an integral part of their programmes; a third, that when USAID was about to ask Congress for a major subvention for the child survival programmes – some of which would be channelled through UNICEF – skilled lobbyists stated that it would 'not be useful' to link these programmes to the question of human numbers.

Similar considerations, it is claimed, strongly influence the attitude of Save the Children Fund in Great Britain, which treads most delicately around this issue. Some within the Fund have been quite frank about the reason: the fragility of their funding base. The profiles of their donors are of people not associated with concerns for human numbers and family planning. However, they do, they insist, believe in and offer this, but quietly – at the country level. At Bellagio III, however, Sai insisted that

UNICEF ought 'to be an advocate through all its field staff, of the importance of family planning . . . and that other agencies working in development, particularly in rural areas, need to appreciate the facts and contribute to the understanding.'

Ralph Henderson has claimed that population issues always were a concern of EPI. He has always identified the population problem as one of the most critical we face. So why didn't WHO offer family planning at the same time as immunization? Because, he replies, what the infrastructure requires is infinitely more complicated than for immunization, and the logistics make those of the cold chain seem like child's play. Three to four contacts are enough for disease protection, but family planning entails a major behavioural change for the whole family. If parents are to make an informed decision, support, education, advice and contacts, as well as massive supplies, are all necessary, and this takes time to deliver.

So because the problem is vast, the politics sensitive, the required infrastructure complex and the finance daunting – though small in terms of current military expenditure – an attack on the population problem is often deferred. Soon it may be too late. For over and beyond the social and economic pressures outlined earlier – not to mention the environmental ones – there is another reason for concern: given the well-established connection between public health and the evolutionary habits of viruses as they exploit overcrowded situations, many people wonder what is going to happen – medically speaking – in the future. The greatest concentration of humans will be found in the slums of megacities in the developing world and in history it was in such overcrowded pockets that new diseases first appeared and epidemics followed.

Set against the complexity of this issue, that of Bellagio's third promissory note, polio eradication, seems comparatively simple. In May 1988 the World Health Organization set the year 2000 as the date by which this should be achieved. But can this be done? Ciro de Quadros insists: 'it is now not a question of can we do it but *will* we do it?'

The global situation is as follows: in Western societies, where polio control is total, transmission of the wild virus has virtually stopped. Control is nearing completion in Korea, in Hong Kong, Singapore and China. Victory is in sight in the Americas, with end game strategies – mopping up, rewards – in action. By June 1990, there were only three cases of polio associated with the wild virus on the continent, one each in Mexico, Ecuador and Peru. All had been confirmed in the spring and by October no further cases had been reported. In December 1990 PAHO expected to announce that transmission had stopped; the wild virus was now impossible to find. Two further years will go by before eradication on the continent is announced, and then only after stringent criteria are fulfilled. But when the announcement does come PAHO will celebrate a second major and thoroughly deserved triumph: they were also the first continent to eradicate smallpox.

The question is, however, how quickly and by what means, can the remaining polio-stricken areas of the world reach the same point? Africa and India present serious problems. Presently India is reporting 60 per cent of all global cases, though this statistic is certainly misleading because Bangladesh is under-reporting and Africa not reporting at all.

India's problems with immunization are not confined to polio. At a time (March 1988) when 90 per cent of the children in Botswana – admittedly a very small country – had been immunized against measles, only 16 per cent had so been immunized in the vastness of India. A survey in the North Arcot district – home for 10 million people – showed many falsifications of the records with the achieved figures being less than one-third of the 96 per cent claimed.

The problems were attributable in part to passivity of the mothers and to the setting of targets. But reports in the press spoke of other problems ranging from the misuse of vaccines by untrained health workers, to consumer resistance against immunization, to consistent failures of the cold chain, with the record of live polio virus vaccine being particularly dismal. India is now set to tackle all these.

However, the numbers to be covered are daunting: the population is 800 million; there are probably nearly 700,000 villages but no more than 120,000 health sub-centres; the proportion of GNP spent on all aspects of health is around 1.8 per cent; and each year 25 million newborn babies must be immunized. Turkey, by contrast, has to cover a mere 1.5 million additionally. Forty per cent of Indian families are living at subsistence level; many children die of malnutrition; there is an urgent need for clean water and good sanitation; many communities have low literacy; because of India's size and great variety the possibilities of extensive social mobilization, as seen in other countries, do not appear to be good, though, as D.A. Henderson reminded us, in the last stage of smallpox eradication in India, every single house in the country was visited. But the Indian government does not believe in campaigns: they set their child survival initiatives squarely within the framework of primary health care and take pride in implementing these themselves. Indians do not want outsiders to tell them what to do. Policies must be developed with their officials; the aid agencies act only as advisors.

Their figures for polio are some of the worst in the world: 500 children contract the disease every day; one in 100 die; 20 per cent of the 500 will have received three doses of oral polio vaccine. Whereas in developing countries three doses are enough to confer immunity, in

India, as in many poor tropical countries, at least six are needed. And in order to achieve total control 98 per cent of the children should be covered . . . and where would the money – for vaccine, equipment, cold chain, training – be coming from?

Yet in some areas of India polio control exists. The North Arcot district is one. Here in 1984, Dr Jacob John, Professor and Head of Virology, and his colleagues, began an excellent surveillance system. Every month data coming in from 500 centres is printed out and appropriate action taken, not only about polio but other diseases too. So even though there was a polio epidemic in 1987, its incidence has quickly and dramatically decreased.

Jacob John, a caring Christian and an internationally regarded virologist, understands viruses really well. Yet he once said to me: 'Remember in the West the truth is what is verifiable; in the East what you want to believe.' His relationship with the Indian government is ambivalent, for many regard him as a Jeremiah, a prophet of doom, who says that everything they are doing is wrong. But this isn't true. Yet he insists that official policy, based on WHO's belief that polio can be controlled with three properly administered doses of oral vaccine, simply does not reflect the realities of public health and the epidemiology of the disease in India. If PAHO's campaign approach were used six doses would achieve success. But India cannot afford such overkill so John is investigating the potential of using the injectible vaccine as well, and, everyone finally agrees, it doesn't really matter which vaccine is used provided the disease disappears.

But will India eradicate polio? The answer to this question may be sought in part in a discussion held in the autumn of 1989, between Dr Mehrotra, the Director of Immunization in India's Ministry of Health, and Ciro de Quadros. They talked at length about ways in which

India could improve coverage. De Quadros's first suggestion – give oral polio vaccine at birth – has now been adopted in the twelve largest cities in India and to every baby born in a government hospital or health centre elsewhere. But so far this is not written into the official schedule and at the time of writing – May 1990 – none of the staff at the primary health care centres in Madras knew about the directive.

De Quadros's second suggestion – to flood an area with polio vaccine when a case is detected – will also be implemented, says Dr Mehrotra. But the third – the strategy of national immunization days – was politically and ideologically more sensitive.

There was an implicit tension here, of course, arising from the fact that polio control in Latin America is way ahead of that on the Indian and African continents. But unless control is rapidly expanded PAHO will have to sustain its programmes for a decade or more, for otherwise cases imported to the Americas will trigger epidemics. Though PAHO is a comparatively rich organization, and could maintain their operations for some time, they would prefer not to have to do so, since their bi-annual vaccination days consume resources that they are now ready to focus on diseases such as measles. 'We are now with measles as we were with polio in 1982,' says de Quadros. 'This is a moment of methodological switch.' Yet if PAHO's proven strategy was adopted in India and Africa, polio might be controlled within two or three years.

Talking to de Quadros – a visionary who looks way beyond target dates and percentage coverages to the eradication of polio and other diseases – his sense of urgency is obvious. But eradication of polio in the rest of the world is ultimately the responsibility of WHO acting in partnership with its member governments. After the World Health Assembly announced its global plan in May 1988, Rotary International immediately gave $5 million for the establishment of a polio eradication team that Dr Nick Ward now directs.

When flatly asked how polio will be eradicated in India and Africa, the answers of Drs Nick Ward and Ralph Henderson – now Deputy Director General of WHO – show that though they are extremely sympathetic and sensitive to the dilemma, and concede that PAHO's policies are working brilliantly, they see difficulty in rigidly applying in other countries the methods used in the Americas.

'Ciro has been extremely effective in being just that tough with his programmes,' says Henderson. 'He's come with good financing; he is able to say you are either with me or against me. He knows that a successful programme is not one that works from ideology of strategies but [as befits an ex-smallpox campaigner] one that keeps asking questions and then modifying and adapting. He has also used an extremely effective technique he calls "mop-up". Where he thinks there is a real danger of polio escaping he goes in house-to-house. He is one of the best managers and epidemiologists we have had. His frustration is that he is standing in front of a door that he sees is open and he is very impatient with the rest of the world for not walking straight through it with him.

'But one of the great challenges in international health is getting a consensus. What we are trying to do is to take the experience and knowledge of PAHO and share that around with our other constituents who at this point are far from seeing where they are going.'

Once more the issue comes back to WHO's original stance towards the EPI programmes. Even given that, wherever possible, they are anxious to merge those aspects of de Quadros's successful policy into their global programme one attitude remains constant: matters must be conducted so that EPI is strengthened and primary health care fostered. Though de Quadros believes that PAHO's methods do just that, nevertheless WHO's policy remains: develop health services on a broad basis, rather than massively delivering one intervention. In Africa, too, this philosophy is widely accepted so Nick Ward is adamant: 'If we went out at this moment knowing what we know, and said to Nigeria for example: we want to do mass vaccination campaigns in polio, their response would be an emphatic no.'

So how does WHO intend to eradicate polio?

'People are not stupid!' says Ward. 'If the countries can achieve 80 per cent coverage of children under one with three doses of OPV – and already they have reached nearly 70 per cent – transmission of polio will drop. Remember, polio is a viral community disease and given the nature of the virus within communities when we have reached 80 per cent coverage then we will have to do a smallpox type of campaign on polio.

This will mean developing good surveillance systems to find outbreaks where transmission of the virus is occurring. Then we must rapidly smother these by vaccinating at a level of 100 per cent children. Anything less would be both unacceptable and ineffective. You do this child by child, house by house, making sure everyone is immunized. A month later this is repeated, and again a month after that. Because there will be vaccine failures and outside visitors and more cases. So you do it again and again until there are none. But you don't call this a campaign. The politically acceptable phrase is "effective containment where transmission is persisting".'

But semantics means nothing to children and some will still develop polio, either from cold chain failure, or through reversion of the vaccine to the wild type, or because on this slow evolving basis, vaccination will not reach them. Ward admits the personal tragedies, but insists we remember the other side of the coin. 'It is already possible to see clearly where in the world the coverage is good and where, by contrast, disease is occurring in any given geographical location and what is the political and managerial potential to do something.'

Yet eradication is a dynamic process and, Ward says, 'by the time polio *is* eradicated we still won't know everything about the disease. We want the practical results of eradication soon and must go for these before we get the knowledge. We can't afford to wait to get the absolutely correct method; we have got to go in and if necessary make mistakes.'

In September 1990, WHO hosted a 'family' meeting, chaired by Dr D.A. 'Smallpox' Henderson, of all those involved to try to resolve several questions of strategy. Several questions were on the agenda: first, given that there is strong resistance at WHO to focusing on one disease alone, at the expense of both the others and primary health care, could PAHO's methods, which, after three years of intense debate, all now acknowledge are the best way to *eradicate* polio, be applied in a way that does not compromise EPI?

Secondly, was not vaccination of all susceptibles *at the same time* a better way to stop transmission than vaccination regularly throughout the year; and, if so, does it not follow that unless this particular strategy is adopted globally polio will not disappear?

For if we compare the situations in Egypt and Brazil, for example, a revealing contrast appears. In both countries nearly 95 per cent of the vulnerable population receives at least three doses of oral polio. In Egypt where these are spread generally over twelve months, polio incidence is not down. But in Brazil, where simultane-ously the children receive vaccine in the concentrated bursts of vaccination days, it is. For then the virus has no place to go and mop-up operations can begin in missed pockets; if polio breaks out the area can be flooded with vaccine.

Ward hoped for a clear statement that firmly endorsed the worth of this strategy. He also hoped for another statement: if this method is followed not only will polio transmission be stopped but EPI will likely be strengthened. However, he was worried that people, stuck in a short-sighted, ideological rut, would rigidly insist that the phrase 'strengthening EPI' only meant increasing coverage of the six antigens and not attacking polio head on.

Actually Ward need not have worried. The atmosphere was exciting for delegates knew that success was within their grasp: de Quadros was the focus of many congratulations; D.A. 'Smallpox' Henderson was buoyant; he remarked on PAHO's incredible achievement; eradication has proceeded faster, better and more effectively than any had thought possible. PAHO's method provided the model and the main architect of success was Ciro; this was another victory for public health and prevention; the strategy for eradication had finally crystallized, though there might be some local variations.

Then as the delegates settled in for detailed discussion they learnt that, primary health care notwithstanding, India had called for a '242 campaign' to eradicate polio. In each year 2 October (Gandhi's birthday), 4 November and 2 December would be intensive polio vaccination days in all urban areas throughout the country. The rural areas pose nothing like the same problem. A new degree of consensus now existed between Jacob John and Ciro de Quadros who in the past had by no means seen eye to eye. The example of Latin America, said John in a burst of generosity, was showing 'that polio virus can be eradicated from large land mass. If it can be done in such a large community there, it can be done globally. This is the greatest story for the rest of the world.'

So the next millennium is likely to receive its fitting gift and officials at WHO made the following prediction: the time frame – completion by the year 2000 – was realistic. Latin America is probably clear; by 1995, polio will have been eradicated in South-east Asia and the western Pacific; by the year 2000 the transmission of the wild polio virus will have been stopped on the African continent, too.

All this supposes that sufficient money comes in to do the job – and in Geneva the lack of donations for eradication was causing concern – and that political will and effort are maintained, and that no jokers in the pack – war or famine – strike. Once completed it could take two or so more years, said Ward, to convince everyone that polio really had gone. Perhaps 2002 was the date. But he hoped for 1996, because that was when he was retiring and he didn't want to leave with any polio around.

While one further promissory note – the potential for new and better vaccines – never carried the same emotive overtones as did population and polio, still the path to its fulfilment may be just as slippery. Given the explosive pace of research and development, the delegates at Bellagio III were told that by the end of the century a whole slew of new vaccines should be available for protection against some old diseases, while existing ones would be vastly improved. Happily, one of the first vaccines to benefit might well be polio, improvements to which could take several forms.

Once the varying epidemiological problems of each geographical location are properly understood, specific vaccines, with different type ratios, could be developed. Others that cannot induce polio may be genetically engineered. Scientists at the Scripps Institute, La Jolla, California, have both deciphered the three-dimensional structure of the virus and identified those particular molecules on Type III that alone revert to the virulent form, and lead to vaccine-induced paralysis. The change is unbelievably minuscule: a mere chemical base is the only difference between harmless and lethal, between a protective vaccine and one that might provoke dangerous disease. Once this molecule is deleted, however, no further cases of vaccine-associated polio should occur.

The cold chain might go. The single greatest blessing for the smallpox campaigners was that their vaccine could be transported freeze-dried. Hopes are now being pinned on a freeze-dried polio vaccine, recently developed by Quadrant, in Cambridge, England, and at the University of Alabama, John Eldridge is working on a one-dose, heat stable polio shot, which releases the equivalent of three doses over a long period.

Such technical advances are only two examples amongst many others that explain scientific optimism. Compared with just ten vaccines developed in the one hundred and fifty years since Jenner, a further twenty to fifty may come on stream in the next decade, giving protection against a range of troubles from malaria, tooth decay to even conception. There is much excitement over a technology which, Dr Lewis Thomas emphasizes, is one of the genuinely decisive ones of modern medicine. So two complementary revolutions are in train this decade: the children's revolution described in this book; and the biotechnology revolution which allows scientists to create vaccines to order.

Theoretical potential is one thing, practical protection another, and once again many pitfalls lie along the path. There are two further aspects to present vaccine research: firstly, modifications of the EPI vaccines; secondly, the creation of new ones against those infections – malaria, respiratory and diarrhoeal diseases – that kill in huge numbers. In both cases it is far easier to specify what is needed than to be certain of what can be delivered.

So far as six diseases are concerned several developments are devoutly to be wished: vaccines of higher potency so that the three-dose schedule of DPT can be reduced to at least two and preferably one; vaccines so heat-stable that the cold chain can go; and a better understanding of an infant's immunological response so we might administer all vaccines at an earlier age. Once measles shots were not given before fifteen months; this is now down to nine; in the Turkish campaign they were given between six and nine months. Measles is rampant in the developing world and spreads rapidly, and since the greatest drop-out rate for children occurs between the second set of shots and a crucial measles shot at nine months, many babies contract measles before they receive protection. It would be a great advantage if we could administer this vaccine much earlier. Finally as neither mothers nor babies really like hypodermics it would be equally nice if all doses could be packed into one single administration. Some people believe that the goals of EPI can never be met until this happens.

The Institut Mérieux has recently developed a method of delivering protection against seven diseases – diphtheria, tetanus, pertussis, polio, measles, mumps, rubella – in a single 0.5 ml dose. Three of the vaccines come as liquid in a phial; the remainder, freeze-dried, are simply added and the mixture drawn up into the needle. This new development is part of a massive programme undertaken by the Institut Mérieux into applied vaccine research, that celebrates the coming of age of vaccinology and the 100th anniversary of the death of Louis Pasteur, with whom Marcel Mérieux, the founder of the Institut, worked.

But there is another way to simplify the process which, if successful, would provide a wonderful twist to a story that began with Jenner, came up through Rahima Banu, and ends with her children being fully protected. For that old immunological war-horse, the vaccinia virus, derived from cowpox and cows (Latin name, *vacca*, hence the word vaccine), may once again be the mechanism for delivering protection. This possibility depends on a technique which did not exist fifteen years ago – splicing genes between organisms. Into the DNA of vaccinia, scientists have now spliced the genes for the antigens of twenty different infectious agents, including those that cause hepatitis B, herpes simplex, one particular form of influenza, malaria and typhoid fever. Though in all cases immune response has been elicited in laboratory animals, what will happen in humans is still unknown.

Massive efforts, mostly inadequately funded, are also being directed towards finding vaccines against the other childhood diseases. Rotaviruses that cause gastrointestinal problems in children kill thousands of infants every year and, as do the respiratory diseases, come in almost as many forms as Heinz soups. Many candidate virus vaccines must be developed against both. The extent of the activity can be judged from the fact that in America the US Army is currently developing forty-two different vaccines, the National Institutes of Health twenty-eight additional ones, the Rockefeller Foundation supporting groups investigating a further six, and the Tropical Diseases Research Programme of WHO supporting not only malaria and leprosy vaccines, but those against tuberculosis, dengue fever, Japanese encephalitis, hepatitis A, meningococcal meningitis, and a number of pulmonary viruses.

So many are being considered that the Institute of Medicine in America was commissioned to establish priorities. Out of a total of twenty-one needed globally, they listed pneumococcal pneumonia, rotavirus, typhoid, bacillary dysentery and malaria as having the highest priority for the developing world.

And this is where our story began. From a gleam in the eye of a scientist, to culture in a laboratory dish, to delivery into the arm of a child there will be the usual wide gaps to bridge. At present the United Nations agencies have no sure way of guaranteeing the necessary investment – whether public or private – to create new vaccines for developing countries. Of the twenty-one vaccines specified as having priority only half are expected to find significant world markets and the production capacity of most commercial vaccine manufacturers is not geared to such commercially unprofitable ventures.

As we saw, all new vaccines cost massive amounts of money for their research and marketing; once they exist the agencies will need more money to pay for them and somehow this will have to be found. Perhaps the United Nations will have to raise funds to purchase vaccines at prices which include development costs, and thus encourage the industry to invest in their research. Agencies that are immunizing all the world's children should by now be able to predict future vaccine use, and, by making long-term commitments for future orders, could easily come up with a reasonable cost which, too, would encourage manufacturers to proceed. But in turn manufacturers will have to be willing to provide the vaccines at, or near, the cost of development and production. It is good to record that initial discussions have been extremely encouraging: many corporations were most willing to discuss vaccine sales of a predetermined volume and at prices approximately equal to marginal production costs.

Alternatively, a public international institution might be created to develop and produce vaccines. Indeed, some people dream of a world institute for applied vaccine research. But, as two delegates to Bellagio III reminded their colleagues, and as this story illustrates: 'The politics of international co-operation are brutal.' Neither do the two existing United Nations biotechnology research centres provide too happy a precedent. Their start-up phase lasted all of five years, during which not one single scientific contribution emerged.

One serious dilemma posed by new vaccines comes from the fact that they are needed fast. Because of this urgency a UN-supported vaccine programme would have no alternative but to spend the money, at least in the short term, on assisting vaccine development in the rich, industrial nations, for only they have commercial institutions capable of scaling up production. Another route would be to take the technology to developing countries but this, too, will take time.

Now, of the twenty-one vaccines given highest priority by the Institute of Medicine, only those against intestinal disease and malaria are expected to generate significant sales in industrial countries. To these AIDS has now been added even though while millions of people die from malaria each year, only thirty thousand die from AIDS. But research into protective vaccines against both is proceeding fast for both are brutal killers on a global scale, and both influence the success of the child survival programmes.

12

The Joker in the Pack

'You can't say civilization don't advance, however,
for in every war they kill you a new way.'

Will Rogers: Autobiography

Shortly after the last naturally occurring case of smallpox
had been identified in March 1976 and the virus finally
banished from history, a distinguished American
specialist in infectious diseases remarked: 'The age of the
great infections is over.'

That very same year, in a remote hospital in Zaire, a
Danish physician contracted a fatal illness whose clinical
symptoms were soon to become frighteningly familiar. In
that same year, too, the disease that provoked these
symptoms was just beginning to infiltrate the gay
communities of New York and Los Angeles. The origins
of the subsequent epidemic were eventually traced to one
man, Gaetan Dugas, a French Canadian airline steward,
since identified as Subject Zero. Travelling widely as he
did, he appears to have contracted the disease in Haiti; he
infected his friends in various places, who infected their
friends. Five years later, an epidemiological pattern
finally emerged when, in 1981, the Center for Disease
Control in Atlanta noticed that clusters of patients were
appearing amongst male homosexuals, showing some
strange symptoms – rare skin cancers, rare pneumonias,
diseases called 'opportunistic' because their agents can

only exploit the body when its immunological defences are compromised. Soon a new disease was recognized Acquired Immuno-deficiency Syndrome (AIDS). Then in January 1984, a team of trained medical researcher travelled to Africa and found the disease already there. In one week, in one single African hospital alone, the described 35 new cases, so concluded that AIDS was firmly established.

Gradually more facts began to emerge. It took only two years from the recognition of AIDS before its major modes of transmission were understood. As the disease continued its rapid spread amongst gay men this pointed to the fact that it was sexually transmitted; when it appeared in haemophiliacs, and in patients who had received blood transfusions, this suggested that infected blood was the main route, a fact confirmed when the disease also erupted with a high incidence in the drug community. Then it was observed that healthy women became infected, so possibly the agent could be transmitted through the semen; its existence in newborn infants showed that infected mothers could infect babies in the womb. Soon it became clear that the infectious agent could remain in a carrier state, with symptoms being delayed for many years. Antibody was produced in patients' blood – a clear indication of the presence of the infection, but not, alas, necessarily of protection.

As often happens in history the pattern of disease transmission was known long before the causal agent was identified. However, in this case the scientific community reacted with remarkable vigour and speed. Within two years of the first recognized cases of AIDS in Los Angeles and New York, a Frenchman, Luc Montagnier of the Pasteur Institute, first identified HIV (Human Immuno-deficiency Virus), followed by an American, Robert C. Gallo of the National Cancer Institute. At first only one species was thought to exist then in October 1985 another. HIV-2 was discovered in

West Africa, where it is mainly confined.

As the Nobel Laureate David Baltimore has pointed out, HIV is a virus with some unusual properties: it is not stable, and can be easily inactivated; it passes from one individual to another only with great difficulty. Whereas many viruses move easily and frequently between people, the transmission of HIV requires deliberately conscious acts that involve the most intimate contact – particularly sexual contact – between two individuals. The sole exception is accidental transmission of infected blood.

But the virus also possesses some very damaging characteristics. HIV is a retro-virus, a group of which has been associated with animal cancers. As a result they have been extensively studied. They and another group, lenti viruses, are closely incorporated into the DNA of most organisms and have probably been so for aeons of evolutionary time. They cause symptoms that take a long time to develop but develop inexorably they do, in spite of every defence the body can mount. The disease takes time to show because the viruses hide from the immune system inside cells or nerves. Perhaps the most insidious thing about HIV is that it has a surface coat which seems totally resistant to the antibodies that usually inactivate viruses. At first there is a battle between the virus and the immune cells that goes on, perhaps for years; a battle which neither wins. But slowly, the virus begins to dominate and an acute phase of AIDS follows, during which the virus finally wipes out the immune system.

To people infected with HIV, death comes with dreadful certainty. About 50 per cent of HIV-infected people will develop full-blown AIDS within 10 years, and possibly close to 100 per cent within 15–20 years. There are three reasons why HIV is more lethal than most other viruses: firstly, because it is designed to avoid the neutralizing effect of antibody; secondly, because the virus can remain dormant in a 'cellular hibernation' when it neither kills cells nor reproduces; thirdly, because it kills the cells of the immune system. But once activated its genetic mechanisms rapidly permit the virus to grow, to produce many progeny and to kill immune cells, specifically certain groups of the T-cells and the macrophages. Not only are these cells eliminated, but also certain of their precursors in the thymus gland and the bone marrow.

Scientists have discovered six possible and simultaneous mechanisms with which HIV depletes the reservoir of immune cells, but no one knows which is the central one. Only a small number of cells need to be infected before the entire immune system collapses; then those opportunistic infections – whether pneumonias, or skin cancers, or even deep brain disorders – can take full advantage and kill the patient.

Whatever the mechanisms at work AIDS has spread rapidly and now verges on the pandemic. In 1981, the year it was first diagnosed, 180 cases were reported by CDC; six months later 403 cases in 24 of America's 50 states, and 200 AIDS cases in Europe, 42 of them in people of African origin who had travelled abroad for treatment. In 1982, WHO reported 1668 cases in 17 countries; in 1983 over 5000 cases in 19 countries. By then several African countries were heavily affected, though only one had reported the disease. During 1984 the global total doubled; in 1985 it doubled again, and for a third time in 1986. By June 1988 there were 100,000 cases in 138 countries. However, one must be cautious in judging the progression of the epidemic from reported cases. There is massive – and uneven – under-reporting in most places. Moreover, due to the long period of asymptomatic infection the numbers do not reflect the state of the epidemic *now*, but only the situation several years back.

By November 1989 the situation had worsened dramatically, and WHO warned that we were in danger of losing the war against AIDS. For in less than ten years at least five million people throughout the world, and possibly double that, had been infected. It was also predicted that in Africa the spread of AIDS could explode, for over three million people across the continent are already carrying the infection. At least half are under the age of twenty-five; just under one-quarter of all AIDS patients are in their twenties. By 1990, it was suspected that globally nearly 600,000 people would show symptoms, and this would be only part of a dramatic surge that would continue as we approached the millennium. By the end of the century, 30 million people and 10 million babies across the world may be infected; well over 6 million people could have died of AIDS.

At the time of writing, in Dar es Salaam, Tanzania, 42 per cent of women working in bars and restaurants are infected, a rate double that found three years ago. One in every twenty Ugandans is now probably carrying the virus; 24 per cent of women at just one ante-natal clinic in Kampala have it. In this town alone 20–30 per cent of all women may be HIV positive. Uganda is the African country that has been most frank about the scale of its problem and its women are now at a higher risk than men, becoming infected at an average age of twenty-six, a situation likely to be typical of many African countries. Kenya has reported more than 6000 confirmed cases; almost one-quarter of the prostitutes in the three main towns have the virus, compared to only 8 per cent of sexually promiscuous men; amongst 400 prostitutes tested in Nairobi, 90 per cent have the virus. In Abidjan, Ivory Coast, 3–4 per cent of adults are infected. Twenty per cent of all deaths in one Kinshasa hospital in Zaire are caused by AIDS; the son of its President, President Kenneth Kaunda, died of the disease; four out of ten prostitutes in the capital have HIV and some seven out of ten have at least one other sexually transmitted disease. The fast spread of the virus in Africa is exceedingly worrying, and no one knows precisely where it will end.

A virus is a virus is a virus, yet globally there are at least three different sets of infective patterns and sub-epidemics. In North America, western Europe and Latin America, those infected at the beginning were predominantly male. The virus was being transmitted through homosexual intercourse and through needle-sharing within the drug community. In some cities the rate of infection in these two groups currently exceeds 50 per cent. Transmission from mother to child, once not serious, is increasing as the disease spreads amongst drug users.

In the United States, however, educational programmes have altered the behaviour of gay men. Being intelligent, many of them now stick to one partner and use condoms. The bath houses have been closed down; the streets of Manhattan, San Francisco and Los Angeles which once provided the opportunity for casual sexual encounters every night no longer hold the same attractions. However, recent reports suggest that the youngest group of gay men, believing that AIDS is a problem of an older generation, are not so restrictive in their behaviour. But as the spread of the disease stabilized in these groups it increased in drug users. Nothing protects from dirty needles. Both women and men are infected equally and it is in this group that educational campaigns seem to have little effect. For the judgement of perpetual drug users is eroded: in the end they care very little about anything. They believe they are going to die one way or another and they don't worry overmuch which way.

This is maybe the standard Western pattern, but pockets of difference are fast emerging. In Mexico City the rate of infection is growing most quickly amongst married women who actually are faithful. The reason is the extent of bisexuality, a fact at first denied but now admitted: in Mexico's culture bisexuality is not regarded as aberrant behaviour for married men. But as a result

AIDS is spilling over to wives, once thought to be risk-free. For on the streets of Mexico City is a world of outcast vulnerable children, boys who have run away or been abandoned. Bisexual men, with whom these homeless, unemployed boys have sex as the only means to earn some money, not only spread the disease among street kids but are taking it home. The children's lifestyle results in repeated exposure to venereal and intestinal diseases; these weaken their immune system, and, furthermore, condoms are rarely used. Seven million children live on the streets in Brazil, infections are spreading rapidly amongst them, and a major epidemic of AIDS is likely.

With the exception of Australia and New Zealand – which have patterns comparable to that of the United States – the second pattern occurs in Asia and the Pacific. This is characterized by the more recent introduction and spread of HIV, and no predominant pattern of transmission is yet apparent. In China and Japan most AIDS victims are the recipients of imported blood products and the virus is spreading only slowly amongst the general population. But in countries like Thailand and the Philippines, a flourishing sex tourist industry could well result in explosive outbreaks. The numbers reported from Thailand – only ten AIDS cases notified in 1989 – are suspected to represent the tip of a very large iceberg, since recent testing of 14,000 drug users showed thousands were HIV positive, 77 per cent of the addicts were sharing needles and only 6 per cent of prostitutes used condoms.

By contrast in sub-Saharan Africa and in the Caribbean, the third pattern shows, with men and women affected in equal numbers, though the latest surveys show that in the Central regions of Africa twice as many women as men are being infected. One cause may be through the use of unsterile needles. Self-destruct, once-only syringes have been developed by WHO, who rigidly insist that the health workers giving immunization are properly trained in sterilization procedures. Yet far more worrying, however, is a practice reported from a number of African countries. Taking advantage of those who believe in the therapeutic value of anything given by injection, unscrupulous people are offering phoney injections with dirty needles. However, though of large public health significance, needle transmission is of minor importance, for worldwide other modes account for 90 per cent of the infective pattern.

The main transmission of HIV in Africa is heterosexual. Just why, and how, the appearance and spread of the virus on this continent should show such a striking difference to that in Western societies remains a mystery. It is far easier to see how a virus that provokes a blood infection can be acquired by contact with infected blood, or by sexual acts like sodomy, which increase the likelihood of the breakdown of membranes, or from mother to child through the placenta, than to understand its spread by the usual heterosexual route.

Species of retro-viruses and lenti-viruses, found in primates and other animals, have been deep in the ubiquitous DNA of life for aeons, so possibly the reason for the explosive and devastating spread of AIDS in Africa will have equally deep origins. Ridiculous suggestions, such as that Africans consort with green monkeys, have led many African governments to react angrily to what they see as attempts to blame the origin of the pandemic on them. The effect on the tourist industry has provoked similar reactions. Two suggestions more frequently offered are that transmission of the virus might have occurred when monkeys were eaten and their infected blood came into contact with human wounds; or secondly, when the men of certain ethnic groups would inject monkey blood under the skin of their thighs, as a way to stimulate, or restore, virility. But however plausible these possibilities, there is no evidence that either of the above played a role.

The reasons must be sought elsewhere. First it must be noted that AIDS may be even older in human history than we at first realized; secondly, the disease is overwhelmingly associated with urbanization. The major cities, always an attractive focus for the rural poor, are growing explosively. People drift, prostitution spreads, the support of family groups weakens, opportunities for promiscuous behaviour appear, and sexually transmitted diseases increase. African males with AIDS certainly will have had more sexual partners, or contact with prostitutes, than those without. In addition the chronic infections of Africa, malaria and measles, which are themselves immuno-suppressive, may render the immune cells more vulnerable to the HIV virus. But probably the most important fact is the extent of sexually transmitted diseases, especially those which ulcerate the genitals; these are at a higher level in tropical Africa than in Europe, and provoke a vicious circle of risk. Syphilis, gonorrhoea, herpes etc., long-established enemies in Africa, are widely prevalent. Where ulceration has occurred, HIV can easily penetrate the skin or the mucosa; the inflammation that follows these sexually transmitted infections provokes an accumulation of those very immune cells that are prime targets for the AIDS virus.

Lack of resources, whether of personnel or of testing laboratories, means that the extent of the AIDS problem is still not clear, but it is likely that the epidemic in Africa is 'riding piggy-back' on others. There is wide under-reporting of sexually transmitted disease, since only a minority of infected people seek medical treatment. As studies in Nigeria show, many prefer to treat themselves, or buy a cheap – or indeed expensive – antibiotic from the thousands of 'pharmacists'. This has contributed to the spread of antibiotic-resistant strains of sexually transmitted diseases that itself compounds the problem.

What are the prospects for treatment of AIDS, and for a vaccine? In neither case are they brilliant. However, pessimism should be tempered by recalling the speed with which the virus was identified and the wealth of scientific resources now being focused on the problem. On the other hand there are few effective cures for viral diseases in general and none for retro-viruses, though palliative treatments exist. Since these viruses reproduce in the immune cells they are difficult to attack without also harming the host; where HIV is spliced into our genetic apparatus a drug likely to destroy it will also kill uninfected immune cells – and we need all the healthy ones we have. HIV also infects brain cells, once again out of reach of the immune system and most drugs. So an effective AIDS therapy will require a whole new field of medicine.

Current anti-AIDS therapy concentrates on compounds that might stop the virus infecting other cells. These drugs will be – are – expensive and need to be taken for the rest of a patient's life. The most useful so far is an anti-cancer drug in use since the early 1960s: AZT, sold as Retrovir. In certain classes of AIDS patients this does seem to improve the functioning of the immune system, and may even reverse damage to the nervous system. But it has serious side-effects, and is extremely expensive, which makes it quite out of the question for treatment in any Third World country. And though the average survival time – at present one year – increases as the cohorts of people treated with AZT increases, AZT does not cure.

Many other drugs are being tested. In October 1989 a group of Japanese scientists reported that they had developed an antibody that would kill infected cells while leaving normal ones untouched. A special protein, Fas-antigen, appears on the surface of HIV-infected cells and scientists developed an antibody to neutralize this. In the laboratory test-tube this quickly eliminated all the

AIDS-infected cells, but as every scientist knows, there are numerous banana skins along the path from laboratory experiment to successful clinical trial.

A vaccine would be the best answer, but from initial optimism scientists moved rapidly to sober caution, and then back to restrained hope. At an international conference in San Francisco (June 1990) a viable vaccine was predicted within ten years. Thirty candidate vaccines are now being tested. One, HGP-30, is now on trial in 24 male volunteers: no side-effects have been reported; immune responses, both antibody and cellular, mounted. As our knowledge of the virus increases designer vaccines become more likely.

What is really needed is a vaccine that completely blocks infection of immune cells. This is a tall order. Before HIV we had little experience with vaccines against retro-viruses: only one had been tested against leukaemia in cats, so there are few precedents to guide the research. The capacity of HIV to splice itself into the cell's DNA and lie dormant for years is one major obstacle. No surface proteins appear, so the immune system cannot see that the cell is infected, and there is nothing 'foreign' for antibodies to bite on. A second problem is that HIV is forever changing its surface coat; a third that the knobs whereby it binds to the immune cells are especially prone to variation. This is highly annoying because such knobs are generally the most promising targets for immune attack: being displayed on both the coat of the virus and an infected cell, they should, in principle, be easily recognized. Given these knobbly variations, a vaccine against one strain might not be effective against others.

Finally, HIV's most exquisite evolutionary adaptation exploits the Trojan horse principle. The virus can enter the cells in an enclosed bubble and from outside the cells look completely normal. Protected by the bubble, the virus can pass between cells, or even to another person, without the immune system being alerted. The virus can even generate a reaction whereby the immune systems destroy their own cells. Ironically, it is not that infected people mount no immune response; generally they mount an impressive one. But although this may hold the disease at bay for years, eventually the immune system collapses and the patient develops clinical and fatal AIDS. Thus it may well prove impossible to remove an HIV infection once it is established. But perhaps, as with malaria, we could make a vaccine that will stop the virus causing disease.

Then in December 1989 a 'breakthrough' was announced when scientists at the National Institutes of Health, USA, reported that they had produced a vaccine against a similar infection in monkeys and had worked out precisely how they were protected. This study, apparently, has dispelled doubts about the feasibility of an AIDS vaccine.

Even when discovered, testing and paying for a vaccine will present further problems. So far only a rare Macaque monkey appears to be susceptible to a human AIDS infection. Scientists in the US did manage to infect over one hundred genetically engineered mice but, following an unfortunate accident during routine laboratory maintenance, they all died. So there is no satisfactory animal in which to test prototype vaccines. Another problem is inherent in the disease. We can predict a vaccine's effectiveness by counting the antibodies or immune cells it provokes. But since these very cells are infected by HIV we have very little idea of what to look for in the blood of someone protected.

There will in any case be a shortage of volunteers for trials. Given the lethal nature of AIDS not many uninfected people will volunteer to test an unproven vaccine, though a group of gallant individuals over the age of seventy have indeed done so. Moreover, although AIDS is spreading fast, there are probably not yet sufficient numbers of patients in the West to conduct an adequate trial. The possibility of conducting this in Africa, where the numbers are considerably greater, is currently under discussion, but there is a genuine ethical dilemma. Would it be proper to conduct trials, whether of drugs or vaccines, in African patients, when because of their impoverished state there is, in the foreseeable future, no way they could possibly benefit? Present consensus among vaccine developers is that preliminary tests should be done in those countries where candidate vaccines have been developed – namely, the West. But since clinical trials always require groups facing a high attack rate, then these will have to be done ultimately in Africa.

AIDS will be devastating for that continent. Initially the disease was focused mainly in urban areas, and in certain countries – Zaire for example – seemed to affect those in the wealthier middle classes more than others, possibly because these could enjoy a more varied lifestyle. Then AIDS moved out of the cities along the highways, and is now reaching into the rural areas. The main routes along Lake Victoria, in Central and East Africa, are marked by various overnight stops where the truck-drivers rest and have sexual contacts with barmaids and prostitutes. From these places the infection has spread to the rural population; the prevalence of HIV infection recently rose here from 10 to 15 per cent and is climbing. Simultaneously, in the urban areas of western and eastern Central Africa, AIDS has spread to housewives, people most unlikely to be sexually promiscuous. Yet in the ante-natal clinics of one country, 25 per cent of all women attending were found to be HIV positive. These young women give birth to a child every two to three years; 30 to 50 per cent of their children are born already infected. By 1992 a quarter of a million children in Africa will have been infected by their mothers.

These children will probably die within the first two

years of life, certainly by the time they are seven, and such deaths will undermine the gains of the Planned Miracle. At the Bellagio III Conference, Bill Foege warned: the moment AIDS reaches 20 per cent of infected infants, the negative effects on infant mortality will begin to show. By the end of 1989 that point had already been reached. Over the years the infection has spread from men to women, then from women to children; now, in proportion to adults, more and more children are coming through with HIV. In years to come child mortality rates may soar to as high as 150 per 1000 live births because of AIDS. This poses a major challenge for the paediatric services in Africa for it will more than offset any reduction from the child survival programmes.

At present AIDS is not yet having a demographic affect on overall population growth rates in Africa, for at this time the group mostly affected is selective. Some children may be infected if their mothers are; those presently not infected are likely to be risk-free until the beginning of their sexually active life. Older people, similarly, are not affected. Although mortality in young adults is high, at present they form only a small section of the demographic pyramid and their deaths will not seriously affect the overall population growth.

But if the disease continues to spread well into the next century at the rate it had spread in the last years of this one, there *will* be major demographic consequences. AIDS could well diminish the expected increase of Africa's urban population by 30 per cent. There will be some dreadful consequences because the groups now seriously affected are also the most intellectually and economically productive and the most socially and politically active. They hold the key to Africa's development, to progress, to socio-economic advancement and they are going to be taken out in large numbers. A recent report from the Zimbabwe Confederation of Industry estimated that currently nearly 20 per cent of the total population (10 million) is infected; in ten years' time 90 per cent of the country's workforce may be dying of AIDS-related diseases.

When challenged as to the point of immunizing Africa's children if they are anyway likely to die of AIDS, Dr Daniel Tarantola, until recently Chief of WHO's National Programme Support in their AIDS Division, replied: 'It would be twice wrong not to do it. These children may have well died in the first five years of their life but the situation is fast evolving: they respond to vaccines very well; the likelihood of a child dying from measles in the first five years of life is still far higher than of it dying from AIDS; thirdly' – and he shows great optimism – 'with drugs coming down the pipeline, possibly these children can eventually be treated.'

But can Africa ever afford this? Whatever the ultimate impact of AIDS, it is going to be far greater in Africa than in the West, blessed with plentiful resources and a sophisticated infrastructure. The statistics reveal stark differences. Each year England spends the equivalent of over $1100 on health care per person, the United States $760, Mexico $11.5, Haiti $3.25, Rwanda $1.6 – an amount that won't buy a bottle of aspirin in London. But the costs of even AIDS prevention are enormous: in Brazil these are estimated to be $28 million, $8 million of which would be used for screening blood for transfusions; in Peru the start-up costs alone of a similar screening programme would be $20 million – a sum sufficient for the annual health care for 1.5 million of the country's citizens; in the USA, treating an AIDS patient with AZT costs $8,000 a year and this does not include the costs of blood transfusions following the consequent anaemia.

Ironically there seems to be a tragic correlation between the amount a particular country can spend per AIDS patient and that country's gross national product. If poor Zaire decided to spend at a level comparable to the rich United States, the entire budget of that nation's largest public hospital, Mama Yemo, would be enough to treat just ten AIDS patients. There are going to be appallingly difficult choices. Diverting resources to AIDS will prejudice the lives of other patients who might be cured. As many as 25 to 50 per cent of hospital beds in certain Central African countries are now occupied by HIV patients; by the mid-1990s the same condition could well apply in Costa Rica, Haiti and Brazil. The current trend is to discharge AIDS patients from health facilities and give preference to those with curable diseases.

WHO responded to the AIDS crisis with a massive worldwide programme and a budget which in 1988 was $65 million. Of that, $45 million was spent in Africa alone. By now all countries in Africa have an AIDS programme, closely linked to their primary health care structures. The activities of these programmes resemble those of fire-fighters, for some things must be done immediately, such as establishing testing facilities at whatever central blood transfusion centres exist – all capital cities in Africa now have one – and providing technical support, consultants and funds.

But these are merely short-term measures. In the long term the linkages between primary health care and AIDS prevention and control become critical. While Daniel Tarantola admits that during the last few years of the child survival initiatives, WHO has learned to be more flexible in its strategic approach towards immunization, he emphasizes: in no country in the world has WHO established vertical programmes for AIDS, for this would be completely inappropriate. However, there are many paths that could be followed by programmes in AIDS prevention and education. The promotion of condoms is important, and in this existing family planning programmes in Africa have not yet been at all successful. But since their use is now a question of preventing both pregnancy and AIDS, the issue of condoms has taken on a new life, as it were. Similarly, the education of pregnant women at ante-natal clinics – a regular activity in the mother and child health services – provides an opportunity at which AIDS education can be infiltrated, as it can also be in the immunization centres.

WHO's experience in Uganda is particularly telling. Ugandans have known for years about the 'slim' disease, and by the time WHO's AIDS programme came in the health care system had been severely affected by the horrific political events preceding the AIDS crisis. AIDS was just one more terrible burden. Donors quickly came in with funds, but much more was needed if the requirements of people – and not only HIV-infected individuals – for quality care were to be met. At the same time the World Bank was helping rehabilitate health care systems, particularly those in district hospitals, and viewed this as a contribution to fighting AIDS. So AIDS did bring visibility to problems in health areas which otherwise might have been neglected; and along with efforts to tackle AIDS came converging efforts to rehabilitate the system and train personnel. The programmes ran fairly smoothly in the towns but mobilizing the rural communities has not been easy.

After four years the education programmes all over Africa have made real impact in terms of awareness. There is an unprecedented level of knowledge about AIDS, even in remote areas. Compared with many other countries there is no discrimination against AIDS patients, no compulsory testing of visitors, and some evidence of behavioural change – but nothing like enough. Many prostitutes carry certificates saying they are AIDS-free (though the authenticity of these may be dubious); apparently men are no longer boasting of the numbers and frequency of their sexual contacts – as a status symbol this is rapidly losing currency. But not, it appears, among the élite, if the example of the Central African Republic holds true. A recent article in the

Sunday Times (1 July 1990) showed that in spite of one of the most enlightened educational programmes, with some levelling off in the incidence of AIDS, those who promoted such education are themselves ignoring the warnings.

As death scythes down the victims, other changes follow. The extended family can now no longer cope. AIDS victims are sent to hospital wherever possible; as AIDS numbers increase, they may be sent straight out again. People turn to a plethora of rationales to account for the deaths that are affecting their communities. In the USA the Moral Majority insists AIDS is a divine punishment for homosexuality; in southwest Uganda, in a village called Mbuye in Rakai district, the Roman Catholics insist that AIDS is a divine punishment for robbery or adultery; in Kasensero, on the shores of Lake Victoria in southern Uganda, the 'powerful witches' of Tanzania are invoked, taking their revenge on Ugandan traders who have traditionally cheated. Every angry African reaction to the suggestion that AIDS originated in Africa because of promiscuous behaviour with green monkeys can be matched by other angry refusals to believe in the existence of the disease at all. In a brothel in the red-light district of Port au Prince, Haiti, the women said: 'There is no such thing. It is a false disease invented by the American government to take advantage of the poor countries. The American President hates the poor people so now he makes up AIDS to take away what little we have.' Some gay men in Canada and America believe that AIDS was created by accident in a secret underground research station at Fort Detrick, Washington. Only because two captive men being used in the experiments escaped, did AIDS come out into the world.

But AIDS is none of these things. AIDS is a virus that, with great success, has exploited a particular ecological niche in the twentieth-century environment, aided in some cases by lifestyle, in others by changing urban patterns in poor, unhealthy, overcrowded populations. The human race has faced and, at the cost of many deaths, survived other epidemics, the greatest of which was probably bubonic plague. In three years, between 1347 and 1350, this may have killed up to 28 million people – one-third to one-half of Europe's population – numbers undoubtedly so vast because most of the population were already starving. In the last year of the First World War an influenza epidemic killed 22 million; measles is still killing 1.5 million people each year, tuberculosis 1 million, pregnancy and childbirth nearly 1 million, the Ethiopian famine killed 1 million and the fifteen years of the Vietnam War nearly 2.35 million.

AIDS may well reach plague dimensions. Already it is a major global problem and a universal human and scientific challenge. 'In a deep and remarkable way,' writes Dr Jonathan Mann, for four years Director of WHO's Global Programme on AIDS, 'the child with AIDS is as the world's child, the man or woman dying with AIDS is the image of our own mortality.'

Civil war left many orphans in Uganda; AIDS is adding many more. A photograph taken in that lakeside village, Kasensero, shows a young girl, Emanuel Lubega, kneeling on fallen palm leaves, next to a single iron cross, one of seven, supported in the earth by rough stones. Every expression except stoic acceptance has been wiped from her face. She tends the graves for her grandfather, Francis Baziwane, who has watched as AIDS killed his son, his daughter and five of his grandchildren. The fourteen-year-old girl and the eighty-year-old patriarch are the sole survivors of the whole family.

Conclusion

'The optimist proclaims that we live in the best of all
possible worlds; and the pessimist fears that this is
so.'

Henry J. Byron, *The Silver Stallion*

This saga had been dubbed the Planned Miracle. Five
years, thousands of miles and millions of words on, it was
time to take stock. Just what was the miracle?

To begin with, the children themselves. From the
moment of protesting appearance and immediate
response to our world, their growth, learning, vulnera-
bility, tenacity, laughter, tears and trust have never
ceased to amaze me. They generate in me some very
ancient emotions: they mitigate the knowledge of my
own mortality; they offer the possibility of doing better
for the world than we ever did. Thus moving from the
children of my family to the world's family of children, I
came passionately to want the same headstart in life for
them all and became impatient when others did not feel
the burden of what everyone at the Harvard Club
meeting, years ago, agreed was a strong moral
imperative.

So at times I became very angry indeed, on behalf of
those small bundles of humanity whom I saw living their
lives on the garbage mountains of rich cities, being sold
into prostitution, exploited economically and sexually by
tough amoral bastards; street boys, street-wise, swept
under the carpet of society's indifference, being killed by

death squads on the sidewalks of Rio; girls married at thirteen burying their first child at fourteen, or sold into virtual slavery, whether domestic or manufacturing – and all this against a backcloth of the arms and drug dealers who are as indifferent to human life as the pimp who offers a nine-year-old child to a tourist. Did the Koran really say, have no more children than you can properly look after? It did. Thus I came to feel also that in the passion for their cause, the right-to-lifers remain woefully inactive – even unconcerned to the point of sin – about the quality of life thereafter. And life was not only harsh beyond belief for the children on the garbage dumps or in the brothels, it was so for their parents too. I remember one blind woman on Lamu Island, her unemployed husband disabled by malaria, who knowing that her children must be immunized, regularly walked the miles to the clinic, the babe in her arms, being guided by one child whose other hand clutched the next toddler in the never-ending brood.

Yet when the anger surged high there were other experiences to reduce its level. UNICEF's phrase, 'the Children's Revolution', while it certainly captures our attention, is perhaps not the most apt because human progress generally occurs through a series of slow, incremental changes, initiated by men and women of vision. And, as Nick Ward said to me, 'the real miracle is the existence of visionaries, like Mahler and Grant. The rest of us are merely technicians.' 'Executants' would be a fairer word to characterize those who are devoting their lives to this cause, and with every fresh practical success, the outlook for children improved.

Yet the realization of their joint vision had been accompanied by much emotion and angst, not all constructive. The echoes of the strategic arguments would probably rumble on for ever, for some people continue to believe that UNICEF simplifies to the point of trivialization, while WHO complicates to the point of impotence. But why, I asked Bill Foege, did Mahler and Grant attract admiration and anger, in roughly equal proportions? He answered in a roundabout fashion.

'I kept out of the initial argument about strategy. A year or so ago I was to give the Presidential Address to the American Public Health Association. So I looked up the history and was intrigued to find that at the turn of this century, precisely the same row developed in New York City over sanitation and water supplies. There were some who said these should be put in immediately; others who insisted one should wait until the whole infrastructure was in place. I suspect that the same form of debate will always recur – as will the admiration and the anger. For you see,' he continued, 'Mahler and Grant are visionaries, and people are afraid of visionaries.'

Looking back over the last five years, with the worst of the dissension passed, Grant now confesses that sustainability of the programmes is turning out to be far harder than anyone realized. Even in Turkey, with its relatively sound economic structure, infant mortality remains high. In some countries it is, because of poverty and debt, higher than when the programmes began. The target for universal coverage may be reached, thanks to major surges of effort in the final months of 1990, but then what? Could the dream slip from Grant's grasp? If it does, apathy, recession, debt, human numbers and continuing indifference to the plight of the poor will be some of the reasons. The lack of a primary health care infrastructure will certainly be another.

For it is also clear that neither will Mahler's vision be fully realized: 'Health For All' by the year 2000 will not be achieved. For a start, and set against the background of a burgeoning population, the costs – calculated at 5 per cent of the countries' GNP – will not be met. Even in 1982, when the downward spiral of the African economies was in full train, the proportion of GNP for health care was only 0.4 per cent in low income countries

and 1.5 per cent in middle income ones. All are in far
worse shape now. In many parts of sub-Saharan Africa
indeed, primary health care simply does not exist.

So unless through some other miracle commitment is
confirmed by a massive degree of funds and effort, the
best we can pray for is a slow continuous decline in infant
mortality with concomitant increases in women's
education and choice.

At a more prosaic level therefore, the large miracle
these people planned for small children has not yet
occurred, though some of it is happening. What
undoubtedly has occurred is that children – their health,
well-being, importance – are now on the political agenda.
Perhaps societies are finally beginning to take this
responsibility seriously and recognize their duty to meet
the needs of their youth. Jim Grant's World Summit for
Children that took place during the last weekend of
September 1990, whose intention was to reinforce the
rights of the child, did not initiate this process but rather
gave international imprimatur to one already in place.
Amid fanfare and media coverage, more than seventy
Heads of State attended, but whether governments will
move beyond rhetoric to action is another question for
the future.

Reporting the Summit, *The Economist* noted that the
agenda was wide. A 'wish list' of actions – most cheap and
simple – to help children survive and flourish had been
drawn up. If these failed to be implemented the blame
should not be placed, the writer felt, so much on cuts in
public spending as on weakness, or indifference, or
conflicts for power amongst a country's would-be rulers.
And UNICEF's good resolutions, the article tartly
concluded, was unlikely to address the main point – that
most children die in countries where women have too
many. This is why Halfdan Mahler was not present.
Though he had, of course, been invited and though he
continues to speak warmly of Jim Grant, finally he came

to feel that UNICEF's concentrated emphasis on survival to the exclusion of almost everything else, was doing more harm than good. Into the discussions of the Summit and the Declaration it would issue, and among references to measles eradication and the elimination of malnutrition or the protection of children from war zones, he sought for some reference to the need for family planning and to guarantee the quality of children's lives from then.

For survival per se is 'no big deal': it is what happens after that really matters – and this is where he hoped the emphasis would be placed. For Mahler was remembering those 200 million young adolescents set to be 600 million in the early years of the next century.

One September, in Washington D.C., a small coda to this saga presented itself when I met Betty Bumpers, wife of Senator Dale Bumpers, of Arkansas. The daughter of a poor farmer in Arkansas, she grew up during the Depression; her father felt he needed four sons but it was his four daughters who helped him plough, milk and muck out.

Many years later, in 1977, when her husband was the State's Senator, Mrs Bumpers was approached by a delegation. Would she help educate the people of Arkansas about immunization. 'I said to 'em, "Hell, we don't need to educate; we need to immunize." When they left I realized what I had done – and Jeez, I'd just said I was going to immunize all the children of Arkansas.

'So we mobilized the National Guard; we activated the agricultural network and the nurses. The doctors wouldn't do anything except lend their presence: there was nothing in it for them.

'Well, one year later, Bill Foege came to Arkansas to present us with a certificate. For we were the first state in the Union ever to achieve 98 per cent of our children immunized.'

'What's the situation like now?' I asked.

'Well, that last goof in the White House closed down all the day care centres and the numbers are down again. They shouldn't be because actually immunization is compulsory before you can attend public school. But we'll have to do it again and now I'd mobilize not only the National Guard but the Joint Chiefs of Staff too!'

If anyone could, she could – and America may have to. In 1986, though America's per capita GNP ranked first amongst the industrialized countries, it was twenty-third in the league table of infant mortality of the under fives. Ahead were Spain, Hong Kong, Singapore, Ireland, Japan, Italy and the United Kingdom. Sweden, Finland and the Scandinavian countries topped the list. The USSR was fiftieth. Afghanistan, Malawi, Ethiopia and Burkina Faso were at the bottom.

Yet though it is indeed a scandal that such a rich country should have such poor figures, another measure – life expectancy relative to income – shows that a country does not have to be rich to achieve a low infant mortality. Now Kerala State, Sri Lanka and China ranked highest; Oman, Iran, Libya, Algeria and Iraq, lowest. Other poor health achievers include some of the richest nations on earth, such as Saudi Arabia. Their per capita GNP is $16,000 per head but their life expectancy only fifty-six.

Two final ironic twists recently appeared. In October 1989 at a conference in Atlanta, delegates pointed out that in certain locations in the United States a mere 50 per cent of vulnerable children were receiving protective immunization. If this situation were to be remedied a major drive would be needed. So perhaps they should look at the strategies of the global childhood immunization programmes to see what lessons could be applied to the slums of Washington, New York, Chicago, Los Angeles and some States in the rural South like Mississippi, or the town of Hinton, Appalachia – where public health is poor. There, as widely reported in the media (the *Independent*, 6 May 1990), Hinton's Public Health Inspector publicly stated that while his home State of Virginia was surrounded by the technology of the affluent West it had pockets with Third World standards of health, income and education.

So he had applied for foreign aid, from the United Nations, and the governments of the USSR, France, Japan and the United Kingdom. The UN response was bureaucratic, the Soviets' polite but edgy, the French charming, the Japanese dismissive. Only the British were kind and helpful, he reports: they contacted several agencies including the World Bank and the International Monetary Fund, but without success. Yet the point of the story is this: if the United States can't maintain simple health standards, can we really expect Burkina Faso to? This is a question I find very difficult to answer.

On the one hand I think we can, for if national politicians are serious about wanting to improve child survival and primary health care, there are plenty of outsiders still willing to help with all kinds of support. For though the larger the developing country the comparatively more expensive the costs, the amount – $2.5 billion per year by the mid-90s – is not impossible, being less than the sum the world spends on arms in one day, what Russians spend on vodka in one month, what the tobacco industry spends on advertising in the USA in one year. Money alone is not really the problem. Mahler still hopes that the North will let go the protective economic blanket a little on behalf of the developing South.

However, the donors and aid agencies now want to be convinced that after the razzmatazz of immunization campaigns is over, these life-saving interventions are firmly part of an ongoing programme of primary health care. USAID is especially concerned about this. They are looking to see if a country's health system is actually and actively working, that its government's commitment has gone beyond verbal rhetoric and photo-opportunities on

television by Presidents, Health Ministers, and Jim Grant,
that there is a specific line item in the national budget. For
even though 80 per cent of present costs are being borne
by the developing countries themselves, low income countries are still spending far more on hospitals than on
primary health care, and much more – $200 billion a year
to be exact – on military establishments, an amount that
greatly exceeds that on health and education combined.

The facts are startling. Soldiers outnumber physicians
at least eightfold. Arms expenditures can add up to 20 per
cent of overall national budgets – in the case of Ethiopia
the figure is 40 per cent. In some cases one-third of a
country's total annual external debt is accounted for by
arms imports. Robert McNamara, when President of the
World Bank, pointed this out in the 1970s and nineteen
years later his successor, Barber Conabel, noted that matters were much the same.

Much of this story, of necessity, has been concerned
with statistics – millions of children immunized, millions
still dying; that silent Hiroshima every three days. Sometimes it is hard to remember that every single child matters
– to its parents, family and community. But those hoping
to bring about the miracle always do. 'Statistics is medicine
with the tears washed off,' wrote Major Greenwood forty
years ago and Bill Foege, routinely caught in an endless
round of conferences, logistics, management, budgets
and research, often observed: 'Behind every one of our
failures lies a human face.'

I wrote the above paragraph after the Berlin Wall had
opened, and in a surge of optimistic joy those hapless captives of a sterile, inhuman ideology were suddenly given a
new freedom and with it the possibility of a new future.
And I asked myself: were the many children of this world,
also hapless captives of circumstance, in the process of
being given a new freedom and a new future? But then I
recalled: the temptation to romanticize was just as insidious
as it had been years back when I first met Rahima Banu.

So what is the reality, what the likely outcome? The reality is that in Africa, especially, the future is very uncertain for reasons that readers of this book will now appreciate. When Incila Diker, speaking of Turkey's triumph said 'Matters cannot end here,' she meant much more than the survival of numbers. 'Survival is all very well, but we must be thinking of what kind of future we can give our children.'

But if we do – and we must – we may ourselves be impaled on a human and moral dilemma starkly enunciated by an American who had worked in Uganda for various aid agencies for over twenty years. Speaking to Thurston Clarke, who reported the conversation in his travel book *Equator: A Journey Round the World* he laid out the dilemma as follows. His views are a stringent antidote to any romanticism.

'Development aid and emergency relief are big business. We sell hope to poor countries, clean consciences to the rich and our corporate logo, our clever marketing tool, is "the starving child"!'

'Are you saying "Let them starve"?'

'See what I mean? See what an effective sales tool they are? What would we do without them? You're right. How can you say no to a starving child? You can't! In the war between economic facts and starving children, the children win every time. But remember that twenty years from now these malnourished children will be malnourished adults, clearing marginal lands, promoting erosion, placing more burdens on their primitive economies, and raising their own huge families of malnourished children. By ensuring they all survive, we're guaranteeing more starvation and suffering. If you want to see the future of Africa, go to Haiti, because that's what this continent is going to become: an overpopulated, eroded wasteland filled with malnourished, terrorized people. And much of the blame will be ours.

'Ask yourself this: If we Europeans decide we have a responsibility to save this particular generation of African children, don't we also have a responsibility to face the consequences of our charity and support the same entirely too large generation throughout its miserable, suffering life? Already the cost is incredible, and we spend too much of the money battling host governments, trying to outwit people living in the capitals who couldn't care less if people starve in the countryside. Thanks to them, it costs a fortune to deliver charity a few hundred miles. And there's no chance the situation will improve. By every economic measurement most African countries are becoming poorer. Every year their factories are less productive and they lose arable land. Their foreign debt is already incredible, and no one seriously believes it can be repaid.

'Eventually the burden of keeping the maximum number of Africans alive at the edge of starvation will become too much. Fifteen or twenty years from now, that Dutch couple who have one child because they can't afford more or because they believe in zero population growth will wonder why they're being taxed to support Rwandan or Ugandan families with ten. And when the rich countries at last rebel against this endless, limitless, destructive charity, then there will be suffering and starvation of incredible magnitude.'

Peter Poore, I remembered, had always insisted that giving aid carries a terrible responsibility – a mutual one, I would argue – and that no one should embark on programmes such as these health initiatives without having thought through the long-term consequences.

The facts are stark. Immunizing a child may cost $5 for the full course but it has been calculated that in sub-Saharan Africa, $500 of matching investment will be needed if that child is to grow to adulthood, a task, as Henry Hobhouse writes, 'far more difficult than keeping the child alive'. Even if there were enough fertile land and food, education and jobs, for a population that increased 25 per cent in the first quarter of the century, 45 per cent in the second, 100 per cent in the third, and, as seems likely, 125 per cent in the fourth, where is the capital to come from? Does 'being compassionate today lay up trouble for tomorrow', to the extent that compassion should be withheld? Are these child survival programmes in truth 'a respectable form of improvidence . . . practised by a veritable army of the good?' Is it inevitable that the consequences will prove to be as dire as Thurston Clarke's 'Samaritan, with his black humor and pessimism' predicted?

Some insist: so dire will be the consequences that, terrible though the choices are, the children should be left to die. Recently, Dr Maurice King of the Department of Public Health at Leeds University, made this explicit, arguing that the recent five-fold increase in human numbers during the last 150 years has imposed irreversible damage on the biosphere; the increasing pressures on resources have led to a rapidly deteriorating environment and the prospect of total ecological collapse in many poor societies. We will see more and more Haitis. UNICEF notwithstanding, reducing infant deaths is not an automatic spur for reduction in human numbers; international family planning campaigns have been inadequate; ecology and compassion are now likely to be incommensurate. So though an individual doctor must rehydrate the individual patient he faces, public health officials should not apply such policies on a global scale, since in the end the communities cannot sustain themselves and are bound to starve.

Thus did an article in *The Lancet* force me to face the ultimate issue, the moral ambush that lay in wait through these years of work. I know the dilemma is real, the dangers appalling. Yet I believe it would be unconscionable, as well as morally unacceptable and politically divisive, to withhold pragmatic compassion. One cannot say to the poor and deprived, 'I am not going to give your existing children vaccination but at the same time here's the technology to limit your families – now use it.'

In both science and everyday life the solution to one set of problems always generates another set of problems and it was ever thus. So I have finally concluded that initiatives in child survival – themselves a fantastic achievement – are likely to be yet another small yet crucial, incremental step towards human progress. But only if further steps follow: democracy and choice – where choice includes having only the number of children parents want; education and empowerment for women; constant pressure upon the inequity that primary health was intended to remedy; and finally, that local governments take a responsibility for their country's destiny at least equal to that they ask the West to assume.

The best stories always have a clear conclusion and a happy ending. Here the final words may never be written, for this is a continuing saga of an extraordinary, moral, human endeavour, whose course I have been privileged to record.

Index